Lonely Planet

ROME

TOP SIGHTS, AUTHENTIC EXPERIENCES

Nicola Williams,
Alexis Averbuck, Duncan Garwood,
Virginia Maxwell

Contents

Villa Borghese & Northern Rome

This is where you'll find the glorious park of Villa Borghese and the city's cultural hub. (Map p252)

Museo e Galleria Borghese

Tivoli (3...)

Tridente, Trevi & the Quirinale

Glamorous, debonair and packed with tourists: this is Rome's designer-clad soul. (Map p245)

...anish ...eps
Palazzo Barberini

Museo Nazionale Romano: Palazzo Massimo alle Terme

Stazione Termini

Monti, Esquilino & San Lorenzo

Busy areas, speckled with glittering churches and cool restaurants and bars. (Maps p245 & p255)

Basilica di Santa Maria Maggiore

...n
...m
...no

Colosseum

Basilica di San Clemente

Acquedotto Neroniano

Basilica di San Giovanni in Laterano

Ancient Rome

No other city has such an evocative ancient heart. The Colosseum, Palatino and Roman Forum are all here. (Map p246)

Terme di Caracalla

Ciampino Airp... (12...

...vanni & ...cio
...ental basilicas, ...g ruins, ...nal trattorias ...mping nightlife. ...255)

Via Ap... Antica

Southern Rome

Encompassing the beautiful, cobbled Via Appia Antica, one of the world's oldest roads, lined with historic catacombs.

Welcome to Rome

An intoxicating cocktail of haunting ruins, iconic monuments, awe-inspiring art and vibrant street life, Italy's hot-blooded capital is one of the world's most charismatic cities. It's la dolce vita (the sweet life) at its Italian best.

Rome's historic cityscape, the result of 3000 years of ad hoc urban development, is an exhilarating spectacle. Ancient icons such as the Colosseum, Roman Forum and Pantheon recall its golden age as *caput mundi* (capital of the world), while barnstorming basilicas testify to its historical role as seat of the Catholic Church.

The city's artistic heritage is also astonishing. Throughout history, Rome has starred in the great upheavals of Western art, drawing the top artists of the day and inspiring them to push the boundaries of creative achievement. The result is a city awash with priceless treasures. Ancient statues adorn world-class museums; Byzantine mosaics and Renaissance frescoes dazzle in art-rich churches; and baroque fountains embellish medieval piazzas. Walk around the centre and without even trying you'll come across masterpieces by the likes of Michelangelo, Caravaggio, Raphael and Bernini.

But a trip to Rome is as much about lapping up the local lifestyle as feasting on art and culture. Whiling away hours on a sun-baked cafe terrace, getting lost in backstreet alleys and hidden piazzas, indulging in sunset *aperitivi* (evening drinks) in on-trend cocktail bars, dining after dark in raucous neighbourhood trattorias – all this, too, is part and parcel of the exquisite Roman experience.

> *...a trip to Rome is as much about lapping up the local lifestyle as feasting on art and culture*

The Colosseum (p36)
F11PHOTO/SHUTTERSTOCK ©

CLOCKWISE FROM TOP RIGHT: KAMIRA/SHUTTERSTOCK ©;
JUSTIN FOULKES/LONELY PLANET ©; VAIVIRGA/SHUTTERSTOCK ©;
S.BORISOV/SHUTTERSTOCK ©; ANYAIVANOVA/SHUTTERSTOCK ©;
MARCO RUBINO/SHUTTERSTOCK ©; TRAVELER1116/GETTY IMAGES ©;
TTSTUDIO/SHUTTERSTOCK ©; NEJRON PHOTO/ SHUTTERSTOCK ©

Plan Your Trip
This Year in Rome

2020

Rome

From religious processions and neighbourhood parties to fashion shows, food fairs, arts festivals and world-class football (soccer) matches, Rome's calendar bursts with events. Many are played out against atmospheric outdoor backdrops, adding a wonderful sense of occasion.

Above and top right: Natale di Rome (p9); Opposite bottom left: Festa de' Noantri (p12); Opposite bottom right: Depeche Mode performing at Estate Romana (p11)

2020

★ Top Festivals & Events

Natale di Roma, April
Estate Romana, June to September
Lungo il Tevere, June to August
Festa de' Noantri, July
Romaeuropa, September to December

Plan Your Trip
This Year in Rome

January

01

As New Year celebrations fade, the winter cold digs in. It's a quiet time of year, but the winter sales are a welcome diversion.

🏊 Tuffo nel Tevere   1 Jan
This New Year's Day tradition dates from 1946; Romans turn out in force to watch a brave soul or two dive into the icy waters of the Tiber from Ponte Cavour after the Gianicolo cannon sounds at midday. This year they will see local lifeguard Maurizio Palmulli's 32nd New Year's dive.

🛍 Shopping Sales   4 Jan
Running from early January, typically the first Saturday of the month, to mid-February, the winter fashion sales offer savings of between 20% and 50%.

✴ Epiphany   6 Jan
A witch known as La Befana delivers gifts to Italian kids for Epiphany, the last day of the Christmas holidays. To mark the occasion, a costumed procession makes its way down Via della Conciliazione to St Peter's Square.

✴ Altaroma Fashion Week   late Jan
Fashionistas swan in for the winter outing of Rome's top fashion event – four good-looking days of dazzling catwalk shows, fashion-driven exhibitions, workshops and parties. Both established designers and new talents preview their seasonal collections (www.altaroma.it).

✴ Festa di Sant'Antonio   17 Jan
Animal lovers take their pets to be blessed at the Chiesa di Sant'Eusebio on Piazza Vittorio Emanuele in honour of St Anthony the Abbot, the patron saint of animals.

☆ Les Étoiles   24–26 Jan
The curtain rises on some of classical ballet's finest dancers, choreographers and ballet companies at this prestigious *internazionale di danza* (international dance gala), staged at Rome's Auditorium Parco della Musica.

Above: Altaroma Fashion Week catwalk show

2020

MZETA/SHUTTERSTOCK ©

February

02

Rome's winter quiet is shattered by colourful carnival celebrations and weekend invasions by cheerful rugby fans in town for the annual Six Nations rugby tournament.

🏉 Six Nations Rugby early Feb–late Mar
The Stadio Olimpico (p198) hosts Italy's home games during the annual Six Nations rugby tournament.

🎭 Valentine's Day 14 Feb
St Valentine (San Valentino in Italian) was a 3rd-century martyr who was executed near Ponte Milvio. His saint's day is widely celebrated – some museums and galleries offer discounted entry, and restaurants prepare romantic menus.

☆ Equilibrio Festival Feb
Performers from Scandinavia take to the stage at the Auditorium Parco della Musica for the year's edition of this contemporary dance festival. Past outings have showcased dance from Germany, France and Scandinavia.

🎭 Carnevale di Romano around 22–23 Feb
Rome runs wild with horse shows, costumed parades, street performers, fireworks and kids in fancy dress hurling *coriandoli* (coloured confetti) at each other during the city's annual carnival, celebrated with gusto for several days prior to *Martedì Grasso* (Shrove Tuesday) on 25 February. Much of the action spills across Piazza del Popolo, Via del Corso, Piazza Navona and Piazza del Campidoglio.

BESTINO/SHUTTERSTOCK ©

Top: Carnevale di Romano;
Bottom: Six Nations Rugby match

Plan Your Trip
This Year in Rome

RONTAV/SHUTTERSTOCK ©

March

The onset of spring brings blooming flowers, rising temperatures and unpredictable rainfall. Unless Easter falls in late March, the city is fairly subdued and low-season prices still apply.

03

✿ Festa della Donna   8 Mar
International Women's Day is celebrated with particular gusto in this traditional city, where Italian men woo their wives, female friends, lovers and colleagues with canary-yellow posies of mimosa flowers; the sweetly perfumed blooms are sold on street corners city-wide.

🚗 Festa di Santa   9 Mar
Devout motorists congregate on Via dei Fori Imperiali to have their cars blessed on the feast day of St Frances of Rome, the patron saint of drivers.

✿ Festa di San Giuseppe   19 Mar
The Feast of St Joseph, which doubles as Father's Day in Italy, is traditionally celebrated by snaffling delicious cream puffs known as *bignè di San Giuseppe*.

⊙ La Settimana dei Musei   early Mar
For the first time last year, during Museum Week (lasting six days in the 1st week in March), gleeful Romans and visitors to Rome revelled in a week of free culture as state museums – the Colosseum and Galleria Borghese included – opened their doors for free. Expect the same in 2020.

⊙ Giornate FAI di Primavera   late Mar
Palazzi (mansions), churches and archaeological sites that are generally closed to the public open their doors for a weekend of special openings, courtesy of Italy's main conservation body, the Fondo Ambiente Italiano (FAI; www.fondoambiente.it).

Above: Spring flowers for sale, Campo de' Fiori (p96)

LUIGI DE POMPEIS/ALAMY STOCK PHOTO ©

04

April

April is a great month in Rome, with lovely, sunny weather, fervent Easter cele-brations, azaleas on the Spanish Steps and Rome's birthday festivities. Expect high-season prices.

🏃 Maratona di Roma   early Apr
Sightseeing becomes sport during Rome's annual marathon, generally held in early April. The 42km route starts and finishes near the Colosseum, taking in many of the city's big sights. Details online at http://maratonainternazionalediroma.it.

🎎 Easter   12 Apr
Easter is a big deal in Rome. On Good Friday the pope leads a candlelit procession around the Colosseum, and there are other smaller parades around the city. At noon on Easter Sunday the pope blesses the crowds in St Peter's Square.

🎎 Mostra delle Azalee   mid-Apr–early May
From mid-April to May, the Spanish Steps are decorated with hundreds of vases of blooming, brightly coloured azaleas.

🍴 La Città della Pizza   mid-Apr
Pizza aficionados: this three-day event, when some of the finest master pizza-makers gather from all over Italy, is for you. Cooking demonstrations, workshops, pop-up pizza trucks and more (www.lacittadellapizza.it).

🎎 Natale di Roma   21 Apr
Rome celebrates its birthday (www.natalidiroma.it) on 21 April with music, processions, historical re-creations and fireworks. Action is centred on Via dei Fori Imperiali and the Circo Massimo.

🎎 Festa della Liberazione   25 Apr
Schools, shops and offices shut as Rome commemorates the WWII liberation of Italy by Allied troops and resistance forces in 1945.

Above: Historical re-creations, Natale di Roma

Plan Your Trip
This Year in Rome

GLORIA IMBROGNO/SHUTTERSTOCK ©

May

May is a busy, high-season month. The weather's perfect – usually warm enough to eat outside – and the city is looking gorgeous with blue skies and spring flowers.

☆ Primo Maggio   1 May
Thousands of fans troop to Piazza di San Giovanni in Laterano for Rome's free May Day rock concert. It's a mostly Italian affair with big-name local performers, but you might catch the occasional foreign guest star.

◉ Open House Roma   early May
Historic and contemporary buildings that are normally closed to the public open their doors for a weekend of visits and guided tours during the Open House Roma event (www.openhouseroma.org), designed to promote Rome's architectural diversity.

🎋 Festival del Verde e del Paesaggio   early May
For three days in early to mid-May, green-fingered Romans gather on the green and flowery rooftop of Rome's Auditorium Parco della Musica for this colourful, springtime garden fest (www.festivaldelverdeedelpaesaggio.it).

🎾 Internazionali BNL d'Italia   early May
The world's top players slug it out on the red courts of the Foro Italico at the Internazionali BNL d'Italia, one of Europe's top tennis tournaments. Details at www.internazionalibnlditalia.com.

☆ Piazza di Siena Showjumping   late May
Set in the attractive confines of Villa Borghese, Piazza di Siena stages Rome's annual international showjumping event (www.piazzadisiena.it) towards the end of the month.

🔒 Gucci Cruise Show   28 May
A complete and utter thrill for Roman fashionistas, the much-vaunted annual cruise show of Italian fashion house Gucci will strut down the catwalk – at Rome's Capitoline Museums, no less.

Above: Brunori Sas performing at the Primo Maggio concert

June

Summer has arrived and with it hot weather and the Italian school holidays. The city's festival season breaks into full stride with many outdoor events.

🏃 UEFA Euro 2020   12, 17 & 21 Jun

One of the biggest tournaments in international football (soccer) kicks off at Rome's Stadio Olimpico at 9pm – the ref blows the whistle on subsequent Group A qualifying matches on 12, 17 and 21 June. Rome will also host one of the quarter finals on 4 July.

☆ Isola del Cinema   mid-Jun–Sep

From mid-June to September, the Isola Tiberina forms the picturesque backdrop for a season of outdoor cinema (p191), featuring Italian and international films, some shown in their original language. Tickets cost €6.

☆ Roma Incontro il Mondo   late Jun–Aug

From late June to August, Villa Ada is transformed into a colourful multi-ethnic village for this popular annual event (www.villaada.org). There's a laid-back party vibe and an excellent program of gigs ranging from reggae to jazz and world music.

🎋 Estate Romana   Jun–Sep

From June to September Rome's big summer festival (www.estateromana.comune.roma.it) involves everything from concerts and dance performances to book fairs, puppet shows and late-night museum openings.

🍺 Birròforum   Jun

Italy's largest craft-beer festival brings three days of al fresco merriment to Lungotevere Maresciallo Diaz, a stone's throw from the river. Taste beers from Italy's top artisan breweries and feast on fantastic street food (www.birroforum.it).

🎋 Festa dei Santi Pietro e Paolo   29 Jun

On 29 June Rome celebrates its two patron saints, Peter and Paul, with flower displays on St Peter's Square and festivities near the Basilica di San Paolo Fuori le Mura.

Above: Floral mosaic for Festa dei Santi Pietro e Paulo

Plan Your Trip
This Year in Rome

STEFANO MONTESI : CORBIS/CORBIS VIA GETTY IMAGES ©

July

07

Hot summer temperatures make sightseeing a physical endeavour, but come the cool of evening, the city's streets burst into life as locals come out to enjoy the summer festivities.

🏃 UEFA Euro 2020 – Quarter Final
4 Jul

The atmosphere at one of the quarter finals of UEFA's buzziest annual football (soccer) tournament, kicking off at Stadio Olimpico at 9pm, promises to be electric.

☆ Opera at the Terme di Caracalla
Jul

The haunting ruins of the 3rd-century Terme di Caracalla (p186) form the spectacular stage for the Teatro dell'Opera's summer season of music and ballet, with shows by big-name Italian and international performers.

🍷 Festa de' Noantri
late Jul

Trastevere celebrates its roots with a raucous street party (www.festadenoantri.it) in the last two weeks of the month. Events kick off with a religious procession and continue with much eating, drinking, dancing and praying.

☆ Concerti del Tempietto
Jul–mid-Oct

The Teatro di Marcello provides the atmospheric venue for classical-music concerts during the Concerti del Tempietto (www.tempietto.it) summer series.

Above: Festa de' Noantri

2020

THOOM/SHUTTERSTOCK ©

August

08

Rome melts in the heat as locals flee the city for their summer holidays. Many businesses shut down around 15 August, but hoteliers offer discounts and there are loads of summer events to enjoy.

✿ Festa della Madonna della Neve
5 Aug

On 5 August rose petals are showered on celebrants in the Basilica di Santa Maria Maggiore to commemorate a miraculous 4th-century snowfall.

✿ Notte di San Lorenzo
10 Aug

It's all about trying to catch a shooting star on this magical date when any Roman who hasn't fled to the seaside gathers outside to watch the Perseids meteor shower cast its magic in the dark night sky.

✿ Ferragosto
15 Aug

The Festival of the Assumption is celebrated with almost total shutdown as what seems like Rome's entire population decamps to the seaside.

♟ Lungo il Tevere
mid-Jun–Aug

Nightly crowds converge on the River Tiber for this popular summer-long event (p175). Stalls, clubs, bars, restaurants, cinemas, even dance floors line the river bank as Rome's nightlife goes al fresco.

DANILO DI GIOVANNI/NURPHOTO VIA GETTY IMAGES ©

⚽ Football Season Opening
Aug

As the rest of the city sizzles in the summer sun, Rome's footballers return. Italy's Serie A gets underway around 20 August and the city's rival AS Roma and SS Lazio fans can once more get their weekly fix.

Top: Lungo il Tevere
Bottom: Football match between AS Roma and Lazio

Plan Your Trip
This Year in Rome

GARI WYN WILLIAMS/ALAMY LIVE NEWS ©

September

Life returns to the city after the August torpor. The kids go back to school and locals return to work, but there's still a relaxed summer vibe and the weather's perfect. High-season rates apply.

🍷 Gay Village
Closing Concert   early Sep
The action-packed season at Rome's summertime gay club – complete with two dance floors, three restaurants, a food truck, a games zone and parties galore – at Testaccio's Città dell'Altra Economia draws to a close with its DJ-hot final concert (https://gayvillage.it).

☆ Roma Fringe Festival   Sep
From cabaret and stand-up comedy to performance art, premieres and contemporary takes on classic plays, independent theatre is celebrated at this fringe fest. Performances by Italian and international companies are staged at Villa Merced in the San Lorenzo neighbourhood (www.roma fringefestival.it).

✖ Taste of Roma   late Sep
A hot date for any Italy-bound, self-respecting foodie, this four-day extrava-ganza at Auditorium Parco della Musica is a hardcore celebration of food in Rome. Expect live cooking sessions, workshops by the city's top chefs, tastings and feasting galore.

🍷 Clubbing   late Sep
The end of the month is a good time for party-goers as Rome's main clubs return to town after their summer exodus. Curtain-raiser events promise new looks and big nights.

🍷 Romaeuropa   late Sep–Dec
Established international performers join emerging stars at Romaeuropa (http://romaeuropa.net), Rome's autumn festival of theatre, opera and dance. Events, staged across town from late September through to early December, range from avant-garde dance to installations, multimedia shows, recitals and readings.

Above: Taste of Roma

2020

TIZIANA FABI/AFP/GETTY IMAGES ©

10

October

Autumn is a good time to visit – the warm weather is holding, Romaeuropa ensures plenty of cultural action and, with the schools back, there are far fewer tourists around.

☆ Santa Cecilia Symphony Season early Oct

Rome's premier orchestra, the Orchestra dell'Accademia Nazionale di Santa Cecilia (www.santacecilia.it), returns to its home stage at the Auditorium Parco della Musica for the inauguration of its symphony season.

☆ Festa del Cinema di Roma mid-Oct

Held at the Auditorium Parco della Musica in late October, Rome's film festival rolls out the red carpet for Hollywood hot shots and bigwigs from Italian cinema. Consult the program on its website (www.romacinema fest.it).

⊙ Friday Night Openings at the Vatican late Apr–mid-Oct

October is your last chance to spend a Friday evening at the Vatican Museums, home of the Sistine Chapel and kilometres of priceless art treasures. Check online for guided-tour and concert ticketing information.

MUHARREMZ/SHUTTERSTOCK ©

Top: Viggo Mortensen at the Festa del Cinema di Roma;
Bottom: Ceiling fresco in the Vatican Museums (p40)

Plan Your Trip
This Year in Rome

November

Although the wettest month, November has its compensations – low-season prices, market stalls laden with bumper autumnal produce and no queues outside the big sights. On the events front, it's a fairly quiet time of year.

☙ Festa di Ognissanti   1 Nov
Celebrated as a national holiday, All Saints' Day is dedicated to all the saints of the Church. It's followed on 2 November by All Souls' Day, when Romans remember their dead by placing flowers on the tombs of loved ones.

☆ Roma Jazz Festival   Nov
Auditorium Parco della Musica and Casa del Jazz are key venues in the city's annual jazz festival, going strong for more than 40 years and luring many an international jazz star as well as homegrown musicians to Auditorium Parco della Musica and Casa del Jazz (www.romajazzfestival.it).

☆ Festival Internazionale di Musica e Arte Sacra   early Nov
The Vienna Philharmonic Orchestra and other top ensembles perform a series of classical concerts in Rome's papal basilicas and other churches. Usually held in early November, it was moved forward to September in 2019. Check programs on www.festivalmusicaeartesacra.net.

☆ Opera Season Opening   mid-Nov
Mid-month, the opera season gets underway at the city's opera house, the Teatro dell'Opera di Roma. The theatre is also home to the city's principal ballet corps, whose performance season starts in December.

Above: Opera performance, Teatro dell'Opera di Roma (p186)

2020

KRAFT74/SHUTTERSTOCK ©

December

The build-up to Christmas is a festive time – the Christmas lights go on, shopping takes on a new urgency and presepi (nativity scenes) appear across town, most spectacularly in St Peter's Square.

🎄 Festa dell'Immacolate Concezione   8 Dec
The pope, in his capacity as the Bishop of Rome, celebrates the Feast of the Immaculate Conception in Piazza di Spagna. Earlier in the day, Rome's fire brigade places a garland of flowers atop the Colonna dell'Immacolata in adjacent Piazza Mignanelli.

🎄 Piazza Navona Christmas Fair   Dec–6 Jan
Rome's showpiece baroque piazza becomes a festive market as fairground stalls set up, selling everything from stuffed toys to teeth-cracking *torrone* (nougat). Tradition dictates that the *befana* (witch) appears on Epiphany (6 January) to hand out sweets to children.

🍷 La Festa di Roma   31 Dec–1 Jan
Rome is a noisy place to be on New Year's Eve thanks to the ever-fabulous Festa di Roma, a massive street party from 9pm that

🎄 Festive Lights   8 Dec
The Mayor of Rome officially starts Rome's festive season by switching on the city's Christmas tree lights in Piazza Venezia. Over the river in the Vatican, a huge tree and life-size *presepe* (nativity scene) adorn St Peter's Square.

STEFANO_VALERI/SHUTTERSTOCK ©

fills downtown piazzas, bridges and streets with fireworks, live music, dancing, acrobatic performances, video installations, theatre shows, DJ sets and all sorts. Circo Massimo is a main stage (www.lafestadiroma.it).

Top: Decorative brooms, Piazza Navona Christmas Fair; Bottom: Festive lights, St Peter's Square (p49)

Plan Your Trip
Hotspots For...

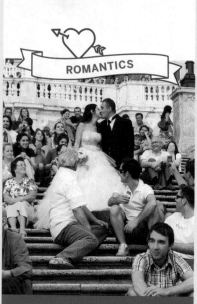

ROMANTICS

👁 **Via Margutta** (p89) Old-world cobbled lane peppered with ivy-laced *palazzi* (mansions), potted plants, old-stone fountains and antique boutiques.

👁 **Spanish Steps** (p94; pictured above) Join just-wedded couples snapping selfies on Rome's most famous staircase.

👁 **Pincio Hill Gardens** (p58) Watch the sun set from this romantic spot in the Villa Borghese.

🍷 **Stravinskij Bar** (p172) Dusk-time cocktails in an elegant courtyard garden.

🍴 **Marco Martini Restaurant** (p140) Gastronomic dining courtesy of Rome's youngest Michelin-starred chef in a lush garden pavilion.

HISTORY NERDS

👁 **Colosseum** (p36; pictured below) Encapsulates the drama of the ancient *caput mundi* (world capital).

👁 **Via Appia Antica** (p76) The first great superhighway, built in the 4th century BC – hike or pedal it.

☆ **Terme di Caracalla** (p186) Catch a summertime ballet or opera in these spectacular 3rd-century baths.

🍴 **La Ciambella** (p124) A laid-back eatery over an ancient bath complex.

🍴 **Antico Caffè Greco** (p130) Rome's oldest cafe, a former haunt of Casanova, Goethe, Wagner, Keats, Byron and Shelley.

ROMAN DOLCE VITA

⊙ **Trevi Fountain** (p86) The iconic fountain that starred in Fellini's 1960 movie *La dolce vita* – toss in a coin.

⊙ **Piazza Navona** (p64) Hub of Roman life, abuzz night and day with packed cafe terraces, hawkers and street artists.

✕ **La Tavernaccia** (p136) Traditional trattoria dining: a passionate affair for every self-respecting Roman.

♟ **Zuma Bar** (p112) Sophisticated hobnobbing over cocktails on the rooftop terrace of Palazzo Fendi.

⚵ **Bici & Baci** (p196) Urban spins by Vespa, Fiat 500 or three-wheeled Ape Calessino.

BARGAIN HUNTERS

🔒 **Mercado de Porta Portese** (p96) Have a Sunday-morning browse at Rome's busiest flea market.

⊙ **Campo de' Fiori** (p96; pictured above) Catch the frenetic sights and smells of this historic market square.

✕ **Bonci Pizzarium** (p129) Rome's best sliced pizza, with an array of gourmet toppings.

✕ **Panella** (p135) Good-value savoury snacks and cakes at this treasure-laden cafe-bakery.

♟ **Bar San Calisto** (p136) Cheap beer and velvety hot chocolate on Trastevere's most atmospheric summertime terrace.

NATURE LOVERS

⊙ **Villa Borghese** (p58) Rome's Central Park: leafy lanes, magnificent museums, and bikes for hire.

⊙ **Vatican Gardens** (p45; pictured above) Grottoes, fountains and fortifications of grandiose papal proportion.

⊙ **Pincio Hill Gardens** (p58) Dreamy balcony gardens above Piazza del Popolo.

⊙ **Orti Farnesiani** (p63) One of Europe's earliest botanical gardens, with breathtaking Forum views.

✕ **Il Giardino di Giulia e Fratelli** (p143) Lunch beneath perfumed orange trees in a bucolic garden along Via Appia Antica.

Plan Your Trip
Top Days in Rome

VIACHESLAV LOPATIN/SHUTTERSTOCK ©

Ancient Rome

The Colosseum is an appropriate high on which to start your odyssey in Rome. Next, head to the nearby crumbling scenic ruins of the Palatino, followed by the Roman Forum. After lunch enjoy 360-degree views from Il Vittoriano and classical art at the Capitoline Museums.

❶ Colosseum (p36)

More than any other monument, it's the Colosseum that symbolises the power and glory of ancient Rome. Visit its broken interior and imagine the roar of the 50,000-strong crowd as the gladiators fought for the spectators' entertainment.

◑ Colosseum to Palatino

🚶 Head south down the Via di San Gregorio to the Palatino.

❷ Palatino (p60)

The gardens and ruins of the Palatino (included with the Colosseum and Forum ticket or SUPER ticket) are an atmospheric place to explore, with great views across the Roman Forum. The Palatino was the most exclusive part of ancient Rome, home of the imperial palace, and is still today a hauntingly beautiful site.

◑ Palatino to Roman Forum

🚶 Still in the Palatino, follow the path down past the Vigna Barberino to enter the Roman Forum near the Arco di Tito.

❸ Roman Forum (p80)

Sprawled beneath the Palatino, the Forum was the empire's nerve centre, a teeming hive of law courts, temples, piazzas and

Day
01

shops. See where the Vestal Virgins lived and senators debated matters of state in the Curia.

○ **Roman Forum to Terre e Domus**

🏃 Exit the Forum on to Via dei Fori Imperiali and head up past the Imperial Forums to Terre e Domus near Trajan's Column.

❹ Lunch at Terre e Domus (p124)

Lunch on earthy Lazio food at this bright modern restaurant just off Piazza Venezia.

○ **Terre e Domus to Il Vittoriano**

🏃 Return to Piazza Venezia and follow it up to the mountainous monument Il Vittoriano.

❺ Il Vittoriano (p75)

Il Vittoriano is an ostentatious, overpowering mountain of white marble; love it or hate it, it's an impressive sight. For an even more mind-blowing vista, take the glass lift to the top and you'll be rewarded with 360-degree views across the whole of Rome.

○ **Il Vittoriano to the Capitoline Museums**

🏃 Descend from Il Vittoriano and head left to the sweeping staircase, La Cordonata. Climb the stairs to reach Piazza del Campidoglio and the Capitoline Museums.

❻ Capitoline Museums (p72)

Marking the summit of the Capitoline Hill (Campidoglio), Piazza del Campidoglio was designed by Michelangelo and is flanked by the world's oldest national museums. The Capitoline Museums harbour some of Rome's most spectacular ancient art, including the iconic depiction of Romulus and Remus sat under the *Lupa capitolina* (Capitoline Wolf).

From left: Ancient Roman busts, Capitoline Museums (p70); Roman Forum (p80)

Plan Your Trip
Top Days in Rome

Vatican City & Centro Storico

With some ancient monuments under your belt, it's time to hit the Vatican. Blow your mind at the Sistine Chapel and Vatican Museums, then complete your tour at St Peter's Basilica. Dedicate the afternoon to exploring the historic centre, including Piazza Navona and the Pantheon.

❶ Vatican Museums (p40)

There are about 7km of exhibits, so you'll never see everything, but try to take in the Pinacoteca, the Museo Pio-Clementino, Galleria delle Carte Geografiche, Stanze di Raffaello (Raphael Rooms) and the Sistine Chapel.

➲ Vatican Museums to Fa-Bìo

🚶 From the Vatican Museums entrance, turn downhill and follow the walls towards Piazza del Risorgimento. Take a left down Via Vespasiano and then the first right to Via Germanico and Fa-Bìo.

❷ Lunch at Fa-Bìo (p128)

Grab a light lunch at this tiny takeaway. It's very popular so you'll need to squeeze through to the counter to order your *panino*, salad or smoothie, all made with quality organic ingredients.

➲ Fa-Bìo to St Peter's Basilica

🚶 Double back to Piazza del Risorgimento, then follow the crowds to reach St Peter's Basilica.

Day
02

BELENOS/SHUTTERSTOCK ©

❸ St Peter's Basilica (p46)

Approaching St Peter's Square from the side, you'll see the basilica as Bernini intended: a surprise. Located at the head of the piazza, it is home to many artistic masterpieces including Michelangelo's *Pietà*. Its breathtaking dome offers magical views.

➲ St Peter's Basilica to Castel Sant'Angelo

🚶 From St Peter's Square, head down the monumental Via della Conciliazione to Castel Sant'Angelo.

❹ Castel Sant'Angelo (p49)

If you still have more energy for sightseeing, visit this landmark castle set around an ancient Roman tomb.

➲ Castel Sant'Angelo to Piazza Navona

🚶 Cross the river via Ponte Sant'Angelo, then follow the river eastwards for around 300m before turning right down Via G Zanardelli to reach Piazza Navona.

❺ Piazza Navona (p64)

This vast baroque square is a showpiece of the historic centre, and full of vibrant life.

The lozenge-shaped space is an echo of its ancient origins as the site of a stadium.

➲ Piazza Navona to the Pantheon

🚶 It's a short walk eastwards from Piazza Navona to Piazza della Rotonda, where you'll find the Pantheon.

❻ Pantheon (p50)

This 2000-year-old temple, now a church, is an extraordinary building; its innovative design has served to inspire generations of architects and engineers.

➲ Pantheon to Pianostrada

🚶 South from Via del Pantheon and Via delle Rotonda to Corso Vittorio Emanuele II, right along the latter, then left (south) along Largo dei Chiavari and its continuations to the restaurant.

❼ Dinner at Pianostrada (p125)

Savour an evening at Pianostrada, with its achingly cool vintage furnishings, modern cuisine and pretty terrace out back.

From left: Galleria delle Carte Geografiche (p43), Vatican Museums; Piazza Navona (p64)

Plan Your Trip
Top Days in Rome

ANDREI RYBACHUK/SHUTTERSTOCK ©

Villa Borghese, Tridente, Trevi & Trastevere

Start your day at the brilliant Museo e Galleria Borghese before a ramble through the shady avenues of Villa Borghese. Next, explore the Tridente neighbourhood, stopping off at the Spanish Steps en route to the Trevi Fountain and an evening in Trastevere.

Day
03

❶ Museo e Galleria Borghese (p56)

Book ahead and start your day at the Museo e Galleria Borghese, one of Rome's best art museums. The highlight is a series of astonishing sculptures by baroque genius Gian Lorenzo Bernini.

◗ Museo e Galleria Borghese to Villa Borghese

✈ Work your way through the leafy paths of Villa Borghese.

❷ Villa Borghese (p58)

Meander through the lovely, rambling park of Villa Borghese, formerly the playground of the mighty Borghese family. Make your way past Piazza di Siena and along tree-shaded lanes to the Pincio, a panoramic terrace offering great views across Rome.

◗ Villa Borghese to Piazza del Popolo

✈ From the Pincio terrace take the ramps and stairs down to Piazza del Popolo.

ANTON ALEKSENKO/GETTY IMAGES ©

❸ Piazza del Popolo (p89)

With its towering Egyptian obelisk, the monumental Piazza del Popolo dates from the 16th century. Nearby, Chiesa di Santa Maria del Popolo is home to remarkable art.

⊙ Piazza del Popolo to Il Margutta

🏃 Head along Via del Babuino, then turn left up pretty Via Margutta.

❹ Lunch at Il Margutta (p131)

Recharge the batteries at this chic art-gallery and lounge restaurant, an ode to modern vegetarian Roma cooking. You won't be disappointed.

⊙ Il Margutta to Spanish Steps

🏃 Head back to Via del Babuino and continue for 900m south to Piazza di Spagna.

❺ Spanish Steps (p94)

This glorious flight of ornamental rococo steps looks over Piazza di Spagna and the glittering, designer district Tridente.

⊙ Spanish Steps to Trevi Fountain

🏃 Take Via dei Due Macelli to Via del Tritone. Cross over to Via in Arcione until it becomes Via del Lavatore.

❻ Trevi Fountain (p86)

Join the crowds at this fantastical baroque fountain, where you can toss in a coin to ensure your return to Rome.

⊙ Trevi Fountain to Trastevere

🏃 Pick up Via del Corso and continue on to Piazza Venezia. Take tram 8 over the river to Trastevere.

❼ Trastevere (p130)

Spend the evening wandering Trastevere's charismatic streets, as popular with locals as they are with visitors. It's a beguiling place for an evening stroll before dinner.

From left: Villa Borghese (p58); Piazza del Popolo (p89)

Plan Your Trip
Top Days in Rome

LEV TSIMBLER/ALAMY STOCK PHOTO ©

Southern Rome & Monti

On your fourth day, venture out to Via Appia Antica and the catacombs. Start the afternoon by visiting the Museo Nazionale Romano: Palazzo Massimo alle Terme, then drop by the Basilica di Santa Maria Maggiore before seeing the day out in boho Monti.

Day

04

❶ Catacombe di San Sebastiano (p78)

Start your day underground on a tour of one of networks of catacombs open to the public. It's fascinating to see the tunnels where early Christians buried their dead.

➲ Catacombe di San Sebastiano to Villa di Massenzio

🏃 Head south about 100m along Via Appia and you'll see Villa di Massenzio on your left.

❷ Villa di Massenzio (p79)

The best-preserved part of Maxentius' 4th-century ruined palace is the Circo di Massenzio, once a racetrack boasting arena space for 10,000 people.

➲ Villa di Massenzio to Mausoleo di Cecilia Metella

🏃 Carry on 50m or so along Via Appia to the tomb of Cecilia Metella.

❸ Mausoleo di Cecilia Metella (p79)

With travertine walls and an interior deco-rated with a sculpted frieze bearing Gaelic

MANJIK/SHUTTERSTOCK ©

shields, ox skulls and festoons, this great, rotund tomb is an imposing sight.

🔵 Mausoleo di Cecilia Metella to Qui Nun Se More Mai

🏃 From the tomb, continue up the road for a few metres to Qui Nun Se More Mai.

④ Lunch at Qui Nun Se More Mai (p143)

Fortify yourself for the afternoon ahead with a lunch of hearty Roman pasta and expertly grilled meat at this rustic restaurant.

🔵 Qui Nun Se More Mai to Palazzo Massimo alle Terme

🚌 After lunch, hop on a bus to Termini station to visit the Palazzo Massimo alle Terme.

⑤ Palazzo Massimo alle Terme (p68)

This light-filled museum holds part of the Museo Nazionale Romano collection, including some superb classical sculpture and an unparalleled collection of ancient Roman frescoes.

🔵 Palazzo Massimo alle Terme to Basilica di Santa Maria Maggiore

🏃 From near the museum pick up Via Cavour and head downhill to reach Santa Maria Maggiore.

⑥ Basilica di Santa Maria Maggiore (p108)

One of Rome's four patriarchal basilicas, this monumental church stands on the hill where snow is said to have miraculously fallen in the summer of AD 358.

🔵 Basilica di Santa Maria Maggiore to Monti

🚌 From Piazza Esquilino, by the back of the basilica, pick up Via Urbana, which runs down to Monti.

⑦ Monti (p172)

There's plenty of evening action in Monti. Take your pick from the wine bars, cafes and restaurants that line its trendy cobbled streets.

From left: Portonaccio Sarcophagus, Palazzo Massimo alle Terme (p68); Basilica di Santa Maria Maggiore (p108)

Plan Your Trip

Need to Know

Daily Costs

Budget: Less than €110

- Dorm bed: €15–45

- Double room in a budget hotel: €60–130

- Pizza plus beer: €15

Midrange: €110–250

- Double room in a hotel: €100–200

- Local restaurant meal: €25–45

- Admission to Vatican Museums: €17

- Roma Pass, a 72-hour card covering museum entry and public transport: €38.50

**Top end:
More than €250**

- Double room in a four- or five-star hotel: €200 plus

- Top restaurant dinner: €45–160

- Opera ticket: €17–150

- City-centre taxi ride: €10–15

- Auditorium concert tickets: €20–90

Advance Planning

Two months before Book high-season accommodation.

One month before Check for concerts at www.auditorium. com. Book tickets for Colosseum tours and visits to the Museo e Galleria Borghese and Palazzo Farnese.

One to two weeks before Reserve tickets for the pope's weekly audience at St Peter's.

Few days before Reserve tables at top restaurants. Book tickets for the Vatican Museums and Colosseum (advisable to avoid queues).

Useful Websites

060608 (www.060608.it) Great for practical details on sights, transport, upcoming events and more.

Coopculture (www.coop culture.it) Information and ticket booking for Rome's monuments.

Lonely Planet (www.lonely planet.com/rome) Destination information, hotel bookings, traveller forum and more.

Romeing (www.romeing.it) English-language magazine with events listings, thematic sections and features.

Turismo Roma (www.turismo roma.it) Rome's official tourist website.

Vatican Museums (www.musei vaticani.va) Book tickets and guided tours to the museums and other Vatican sites.

Currency

euro (€)

Language

Italian

Visas

Not required by EU citizens. Not required by nationals of Australia, Canada, New Zealand and the USA for stays of up to 90 days.

Money

ATMs are widespread. Major credit cards are widely accepted but some smaller shops, trattorias and hotels might not take them.

Mobile Phones

Local SIM cards can be used in European, Australian and unlocked US phones. Other phones must be set to roaming.

Time

Western European Time (GMT/UTC plus one hour)

For more, see the
Survival Guide (p229)

When to Go

Spring and autumn are the best times – the weather's good and there are many festivals and outdoor events on. But it's also busy and peak rates apply.

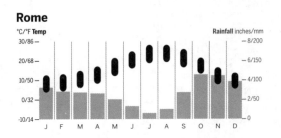

Arriving in Rome

Leonardo da Vinci (Fiumicino) Airport Leonardo Express trains to Stazione Termini 6.08am to 11.23pm, €14; slower FL1 trains to Trastevere, Ostiense and Tiburtina stations 5.57am to 10.42pm, €8; buses to Stazione Termini 6.05am to 12.40am, €6-6.90; airport-to-hotel shuttles from €22 per person; taxis €48 (fixed fare to within the Aurelian walls that mark out the city centre).

Ciampino Airport Buses to Stazione Termini 4am to 12.15am, €6; airport-to-hotel shuttles €25 per person; taxis €30 (fixed fare to within the Aurelian walls).

Stazione Termini Airport buses and trains, and international trains, arrive at Stazione Termini. From there, continue by bus, metro or taxi.

Getting Around

Public transport includes buses, trams, the metro and a suburban train network. The main hub is Stazione Termini. Tickets, which come in various forms, are valid for all forms of transport. Children under 10 travel free.

Metro The metro is quicker than surface transport, but the network is limited. Two main lines serve the centre, A (orange) and B (blue), crossing at Stazione Termini. Trains run between 5.30am and 11.30pm (to 1.30am on Fridays and Saturdays).

Buses Most routes pass through Stazione Termini. Buses run from approximately 5.30am until midnight, with limited services throughout the night.

Foot Walking is the best way of getting around the *centro storico* (historic centre).

What to Take

o Purse with strap – petty theft can be a problem.

o Water bottle – refill it at drinking fountains.

o Electrical adapter and phone charger.

What to Wear

o Dress comfortably – you'll be walking a lot. Trainers or comfy shoes will help on the cobbled streets.

o Appearances matter in Rome. Suitable wear for men is generally trousers (pants) and shirts or polo shirts; for women, skirts, trousers or dresses.

o Shorts, T-shirts and sandals are fine in summer, but strict dress codes apply at St Peter's Basilica and the Vatican Museums.

o Smart casual is the evening-wear norm. A waterproof jacket is useful in spring and autumn.

Plan Your Trip
What's New

ALEXANDRA BRUZZESE/LONELY PLANET ©

SUPER Ticket

The snappily titled **SUPER Ticket** is a new pass covering the Colosseum, Palatino and Roman Forum. Costing €6 more than the regular entrance ticket, it's valid for two days and gives access to a series of extra 'internal' sights, such as the Museo Palatino, which are off-limits to regular ticket-holders.

Wine Culture

Wine aficionados on the lookout for new labels will enjoy Rimessa Roscioli (p170). Brought to you by Rome's foodie Roscioli family, it's a wine bar–bistro where tastings are tailored to your preferences and wines are paired with excellent Italian food. In Testaccio, natural-wine specialist Barnaba (p177) is the 'hood's new hot ticket.

VyTa Enoteca Regionale del Lazio

Roman architect Daniela Colli is the contemporary design talent behind VyTA Enoteca Regionale del Lazio (p133), a

superglam wine bar–restaurant with sleek interiors and gourmet food and wine from Rome's surrounding Lazio region.

Niji Roma

Rome's love affair with craft cocktails shows no sign of waning, as witnessed by Niji Roma (p112), a mellow, stylish and tastefully cool Trastevere bar.

Fashion Openings

Ladies yearning for elegant yet comfortable fashions are well served at Roman designer Livia Risi's new Trastevere boutique. In the historic centre, effortlessly chic new concept store Chez Dede (p151) showcases everything from bags and ceramics to limited-edition perfumes.

Above: Rimessa Roscioli (p170)

Plan Your Trip
For Free

Need to Know

Transport Holders of the Roma Pass (48/72 hours €28/38.50) are entitled to free public transport.

Wi-fi Free wi-fi is available in many hostels, hotels, bars and cafes.

Tours To take a free tour check out www.newrome freetour.com.

Free Art

Churches All free to enter, including showstoppers St Peter's Basilica (p46), Basilica di San Pietro in Vincoli (p109), Chiesa di San Luigi dei Francesi (p67) and Basilica di Santa Maria del Popolo (p88).

Vatican Museums The Vatican Museums (p41) are free on the last Sunday of the month.

State Museums All state-run museums are *gratis* on the first Sunday of the month.

Street Art Rome boasts many magnificent pieces, such as *Triumphs & Laments* (p197) illustrating scenes from Roman history along the Tiber, and they're all free.

Free Monuments

Trevi Fountain You don't have to spend a penny to admire the Trevi Fountain (p86), although most people throw a coin into the water to ensure their return to Rome.

Bocca della Verità According to legend, if you tell a lie with your hand in the Mouth of Truth (p75), it'll bite it off.

Spanish Steps The ideal perch for a sightseeing time-out, the Spanish Steps (p94) have long been a favourite visitor hang-out.

Piazzas & Parks

Piazzas People-watching on Rome's piazzas is a signature city experience. Top spots include Piazza Navona (p64), Campo de' Fiori (p96), Piazza di Spagna (p95) and Piazza del Popolo (p89).

Parks Stroll for free in lush green parks such as Villa Borghese (p58) and Villa Celimontana (p103).

Above: *Moses* by Michelangelo, Basilica di San Pietro in Vincoli (p109)

Plan Your Trip
Family Travel

IMGORTHAND/GETTY IMAGES ©

Need to Know

Getting Around Cobbled streets make getting around with a pram or pushchair difficult.

Eating Out In a restaurant ask for a *mezza porzione* (child's portion) and *seggiolone* (high chair).

Supplies Buy baby formula and sterilising solution at pharmacies. Disposable nappies (diapers; *pannolini*) are available from supermarkets and pharmacies.

Discounts Visitors aged under 18 years get in free at state-run museums, while city-run museums are free for children under six years, and discounted for six- to 25-year-olds.

Transport Children under 10 years travel free on all public transport in the city.

History for Kids

Everyone wants to see the Colosseum (p36) and it doesn't disappoint, especially if accompanied by tales of bloodthirsty gladiators and hungry lions. For maximum effect, prep your kids beforehand with a Rome-based film.

Virtual reality brings the Terme di Caracalla (p102) back to life courtesy of headsets that re-create the massive baths as they looked in their heyday.

Parents and older kids will enjoy the multimedia tour of Roman excavations beneath **Palazzo Valentini** (Map p246; ☑06 2276 1280; www.palazzovalentini.it; Via Foro Traiano 85; adult/reduced €12/8; ⊙9.30am-6.30pm Wed-Mon; 👪; ⓂBarberini).

Hands-on Activities

Kids love throwing things, so they'll enjoy tossing coins into the Trevi Fountain (p86). And if they ask, an average of about €3000 is thrown in daily.

Another favourite is putting your hand in the Bocca della Verità (Mouth of Truth; p75). Local legend has it that if you tell a fib, the mouth will slam shut and bite your hand off.

Near Piazza del Popolo, Explora – Museo dei Bambini di Roma (p59) is a hands-on museum for kids under 12, with interactive displays and a free play park.

NIPPICH SOMSAARD/SHUTTERSTOCK ©

Run in the Park

When the time comes to let the kids off the leash, head to Villa Borghese (p58), the most central of Rome's main parks. There's plenty of space to run around in – though it's not absolutely car-free – and you can hire bicycles, including four-seater family bikes.

The lovely park at Villa Celimontana (p103) on Celio Hill is a peaceful spot for a game of tag and a relaxed family picnic on grassy banks.

How to Scare Teens

Spook your teens with a trip to the Via Appia Antica (p76) catacombs, with tunnels full of creepy tombs and ancient burial chambers.

Definitely for older kids only, the crypt under the Convento dei Cappuccini (p115) is a decidedly scary place where everything is artfully crafted from human bones.

★ Best Snack Joints

Bonci Pizzarium (p129)

Trapizzino (p140)

Forno Roscioli (p125)

Antica Norcineria Iacozzilli (p137)

Gelateria dei Gracchi (p129)

Food for Kids

Roman-style fast food is always a hit. *Pizza al taglio* (pizza by the slice) is cheap (about €1 buys two small slices of pizza *bianca* – with salt and olive oil) and easy to buy from one of hundreds of takeaways around town.

Or keep the whole family sweet with some gelato (a type of ice cream), made in a rainbow of colourful flavours and served in *coppette* (tubs), *coni* (cones) or coated in chocolate to become a rather irresistible gelato bar.

From left: Throwing coins into the Trevi Fountain (p86); Gelato

TOP EXPERIENCES

The very best to see and do

Colosseum

A monument to raw, merciless power, the Colosseum is the most thrilling of Rome's ancient sights. It was here that gladiators met in mortal combat and condemned prisoners fought off wild beasts in front of baying, bloodthirsty crowds. Two thousand years on and it's Italy's top tourist attraction, drawing more than six million visitors a year.

Great for...

❶ Need to Know

Colosseo; Map p246; ☏06 3996 7700; www.parcocolosseo.it; Piazza del Colosseo; adult/reduced incl Roman Forum & Palatino €16/7.50, SUPER ticket €22/13.50; ⊘8.30am-1hr before sunset; ⓂColosseo

★ **Top Tip**

Beat the queues: buy your ticket at the Palatino (Via di San Gregorio 30).

Built by Vespasian (r AD 69–79) in the grounds of Nero's vast Domus Aurea complex, the arena was inaugurated in AD 80, eight years after it had been commissioned. To mark the occasion, Vespasian's son and successor, Titus (r AD 79–81), staged games that lasted 100 days and nights, during which 5000 animals were slaughtered. Trajan (r AD 98–117) later topped this, holding a marathon 117-day killing spree involving 9000 gladiators and 10,000 animals.

The 50,000-seat arena was originally known as the Flavian Amphitheatre, and although it was Rome's most fearsome arena it wasn't the biggest – the Circo Massimo could hold up to 250,000 people. The name Colosseum, when introduced in medieval times, was a reference not to its size but to the Colosso di Nerone, a giant statue of Nero that stood nearby.

With the fall of the Roman Empire in the 5th century, the Colosseum was abandoned and gradually became overgrown. In the Middle Ages it served as a fortress for two of the city's warrior families, the Frangipani and the Annibaldi. Later, during the Renaissance and baroque periods, it was plundered of its precious travertine, and the marble stripped from it was used to make huge palaces such as Palazzo Venezia, Palazzo Barberini and Palazzo Cancelleria.

More recently, pollution and vibrations caused by traffic and the metro have taken a toll. To help counter this, it was given a major clean-up between 2014 and 2016, the first in its 2000-year history, as part of a

€25-million restoration project sponsored by the luxury shoemaker Tod's.

Exterior

The outer walls have three levels of arches, framed by Ionic, Doric and Corinthian columns. These were originally covered in travertine, and marble statues filled the niches on the 2nd and 3rd storeys. The upper level, punctuated with windows and slender Corinthian pilasters, had supports for 240 masts that held up a huge canvas awning over the arena, shielding spectators from sun and rain. The 80 entrance arches, known as *vomitoria*, allowed the spectators to enter and be seated in a matter of minutes.

Arena

The stadium originally had a wooden floor covered in sand – *harena* in Latin, hence the word 'arena' – to prevent combatants from slipping and to soak up spilt blood.

From the floor, trapdoors led down to the hypogeum, a subterranean complex of corridors, cages and lifts beneath the arena floor.

Stands

The *cavea,* for spectator seating, was divided into three tiers: magistrates and senior officials sat in the lowest tier, wealthy citizens in the middle, and the plebeians in the highest tier. Women (except for Vestal Virgins) were relegated to the cheapest sections at the top. As in modern stadiums, tickets were numbered and spectators assigned a seat in a specific sector. The podium, a terrace in front of the tiered seating, was for the emperor, senators and other VIPs.

Hypogeum

The hypogeum served as the stadium's backstage area. Sets for the various battle scenes were prepared here and hoisted up to the arena by a complicated system of pulleys. The hypogeum is also where caged animals were kept and where gladiators would gather before showtime, having come in through an underground corridor from the nearby Ludus Magnus (gladiator school).

> ★ **Don't Miss**
>
> The Belvedere (top three tiers) and the hypogeum's network of dank tunnels beneath the main arena. Visits require advance booking and cost an extra €9.

ADISA/SHUTTERSTOCK ©

> ✕ **Take a Break**
>
> Quench your thirst post-Colosseum over a chilled bottle of craft beer at **BrewDog Roma** (Map p246; ☏06 4555 6932; www.brewdog.com/bars/worldwide/roma; Via delle Terme di Tito 80; ☉noon-1am Sun-Thu, to 2am Fri & Sat; Ⓜ Colosseo).

Modern Bramante Staircase, Museo Pio-Clementino

LUBOSLAV TILES/SHUTTERSTOCK ©

Vatican Museums

Founded in the 16th century, the Vatican Museums boast one of the world's greatest art collections. Highlights include spectacular classical statuary, rooms frescoed by Raphael, and the Michelangelo-decorated Sistine Chapel.

Housing the museums are the lavishly decorated halls and galleries of the Palazzo Apostolico Vaticano. This vast 5.5-hectare complex consists of two palaces – the Vatican palace (nearer to St Peter's) and the Palazzetto di Belvedere – joined by two long galleries. Inside are three courtyards: the Cortile della Pigna, the Cortile della Biblioteca and, to the south, the Cortile del Belvedere. You'll never cover it all in one day, so it pays to be selective.

Pinacoteca

Often overlooked by visitors, the papal picture gallery contains Raphael's last work, *La Trasfigurazione* (Transfiguration; 1517–20), actually completed by his students after his death in 1520. There are also paintings by Giotto, Fra Angelico, Filippo

---

Great for...

Don't Miss

Raphael's last painting, *La Trasfigurazione* (Transfiguration), in the Pinacoteca.

Stained glass, Vatican Museums

ℹ Need to Know

Musei Vaticani; Map p253; ☎06 6988 4676;
www.museivaticani.va; Viale Vaticano; adult/
reduced €17/8; ⊘9am-6pm Mon-Sat, to 2pm
last Sun of month, last entry 2hr before close;
🚇Piazza del Risorgimento, ⓂOttaviano-San
Pietro

✕ Take a Break

Snack on scissor-cut squares of
gourmet pizza at Bonci Pizzarium
(p129).

★ Top Tip

To avoid queues, book tickets online
(http://biglietteriamusei.vatican.va/
musei/tickets/do; plus €4 booking fee).

Lippi, Perugino, Titian, Pietro da Cortona
and Caravaggio. Leonardo da Vinci's haunting *San Gerolamo* (St Jerome; c 1480) was
never finished.

Museo Chiaramonti & Braccio Nuovo

The Museo Chiaramonti is effectively the
long corridor that runs down the eastern
side of the Palazzetto di Belvedere. Its walls
are lined with thousands of statues and
busts representing everything from immor-
tal gods to playful cherubs and unattractive
Roman patricians. Near the end of the hall,
off to the right, is the Braccio Nuovo (New
Wing), which contains a famous statue
of the Nile as a reclining god covered by
16 babies.

Museo Pio-Clementino

This stunning museum contains some
of the Vatican Museums' finest classical
statuary, including the peerless *Apollo
Belvedere* and the 1st-century *Laocoön,*
both in the **Cortile Ottagono** (Octagonal Courtyard). Before you go into the
courtyard, take a moment to admire the
1st-century *Apoxyomenos,* one of the
earliest known sculptures to depict a figure
with a raised arm.

To the left as you enter the courtyard,
the *Apollo Belvedere* is a 2nd-century
Roman copy of a 4th-century-BC Greek
bronze. A beautifully proportioned
representation of the sun god Apollo, it's
considered one of the great masterpieces
of classical sculpture. Nearby, the *Laocoön*
depicts a muscular Trojan priest and his
two sons in mortal struggle with two sea
serpents.

Back inside, the **Sala degli Animali** is filled with sculpted creatures and some magnificent 4th-century mosaics. Continuing on, you come to the **Sala delle Muse**, centred on the *Torso Belvedere*, another of the museum's must-sees. A fragment of a muscular 1st-century-BC Greek sculpture, it was found in Campo de' Fiori and used by Michelangelo as a model for his *ignudi* (male nudes) in the Sistine Chapel.

The next room, the **Sala Rotonda**, contains a number of colossal statues, including a gilded-bronze *Ercole* (Hercules) and an exquisite floor mosaic. The enormous basin in the centre of the room was found at Nero's Domus Aurea and is made out of a single piece of red porphyry stone.

Museo Gregoriano Egizio

Founded by Gregory XVI in 1839, this museum contains pieces taken from Egypt in Roman times. The collection is small but there are fascinating exhibits, including a fragmented statue of the pharaoh Ramses II on his throne, vividly painted sarcophagi dating from around 1000 BC, and a macabre mummy.

Museo Gregoriano Etrusco

At the top of the 18th-century Simonetti staircase, this museum displays artefacts unearthed in the Etruscan tombs of northern Lazio, as well as a superb collection of vases and Roman antiquities. In Room III admire the *Marte di Todi* (Mars of Todi), a black bronze of a warrior dating to the late 5th century BC.

Braccio Nuovo (p41)

Galleria delle Carte Geografiche & Sala Sobieski

The last of three galleries on the upper floor – the other two are the **Galleria dei Candelabri** (Gallery of the Candelabra) and the **Galleria degli Arazzi** (Tapestry Gallery) – the 120m-long Galleria delle Carte Geografiche is hung with 40 huge topographical maps. These were created between 1580 and 1583 for Pope Gregory XIII based on drafts by Ignazio Danti, one of the leading cartographers of his day.

> **★ Minimising the Crowds**
>
> Tuesdays and Thursdays are the quietest days to visit. Wednesday mornings are also good; on other days afternoons are better than mornings. Avoid Mondays, when many other museums are shut, and rainy days.

Beyond the gallery, the **Sala Sobieski** is named after an enormous 19th-century painting depicting the victory of the Polish king John III Sobieski over the Turks in 1683.

Stanze di Raffaello

These four frescoed chambers, currently undergoing partial restoration, were part of Pope Julius II's private apartments. Raphael himself painted the Stanza della Segnatura (1508–11) and the Stanza d'Eliodoro (1512–14), while the Stanza dell'Incendio (1514–17) and Sala di Costantino (1517–24) were decorated by students following his designs.

The first room you come to is the **Sala di Costantino**, which features a huge fresco depicting Constantine's defeat of Maxentius at the battle of Milvian Bridge.

The **Stanza d'Eliodoro**, which was used for private audiences, takes its name from the *Cacciata d'Eliodoro* (Expulsion of Heliodorus from the Temple), an allegorical work reflecting Pope Julius II's policy of forcing foreign powers off Church lands. To its right, the *Messa di Bolsena* (Mass of Bolsena) shows Julius paying homage to the relic of a 13th-century miracle at the lakeside town of Bolsena. Next is the *Incontro di Leone Magno con Attila* (Encounter of Leo the Great with Attila) by Raphael and his school, and, on the fourth wall, the *Liberazione di San Pietro* (Liberation of St Peter), a brilliant work illustrating Raphael's masterful ability to depict light.

The **Stanza della Segnatura**, Julius' study and library, was the first room that Raphael painted, and it's here that you'll find his great masterpiece, *La Scuola di Atene* (The School of Athens), featuring philosophers and scholars gathered around Plato and Aristotle. The seated figure in

> **★ Top Tip**
>
> Exhibits are simply labelled: hire an audio guide (€8) or buy the excellent *Guide to the Vatican Museums and City* (€13).

MISTERVLAD/SHUTTERSTOCK ©

front of the steps is believed to be Michelangelo, while the figure of Plato is said to be a portrait of Leonardo da Vinci, and Euclid (the bald man bending over) is Bramante. Raphael also included a self-portrait in the lower right corner – he's the second figure from the right.

The most famous work in the **Stanza dell'Incendio di Borgo** is the *Incendio di Borgo* (Fire in the Borgo), which depicts Pope Leo IV extinguishing a fire by making the sign of the cross. The ceiling was painted by Raphael's master, Perugino.

Sistine Chapel

The jewel in the Vatican's crown, the Sistine Chapel (Cappella Sistina) is home to two of the world's most famous works of art: Michelangelo's ceiling frescoes and his *Giudizio Universale* (Last Judgment).

The chapel was originally built for Pope Sixtus IV, after whom it's named, and was consecrated on 15 August 1483. However, apart from the wall frescoes and floor, little remains of the original decor, which was sacrificed to make way for Michelangelo's two masterpieces. The first, the ceiling, was commissioned by Pope Julius II and painted between 1508 and 1512; the second, the spectacular *Giudizio Universale,* was painted between 1535 and 1541.

Michelangelo's ceiling design, best viewed from the chapel's main entrance in the far east wall, covers the entire 800-sq-metre surface. With painted architectural features and a cast of colourful biblical characters, it's centred on nine panels depicting stories from the book of Genesis.

As you look up from the east wall, the first panel is the *Drunkenness of Noah,* followed by *The Flood* and the *Sacrifice of Noah.* Next, *Original Sin & Banishment from the Garden of Eden* famously depicts Adam and Eve being sent packing after accepting the forbidden fruit from Satan, represented by a snake with the body of a woman coiled around a tree. The *Creation of Eve* is then followed by the *Creation of Adam.* This, one of the most famous im-

ages in Western art, shows a bearded God pointing his finger at Adam, thus bringing him to life. Completing the sequence are the *Separation of Land from Sea;* the *Creation of the Sun, Moon & Plants;* and the *Separation of Light from Darkness,* featuring a fearsome God reaching out to touch the sun. Set around the central panels are 20 athletic male nudes, known as *ignudi.*

Opposite, on the west wall, is Michelangelo's mesmeric *Giudizio Universale,* showing Christ – in the centre near the top – passing sentence over the souls of the dead as they are torn from their graves to face him. The saved get to stay in heaven (in the upper right); the damned are sent down to face the demons in hell (in the bottom right).

Near the bottom, on the right, you'll see a man with donkey ears and a snake wrapped

Ceiling of the Sistine Chapel

around him. This is Biagio de Cesena, the papal master of ceremonies, who was a fierce critic of Michelangelo's composition. Another famous figure is St Bartholomew, just beneath Christ, holding his own flayed skin. The face in the skin is said to be a self-portrait of Michelangelo, its anguished look reflecting the artist's tormented faith.

The chapel's walls also boast superb frescoes. Painted between 1481 and 1482 by a crack team of Renaissance artists, including Botticelli, Ghirlandaio, Pinturicchio, Perugino and Luca Signorelli, they represent events in the lives of Moses (to the left looking at the *Giudizio Universale*) and Christ (to the right). Highlights include Botticelli's *Temptations of Christ* and Perugino's *Handing over of the Keys*.

As well as providing a showcase for priceless art, the Sistine Chapel serves an important religious function as the place where the conclave meets to elect a new pope.

★ **Did You Know?**

A popular Sistine Chapel myth is that Michelangelo painted the ceilings lying down. In fact, he designed a curved scaffolding that allowed him to work standing up.

★ **Top Tip**

Up to a third of the Vatican is covered by the perfectly manicured **Vatican Gardens** (Map p253; adult/reduced incl Vatican Museums €33/24, by open-air bus €37/23; ⊙ by reservation only). Visits are by guided tour only – either on foot (two hours) or by open-air bus (45 minutes). Book at least a week in advance.

S-F/SHUTTERSTOCK ©

View along Via della Conciliazione to the basilica

St Peter's Basilica

In this city of outstanding churches, none can hold a candle to St Peter's, Italy's largest, richest and most spectacular basilica.

The original church was commissioned by the emperor Constantine and built around 349 on the site where St Peter is said to have been buried between AD 64 and 67. Like many medieval churches, it fell into disrepair and it wasn't until the mid-15th century that it was restored, first by Pope Nicholas V and then, more successfully, by Julius II.

In 1506 construction began on a design by Bramante, but building ground to a halt when the architect died in 1514. In 1547 Michelangelo took on the project, simplifying Bramante's plans and creating designs for what would become his greatest architectural achievement: the dome. But he didn't live to see it built: Giacomo della Porta, Domenico Fontana and Carlo Maderno completed the basilica, finally consecrated in 1626.

Great for...

Don't Miss

Climbing the (numerous, steep and tiring, but worth it) steps of the dome for views over Rome.

Michelangelo's *Pietà*

DROP OF LIGHT/SHUTTERSTOCK ©

❶ Need to Know

Basilica di San Pietro; Map p253; ☑06 6988 3731; www.vatican.va; St Peter's Sq; ⏱7am-7pm Apr-Sep, to 6pm Oct-Mar; ⛟Piazza del Risorgimento, ⓂOttaviano-San Pietro; FREE

✕ Take a Break

For a salad or tasty *panino* stop off at hit organic takeaway Fa-Bìo (p128).

★ Top Tip

Strict dress codes are enforced: no shorts, miniskirts or bare shoulders.

Facade

Built between 1608 and 1612, Maderno's immense facade is 48m high and 115m wide. Eight 27m-high columns support the upper attic on which 13 statues stand representing Christ the Redeemer, St John the Baptist and the 11 apostles. The central balcony, the **Loggia della Benedizione**, is where the pope stands to deliver his *Urbi et Orbi* blessing at Christmas and Easter.

Interior

At the beginning of the right aisle is Michelangelo's hauntingly beautiful *Pietà*. Sculpted when the artist was 25 (in 1499), it's the only work he ever signed; his signature is etched into the sash across the Madonna's breast.

On a pillar just beyond the *Pietà,* Carlo Fontana's gilt and bronze **monument to Queen Christina of Sweden** commemorates the far-from-holy Swedish monarch who converted to Catholicism in 1655.

Moving on, you'll come to the **Cappella di San Sebastiano**, home of Pope John Paul II's tomb, and the **Cappella del Santissimo Sacramento**, a sumptuously decorated baroque chapel.

Dominating the centre of the basilica is Bernini's 29m-high **baldachin**. Supported by four spiral columns and made with bronze taken from the Pantheon, it stands over the **papal altar**, which itself stands over St Peter's original grave.

Above the baldachin, Michelangelo's **dome** soars to a height of 119m. Based on Brunelleschi's cupola in Florence, it's supported by four massive stone **piers** named after the saints whose statues adorn the Bernini-designed niches – Longinus, Helena, Veronica and Andrew.

At the base of the **Pier of St Longinus** is Arnolfo di Cambio's much-loved 13th-century bronze **statue of St Peter**, whose right foot has been worn down by centuries of caresses.

Dominating the tribune behind the altar is Bernini's extraordinary **Cattedra di San Pietro**, centred on a wooden seat that was once thought to have been St Peter's, but in fact dates to the 9th century.

Right of the throne, Bernini's **monument to Urban VIII** depicts the pope flanked by Charity and Justice.

Near the head of the left aisle are the so-called **Stuart monuments**. On the right is the monument to Clementina Sobieska, wife of James Stuart, by Filippo Barigioni, and on the left is Canova's vaguely erotic monument to the last three members of the Stuart clan, the pretenders to the English throne who died in exile in Rome.

Dome

From the **dome** (Map p253; with/without lift €10/8; ☉8am-6pm Apr-Sep, to 5pm Oct-Mar) entrance on the right of the basilica's main portico, you can walk the 551 steps to the top or take a small lift halfway and then follow on foot for the last 320 steps. Either way, it's a long, steep climb. But the top rewards with stunning views.

Museo Storico Artistico

Accessed from the left nave, the **Museo Storico Artistico** (Tesoro, Treasury; Map p253; ☑06 6988 1840; €5 incl audioguide; ☉9am-6.10pm Apr-Sep, to 5.10pm Oct-Mar, last entrance 30min before closing) sparkles with sacred relics. Highlights include a tabernacle by Donatello and the 6th-century *Crux Vaticana* (Vatican Cross).

Interior of St Peter's Basilica

Vatican Grottoes

Extending beneath the basilica, the **Vatican Grottoes** (Map p253; ⏱8am-5pm Apr-Sep, to 4pm Oct-Mar) `FREE` contain the tombs and sarcophagi of numerous popes, as well as several columns from the original 4th-century basilica. The entrance is in the Pier of St Andrew.

St Peter's Tomb

Excavations beneath the basilica have uncovered part of the original church and what archaeologists believe is the **Tomb**

> ★ **Local Knowledge**
>
> Near the main entrance, a red floor disc marks the spot where Charlemagne and later Holy Roman emperors were crowned by the pope.

MANJIK/SHUTTERSTOCK ©

of St Peter (Map p253; ☎06 6988 5318; www. scavi.va; €13). Visits are by guided tour.

What's Nearby?

St Peter's Square   Piazza

(Piazza San Pietro; Map p253; 🚇Piazza del Risorgimento; Ⓜ️Ottaviano-San Pietro) Overlooked by St Peter's Basilica, the Vatican's central square was laid out between 1656 and 1667 to a design by Gian Lorenzo Bernini. Seen from above, it resembles a giant keyhole with two semicircular colonnades, each consisting of four rows of Doric columns, encircling a giant ellipse that straightens out to funnel believers into the basilica. The effect was deliberate – Bernini described the colonnades as representing 'the motherly arms of the church'.

Castel Sant'Angelo   Museum, Castle

(Map p250; ☎06 681 91 11; www.castelsant angelo.beniculturali.it; Lungotevere Castello 50; adult/reduced €14/7, free 1st Sunday of the month Oct-Mar; ⏱9am-7.30pm, ticket office to 6.30pm; 🚇Piazza Pia) With its chunky round keep, this castle is an instantly recognisable landmark. Built as a mausoleum for the emperor Hadrian, it was converted into a papal fortress in the 6th century and named after an angelic vision that Pope Gregory the Great had in 590. Nowadays, the castle houses the **Museo Nazionale di Castel Sant'Angelo** and its eclectic collection of paintings, sculpture, military memorabilia and medieval firearms.

> ★ **Free Tours**
>
> October to late May, free two-hour basilica tours in English are run by seminarians from the Pontifical North American College (www.pnac.org), usually departing 2.15pm Monday, Wednesday and Friday from the Ufficio Pellegrini e Turisti (p233).

Pantheon

A striking 2000-year-old temple, now a church, the Pantheon is Rome's best-preserved ancient monument and one of the Western world's most influential buildings. Its greying, pockmarked exterior may look aged, but inside it's a different story: it is both unique and exhilarating to pass through its vast bronze doors and gaze up at the largest unreinforced concrete dome ever built.

Great for...

ℹ **Need to Know**

Map p250; www.pantheonroma.com; Piazza della Rotonda; ⏰8.30am-7.30pm Mon-Sat, 9am-6pm Sun; 🚌Largo di Torre Argentina; FREE

★ **Top Tip**

Mass is celebrated at the Pantheon at 5pm on Saturdays and 10.30am on Sundays.

In its current form the Pantheon dates to around AD 125. The original temple, built by Marcus Agrippa in 27 BC, burnt down in AD 80, and although it was rebuilt by Domitian, it was struck by lightning and destroyed for a second time in AD 110. The emperor Hadrian had it reconstructed between AD 118 and 125, and it's this version that you see today.

Hadrian's temple was dedicated to the classical gods – the name Pantheon is a derivation of the Greek words *pan* (all) and *theos* (god) – but in 608 it was consecrated as a Christian church and it's now officially known as Basilica di Santa Maria ad Martyres.

Thanks to this consecration, it was spared the worst of the medieval plundering that reduced many of Rome's ancient buildings to near dereliction. But it didn't escape entirely unscathed – gilded-bronze roof tiles were removed and bronze from the portico was used by Bernini for the baldachin at St Peter's Basilica.

Exterior

The dark-grey pitted exterior faces on to busy, cafe-lined Piazza della Rotonda. And while its facade is somewhat the worse for wear, it's still an imposing sight. The monumental entrance **portico** consists of 16 Corinthian columns, each 11.8m high and made of Egyptian granite, supporting a triangular **pediment**. Behind the columns, two 20-tonne **bronze doors**, 16th-century restorations of the original portal, give on to the central rotunda. Rivets and holes in the building's brickwork indicate where marble-veneer panels were originally placed.

Interior of the Pantheon

Inscription

For centuries the inscription under the pediment – M:AGRIPPA.L.F.COS.TERTIUM.FECIT or 'Marcus Agrippa, son of Lucius, in his third consulate built this' – led scholars to think that the current building was Agrippa's original temple. However, 19th-century excavations revealed traces of an earlier temple and historians realised that Hadrian had simply kept Agrippa's original inscription.

Interior

Though impressive from outside, it's only when you get inside that you can appreciate the Pantheon's full size. With light

IN GREEN/SHUTTERSTOCK ©

streaming in through the **oculus** (the 8.7m-diameter hole in the centre of the dome), the cylindrical marble-clad interior seems vast.

Opposite the entrance is the church's main **altar**, over which hangs a 7th-century icon of the *Madonna col Bambino* (Madonna and Child). To the left are the tombs of the artist Raphael, King Umberto I and Margherita of Savoy. Over on the opposite side of the rotunda is the tomb of King Vittorio Emanuele II.

Dome

The Pantheon's dome, considered to be the Romans' most important architectural achievement, was the largest dome in the world until the 15th century when Brunelleschi beat it with his Florentine cupola. Its harmonious appearance is due to a precisely calibrated symmetry – its diameter is exactly equal to the building's interior height of 43.3m. At its centre, the oculus, which symbolically connected the temple with the gods, plays a vital structural role by absorbing and redistributing the dome's huge tensile forces.

What's Nearby?

Basilica di Santa Maria Sopra Minerva   Basilica

(Map p250; www.santamariasopraminerva.it; Piazza della Minerva 42; ⏰6.55am-7pm Mon-Fri, 10am-12.30pm & 3.30-7pm Sat, 8.10am-12.30pm & 3.30-7pm Sun; 🚇Largo di Torre Argentina) Built on the site of three pagan temples, including one dedicated to the goddess Minerva, the Dominican Basilica di Santa Maria Sopra Minerva is Rome's only Gothic church. However, little remains of the original 13th-century structure and these days the main drawcard is a minor Michelangelo sculpture and the magisterial, art-rich interior.

Walking Tour: Centro Storico Piazzas

Rome's historic centre boasts some of the city's most celebrated piazzas, and several lovely but lesser-known squares. Each has its own character but together they encapsulate much of the city's beauty, history and drama.

Start Piazza Colonna

Distance 1.5km

Duration 2½ to three hours

Classic Photo Pantheon

4 It's a short walk along Via del Seminario to **Piazza della Rotonda**, where the **Pantheon** (p50) needs no introduction.

5 Piazza Navona (p64) is Rome's great showpiece square, where you can compare the two giants of Roman baroque – Gian Lorenzo Bernini and Francesco Borromini.

Corso del Rinascimento

Piazza Navona ⑤

Salita dei Crescenzi ④

Via della Rotonda

Via degli Staderari

Via dei Canestrari

Piazza di San Pantaleo

Via Monterone

Via dei Cappellari

Corso Vittorio Emanuele II

Via del Monserrato

Lgt dei Tebaldi

Via dei Farnesi

Via dei Baullari

⑥

⑦ **FINISH**

Via dei Giubbonari

Take a Break... Those in the know head to **Forno di Campo de' Fiori** (www.fornocampodefiori.com) for some of Rome's best *pizza bianca* ('white' pizza with olive oil and salt).

7 Just beyond the Campo, the more sober **Piazza Farnese** is overshadowed by the austere facade of the Renaissance Palazzo Farnese.

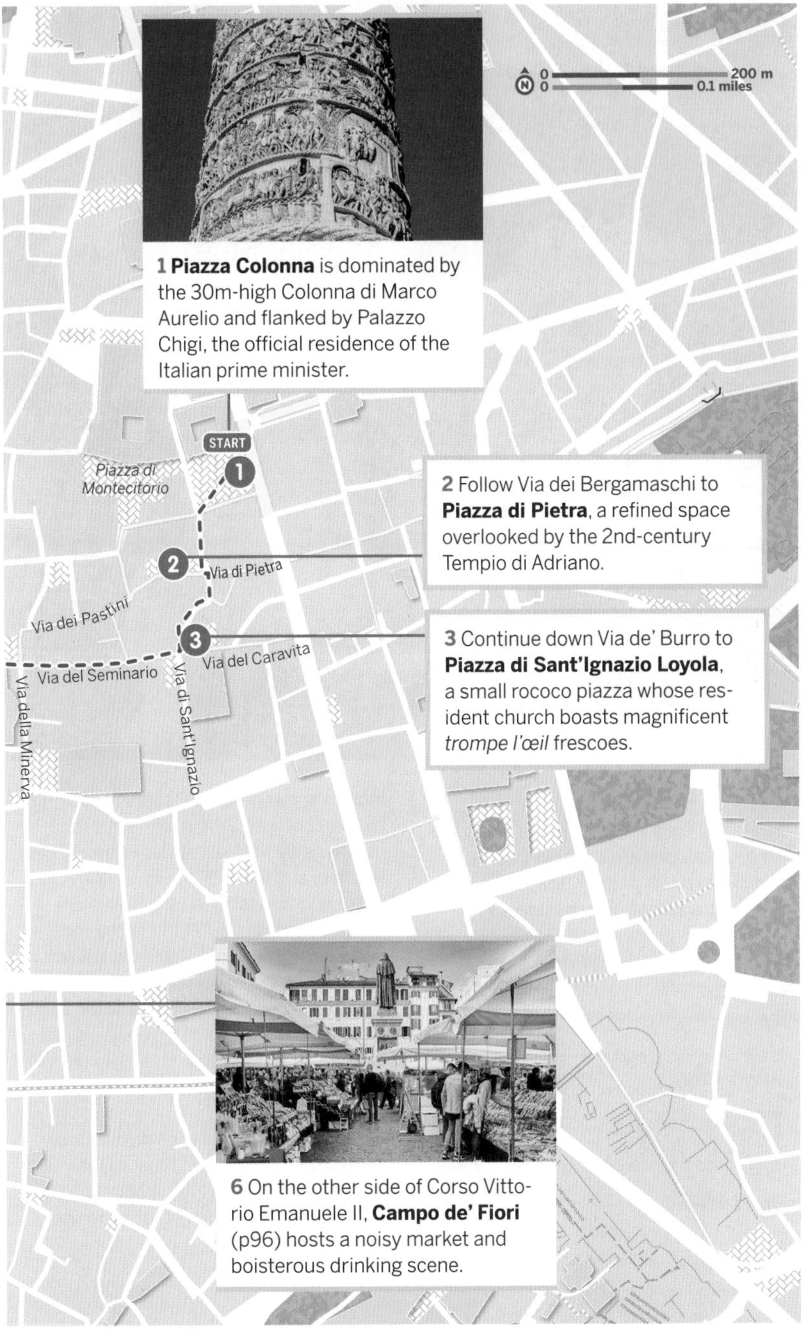

1 Piazza Colonna is dominated by the 30m-high Colonna di Marco Aurelio and flanked by Palazzo Chigi, the official residence of the Italian prime minister.

START

Piazza di Montecitorio

Via di Pietra

Via dei Pastini

Via del Seminario

Via del Caravita

Via della Minerva

Via di Sant'Ignazio

2 Follow Via dei Bergamaschi to **Piazza di Pietra**, a refined space overlooked by the 2nd-century Tempio di Adriano.

3 Continue down Via de' Burro to **Piazza di Sant'Ignazio Loyola**, a small rococo piazza whose resident church boasts magnificent *trompe l'œil* frescoes.

6 On the other side of Corso Vittorio Emanuele II, **Campo de' Fiori** (p96) hosts a noisy market and boisterous drinking scene.

0 200 m
0 0.1 miles

Bernini's *Ratto di Proserpina*

Museo e Galleria Borghese

Housing what's often referred to as the 'queen of all private art collections', this spectacular gallery boasts some of the city's finest art treasures. Find it, moreover, gracefully languishing in the green beauty of Rome's most celebrated park.

Great for...

Don't Miss

Canova's *Venere vincitrice,* his sensual portrayal of Paolina Bonaparte Borghese.

Including a series of sensational sculptures by Gian Lorenzo Bernini and important paintings by the likes of Caravaggio, Titian, Raphael and Rubens, the museum's collection was formed by Cardinal Scipione Borghese (1579–1633), the most knowledgeable and ruthless art collector of his day. It was originally housed in his residence near St Peter's, but in the 1620s he had it transferred to his new villa just outside Porta Pinciana. And it's in the villa's central building, the Casino Borghese, that you'll see it today.

Over the centuries the villa has undergone several overhauls, most notably in the late 1700s when Prince Marcantonio Borghese added much of the lavish neoclassical decor.

Villa Borghese (p58)

KIEV.VICTOR/SHUTTERSTOCK ©

Museo e Galleria Borghese

ℹ Need to Know

Map p252; ☏ 06 3 28 10; http://galleria borghese.beniculturali.it; Piazzale del Museo Borghese 5; adult/child €15/8.50; ⏱9am–7pm Tue-Sun; 🚃Via Pinciana

✕ Take a Break

Enjoy coffee or a full meal at the grand neoclassical Caffè delle Arti (p141), inside La Galleria Nazionale.

★ Top Tip

Prebook your ticket; bring ID to collect it 30 minutes before your preallocated entry time.

The villa is divided into two parts: the ground-floor museum and the upstairs picture gallery.

Ground Floor

Stairs lead up to a portico flanking the grand entrance hall, decorated with 4th-century floor mosaics of fighting gladiators and a 2nd-century *Satiro combattente* (Fighting Satyr).

The scene-stealer in **Sala I** is Antonio Canova's daring depiction of Napoleon's sister, Paolina Bonaparte Borghese, reclining topless as *Venere vincitrice* (1805–08). Further on, in **Sala III**, Gian Lorenzo Bernini's *Apollo e Dafne* (1622–25), one of a series depicting pagan myths, captures the exact moment Daphne's hands start morphing into leaves. **Sala IV** is home to Bernini's masterpiece *Ratto di Proserpina*

(1621–22). This flamboyant sculpture brilliantly reveals the artist's virtuosity – just look at Pluto's hand pressing into the seemingly soft flesh of Persephone's thigh.

Caravaggio dominates **Sala VIII** with a dissipated *Bacchino malato* (Young Sick Bacchus; 1593–94), the strangely beautiful *La Madonna dei Palafrenieri* (Madonna of the Palafrenieri; 1605–06), and *San Giovanni Battista* (St John the Baptist; 1609–10), probably the artist's last work.

Pinacoteca

Upstairs, the picture gallery offers a wonderful snapshot of Renaissance art. Don't miss Raphael's extraordinary *La deposizione di Cristo* (The Deposition; 1507) in **Sala IX**, and his *Dama con liocorno* (Lady with a Unicorn; 1506). In the same room is Fra Bartolomeo's superb *Adorazione del Bambino* (Adoration of the Christ Child; 1495) and Perugino's *Madonna con Bambino* (Madonna and Child; first quarter of the 16th century).

Next door in **Sala X**, Correggio's *Danäe* (1530–31) shares the room with a willowy Venus, as portrayed by Cranach in his *Venere e Amore che reca il favo do miele* (Venus and Cupid with Honeycomb; 1531).

Other highlights include Bernini's two self-portraits in **Sala XIV**, and Titian's early masterpiece, *Amor sacro e amor profano* (Sacred and Profane Love; 1514) in **Sala XX**.

What's Nearby?

Villa Borghese   Park

(Map p252; entrances at Piazzale San Paolo del Brasile, Piazzale Flaminio, Via Pinciana, Via Raimondo, Largo Pablo Picasso; ☼sunrise-sunset; 🚃Via Pinciana) Locals, lovers, tourists, joggers – no one can resist Rome's finest park. Originally the 17th-century estate of Cardinal Scipione Borghese, it covers about

80 hectares of wooded glades, gardens, grassy banks, the landscaped **Giardino del Lago** (Map p252) and **Piazza di Siena** (Map p252), a dusty arena used for Rome's top equestrian event in May.

Pincio Hill Gardens   Gardens

(Map p252; Ⓜ︎Flaminio) Strike out to explore 19th-century Pincio Hill, named after the Pinci family who owned this part of Rome in the 4th century. It's quite a climb up but at the top you're rewarded with lovely views over to St Peter's and the Gianicolo Hill.

Museo Nazionale Etrusco
di Villa Giulia   Museum

(Map p252; ☎06 322 65 71; www.villagiulia.beni culturali.it; Piazzale di Villa Giulia; adult/reduced €8/4; ☼9am-8pm Tue-Sun; 🚃Via delle Belle Arti) Pope Julius III's 16th-century villa provides the charming setting for Italy's finest

Museo e Galleria Borghese

collection of Etruscan and pre-Roman treasures. Exhibits, many of which came from tombs in the surrounding Lazio region, range from bronze figurines and black *bucchero* tableware to temple decorations, terracotta vases and a dazzling display of sophisticated jewellery.

La Galleria Nazionale Gallery

(Galleria Nazionale d'Arte Moderna e Contemporanea; Map p252; ☑06 3229 8221; http://lagallerianazionale.com; Viale delle Belle Arti 131, accessible entrance Via Antonio Gramsci 71; adult/reduced €10/5; ☉8.30am-7.30pm

> **★ Top Tip**
>
> Monday is not a good time for exploring Villa Borghese. Sure, you can walk in the park, but its museums and galleries are all shut – they are only open Tuesday to Sunday.

PHOTOKANTO/SHUTTERSTOCK ©

Tue-Sun; ☒Piazza Thorvaldsen) ✔ Housed in a vast belle-époque palace, this oft-overlooked modern art gallery, known locally as GNAM, is an unsung gem. Its superlative collection runs the gamut from neoclassical sculpture to abstract expressionism with works by many of the most important exponents of 19th- and 20th-century art.

Museo d'Arte Contemporanea di Roma Arts Centre

(MACRO; ☑06 69 62 71; www.museomacro.org; Via Nizza 138, cnr Via Cagliari; ☉10am-8pm Tue-Fri & Sun, to 10pm Sat; ☒Via Nizza) **FREE** Along with MAXXI, this is Rome's most important contemporary art gallery. Vying with the exhibits for your attention is the museum's sleek black-and-red interior design. Occupying a former Peroni brewery, the conversion by French architect Odile Decq retains much of the building's original structure while also incorporating a sophisticated steel-and-glass finish.

Explora – Museo dei Bambini di Roma Museum

(Map p252; ☑06 361 37 76; www.mdbr.it; Via Flaminia 80-86; adult €8, children 1-3yr €5, under 1yr free; ☉entrance 10am, noon, 3pm & 5pm Tue-Sun, no 10am entrance in Aug; ☒Flaminio) Rome's only dedicated kids' museum, Explora is aimed at the under-12s. It's divided into thematic sections and is a hands-on, feet-on, full-on experience. Outside there's also a free play park open to all. Booking is recommended for the timed entrances and is required on weekends.

> **★ Local Knowledge**
>
> For unforgettable views over Rome's rooftops and domes, make your way to the Pincio Hill Gardens in the southwest of Villa Borghese.

Domus Augustana (p62)

Palatino

Rising above the Roman Forum, the Palatino (Palatine Hill) is an atmospheric area of towering pine trees, majestic ruins and memorable views. According to legend, this is where Romulus and Remus were saved by a wolf and where Romulus founded Rome in 753 BC. Archaeological evidence can't prove the myth, but it has dated human habitation here to the 8th century BC.

Great for...

❶ Need to Know

Palatine Hill; Map p246; ☑06 3996 7700; www.parcocolosseo.it; Via di San Gregorio 30, Piazza di Santa Maria Nova; adult/reduced incl Colosseum & Roman Forum €12/7.50, SUPER ticket €18/13.50; ⏱8.30am-1hr before sunset, some SUPER ticket sites Mon, Wed, Fri & morning Sun only; Ⓜ Colosseo)

★ **Top Tip**

Access to Casa di Livia and Casa di Augusto requires the SUPER ticket and is by guided tour only. Numbers are limited: book an entry time when buying your ticket.

The Palatino was ancient Rome's most exclusive neighbourhood. The emperor Augustus lived here all his life and successive emperors built increasingly opulent palaces. But after Rome's fall, it fell into disrepair, and in the Middle Ages churches and castles were built over the ruins. Later, wealthy Renaissance families had landscaped gardens laid out on the site.

Most of the Palatino as it appears today is covered by the ruins of the emperor Domitian's 1st-century complex, which served as the main imperial palace for 300 years.

Stadio

On entering the Palatino from Via di San Gregorio, head uphill until you come to the first recognisable construction, the *stadio*. This sunken area, which was part of

the main imperial palace, was used by the emperor for private games. A path to the side of the *stadio* leads to the remains of a complex built by Septimius Severus, comprising baths (**Terme di Settimio Severo**) and a palace (**Domus Severiana**) where, if they're open, you can visit the **Arcate Severiane** (Severian Arches; Map p246; admission incl in Palatino ticket; ⊘8.30am-6.45pm Tue & Fri summer, shorter hours Tue & Fri winter), a series of arches built to facilitate further development.

Domus Augustana, Museo Palatino & Domus Flavia

Next to the *stadio* are the ruins of the **Domus Augustana** (Emperor's Residence; Map p246), the emperor's private quarters in the imperial palace. Also here is the **Aula Isiaca** (Map p246; SUPER ticket adult/reduced

The *stadio*

€18/13.50; ⏰9am-6.30pm Mon, Wed & Fri, to 2pm Sun summer, 9am-3.30pm Mon, Wed & Fri, to 1pm Sun winter), a frescoed room from a luxurious Republican-era house, and the **Loggia Mattei**, a Renaissance loggia decorated by Baldassarre Peruzzi.

The white building next to the Domus Augustana houses the **Museo Palatino** (Map p246; SUPER ticket adult/reduced €18/13.50; ⏰8.30am-1½hr before sunset), charting the development of the Palatino through video presentations, models and archaeological finds. North is **Domus Flavia** (Map p246), the public part of the palace centred on a grand columned

peristyle – the grassy area with the base of an octagonal fountain – off which the main halls led.

Casa di Livia & Casa di Augusto

Among the best-preserved buildings is the **Casa di Livia** (Map p246; SUPER ticket adult/reduced €18/13.50; ⏰9am-6.30pm Mon, Wed & Fri, to 2pm Sun summer, 9am-3.30pm Mon, Wed & Fri, to 1pm Sun winter). Home to Augustus' wife Livia, it was built around an atrium leading on to what were once frescoed reception rooms. Nearby, **Casa di Augusto** (Map p246; SUPER ticket adult/reduced €18/13.50; ⏰9am-6.30pm Mon, Wed & Fri, to 2pm Sun summer, 9am-3.30pm Mon, Wed & Fri, to 1pm Sun winter), the private residence of Augustus, features some superb frescoes in vivid reds, yellows and blues.

Criptoportico Neroniano

Northeast of Casa di Livia is **Criptoportico Neroniano** (Map p246; SUPER ticket adult/reduced €18/13.50; ⏰8.30am–1hr before sunset), a 130m tunnel where Caligula is said to have been murdered. Nero used it to connect his Domus Aurea with the Palatino.

Orti Farnesiani

Covering the Domus Tiberiana (Tiberius' palace) in the northwest of the Palatino, the **Orti Farnesiani** (Map p246) is one of Europe's earliest botanical gardens. It was named after Cardinal Alessandro Farnese, who had it laid out in the mid-16th century.

> ★ **Don't Miss**
>
> The sight of the Roman Forum laid out beneath you from the balcony in the Orti Farnesiani is spectacular.

HERCULES MILAS/ALAMY STOCK PHOTO ©

> ✕ **Take a Break**
>
> Picnic with a *panino* from Alimentari Pannella Carmela (p125) on the grassy Vigna Barberini near the Orti Farnesiani.

Fontana del Nettuno (p66) on the Piazza Navona

Piazza Navona

With its showy fountains, exuberant baroque palazzi (mansions) and busy pavement cafes, Piazza Navona is central Rome's elegant showcase square. Long a hub of local life, it hosted Rome's main market for close on 300 years, and today attracts a colourful daily circus of street performers, hawkers, artists, tourists, fortune tellers and pigeons.

Great for...

ℹ️ Need to Know

Map p250; 🚌 Corso del Rinascimento

★ **Top Tip**

Each December (until 6 January) the piazza hosts a traditional Christmas market.

Stadio di Domiziano

Like many of Rome's landmarks, the piazza sits over an ancient monument, in this case the 1st-century-AD **Stadio di Domiziano** (Domitian's Stadium; Map p250; 06 6880 5311; www.stadiodomiziano.com; Via di Tor Sanguigna 3; adult/reduced €8/6; 10am-6.30pm Sun-Fri, to 7.30pm Sat). This 30,000-seat stadium, the subterranean remains of which can be accessed from Via di Tor Sanguigna, hosted athletic meets – hence the name Navona, a corruption of the Greek word *agon*, meaning public games.

Fountains

The piazza's grand centrepiece is Bernini's **Fontana dei Quattro Fiumi** (Fountain of the Four Rivers; Map p250), a showy fountain featuring four muscular personifica-tions of the rivers Nile, Ganges, Danube and Plata.

The **Fontana del Moro** at the southern end of the square was designed by Giacomo della Porta in 1576.

At the northern end of the piazza, the 19th-century **Fontana del Nettuno** depicts Neptune fighting with a sea monster, surrounded by sea nymphs.

Main Buildings

Overlooking Bernini's Fontana dei Quattro Fiumi is the Chiesa di Sant'Agnese in Agone (p186), an elaborate baroque church designed by Francesco Borromini.

Further down, the 17th-century **Palazzo Pamphilj** (Map p250; http://roma.itamaraty. gov.br/it; Piazza Navona 10; by reservation only) was built for Pope Innocent X and now houses the Brazilian Embassy.

Fontana dei Quattro Fiumi

What's Nearby?

Chiesa di San Luigi dei Francesi — Church

(Map p250; ☎06 68 82 71; Piazza di San Luigi dei Francesi 5; ⊗9.30am-12.45pm & 2.30-6.30pm Mon-Fri, 9.30am-12.15pm & 2.30-6.45pm Sat, 11.30am-12.45pm & 2.30-6.45pm Sun; ☐Corso del Rinascimento) Church to Rome's French community since 1589, this opulent baroque *chiesa* (church) is home to a celebrated trio of Caravaggio paintings: the *Vocazione di San Matteo* (The Calling of Saint Matthew), the *Martirio di San Matteo* (The Martyrdom of Saint Matthew) and *San Matteo e l'angelo* (Saint Matthew and the Angel), known collectively as the St Matthew cycle.

> ★ **Don't Miss**
> Bernini's Fontana dei Quattro Fiumi, the piazza's high-camp central fountain.

Museo Nazionale Romano: Palazzo Altemps — Museum

(Map p250; ☎06 68 48 51; www.museonazionale romano.beniculturali.it; Piazza Sant'Apollinare 46; adult/reduced €10/5, incl Palazzo Massimo alle Terme, Crypta Balbi & Terme di Diocleziano €12/6; ⊗9am-7.45pm Tue-Sun; ☐Corso del Rinascimento) Just north of Piazza Navona, Palazzo Altemps is a beautiful late-15th-century *palazzo* housing the best of the Museo Nazionale Romano's formidable collection of classical sculpture. Many pieces come from the celebrated Ludovisi collection, amassed by Cardinal Ludovico Ludovisi in the 17th century.

Basilica di Sant'Agostino — Basilica

(Map p250; ☎06 6880 1962; Piazza di Sant'Agostino 80; ⊗7.45am-noon & 4-7.30pm; ☐Corso del Rinascimento) The plain white facade of this early Renaissance church, built in the 15th century and renovated in the late 1700s, gives no indication of the impressive art inside. The most famous work is Caravaggio's *Madonna dei pellegrini* (Madonna of the Pilgrims), in the first chapel on the left, but you'll also find a fresco by Raphael and a much-venerated sculpture by Jacopo Sansovino.

Chiesa di Sant'Ignazio di Loyola — Church

(Map p250; ☎06 679 44 06; https://santignazio. gesuiti.it; Piazza di Sant'Ignazio; ⊗7.30am-7pm Mon-Sat, from 9am Sun; ☐Via del Corso) Flanking a delightful rococo piazza, this important Jesuit church boasts a Carlo Maderno facade and two celebrated *trompe l'œil* frescoes by Andrea Pozzo (1642–1709). One cleverly depicts a fake dome, while the other, on the nave ceiling, shows St Ignatius Loyola being welcomed into paradise by Christ and the Madonna.

> ✕ **Take a Break**
> In Palazzo Braschi, at the southern end of the piazza, Vivi Bistrot (p128) is a charming spot for a lunchtime bite.

Frescoes from an ancient Roman villa (p70)

Museo Nazionale Romano: Palazzo Massimo alle Terme

Every day, thousands of passers-by hurry past this towering neo-Renaissance palazzo without giving it a second glance. They don't know what they're missing. This is one of Rome's finest museums, a light-filled treasure trove packed with spectacular classical art. The sculpture is truly impressive, but what really takes the breath away is its collection of vibrantly coloured frescoes and mosaics.

Great for...

ℹ️ Need to Know

Map p245; ☎06 3996 7700; www.coop culture.it; Largo di Villa Peretti 1; adult/ reduced €10/5; ☉9am-7.45pm Tue-Sun; Ⓜ Termini

★ **Top Tip**
Buy a combo ticket, valid three days, covering admission to the Terme di Diocleziano, Palazzo Altemps and the Crypta Balbi.

Sculpture

The ground and 1st floors are devoted to sculpture, examining imperial portraiture as propaganda and including some breathtaking works of art, including the 2nd-century-BC Greek bronzes the *Boxer* and the *Prince,* a crouching *Aphrodite* from Villa Adriana, the 2nd-century-BC *Sleeping Hermaphrodite,* and the idealised vision of the *Discus Thrower.* Also fascinating are the elaborate bronze fittings that belonged to Caligula's ceremonial ships.

Frescoes & Mosaics

On the 2nd floor, magnificent and vibrantly coloured frescoes include scenes from nature, mythology, and domestic and sensual life, using rich, vivid (and expensive) colours. These magnificent panels, originally used as

interior decor, give a more complete picture of the inside of an ancient Roman villa than you'll see anywhere else in the world.

Particularly breathtaking, in Room 2, are the frescoes (dating from 30 BC to 20 BC) from Villa Livia, one of the homes of Augustus' wife Livia Drusilla. They depict a paradisiacal garden full of a wild tangle of roses, pomegranates, irises and camomile under a deep-blue sky. They once decorated a summer *triclinium*, a large living and dining area built half underground to provide protection from the heat.

The 2nd floor also features some exquisitely fine floor mosaics and rare inlay work.

Coins & Jewels

The basement contains an absorbing coin collection tracing the Roman Empire's use of coins for propaganda purposes. There's

Sculptures, including the *Discus Thrower* (far left)

also jewellery dating back several millennia, and the disturbing remains of a mummified eight-year-old girl, the only known example of mummification dating from the Roman Empire.

What's Nearby?

Museo Nazionale Romano: Terme di Diocleziano
Museum

(Map p245; ☎06 3996 7700; www.coopculture. it; Viale Enrico de Nicola 78; adult/reduced €10/5; ⊙9am-6.30pm Tue-Sun; ⓂTermini) The Terme di Diocleziano was ancient Rome's largest bath complex, covering about 13 hectares and able to accommodate some 3000

people. Today its ruins house a branch of the impressive Museo Nazionale Romano. Exhibits, which include memorial inscriptions, bas-reliefs and archaeological artefacts, provide a fascinating insight into Roman life. Outside, the vast cloister, constructed from drawings by Michelangelo, is lined with classical sarcophagi, headless statues and huge sculpted animal heads, thought to have come from the Foro di Traiano.

Chiesa di Santa Maria della Vittoria
Church

(Map p245; ☎06 4274 0571; www.chiesasanta mariavittoriaroma.it; Via XX Settembre 17; ⊙7am-noon & 3.30-7.15pm; ⓂRepubblica) This modest church is an unlikely setting for an extraordinary work of art – Bernini's extravagant and sexually charged *Santa Teresa trafitta dall'amore di Dio* (Ecstasy of St Teresa). This daring sculpture depicts Teresa, engulfed in the folds of a flowing cloak, floating in ecstasy on a cloud while a teasing angel pierces her repeatedly with a golden arrow.

Palazzo delle Esposizioni
Cultural Centre

(Map p245; ☎06 3996 7500; www.palazzoespo sizioni.it; Via Nazionale 194; ⊙10am-8pm Tue-Thu & Sun, to 10.30pm Fri & Sat; ☐Via Nazionale) This huge neoclassical palace was built in 1882 as an exhibition centre, though it has since served as headquarters for the Italian Communist Party, a mess hall for Allied servicemen, a polling station and even a public loo. Nowadays it's a splendid cultural hub, with cathedral-scale exhibition spaces hosting blockbuster art exhibitions and sleekly designed art labs, as well as a bookshop, cafe and upmarket **restaurant** serving weekend brunch beneath a dazzling all-glass roof. Occasional concerts, performances and film screenings are also held here.

> ★ **Don't Miss**
> The athletic pose of the *Discus Thrower*, *Il discobolo*, a stirring homage to the male physique.

ADAM EASTLAND/ALAMY STOCK PHOTO ©

> ✕ **Take a Break**
> Head to the Mercato Centrale (p133) at Termini station for a range of tempting food stalls.

Capitoline Museums

Dating to 1471, the Capitoline Museums are the world's oldest public museums. Their collection of classical sculpture is one of Italy's finest, including crowd-pleasers such as the iconic Lupa capitolina (Capitoline Wolf), and the formidable picture gallery includes masterpieces by the likes of Titian, Tintoretto, Rubens and Caravaggio.

Great for...

❶ Need to Know

Musei Capitolini; Map p246; ☑06 06 08; www. museicapitolini.org; Piazza del Campidoglio 1; adult/reduced €11.50/9.50; ⊘9.30am-7.30pm, last admission 6.30pm; ➈Piazza Venezia

★ **Top Tip**

In a tunnel between the two *palazzi*, the Tabularium commands inspiring views over the Roman Forum.

The museums occupy two stately *palazzi* (mansions) on **Piazza del Campidoglio**. The entrance is in **Palazzo dei Conservatori**, where you'll find the original core of the sculptural collection and the Pinacoteca (picture gallery).

Palazzo dei Conservatori: 1st Floor

Before you start on the sculpture collection proper, check out the marble body parts littered around the ground-floor **courtyard**. The mammoth head, hand and feet all belonged to a 12m-high statue of Constantine that once stood in the Basilica di Massenzio in the Roman Forum.

Of the sculpture on the 1st floor, the Etruscan *Lupa capitolina* (Capitoline Wolf) is the most famous. Dating to the 5th century BC, the bronze wolf stands over her

suckling wards, Romulus and Remus, who were added in 1471.

Other highlights include the *Spinario*, a delicate 1st-century-BC bronze of a boy removing a thorn from his foot, and Gian Lorenzo Bernini's *Medusa* bust.

Palazzo dei Conservatori: 2nd Floor

The 2nd floor is given over to the **Pinacoteca**, the museum's picture gallery. Each room harbours masterpieces, but two stand out: the **Sala Pietro da Cortona**, which features Pietro da Cortona's famous depiction of the *Ratto delle Sabine* (Rape of the Sabine Women; 1630); and the **Sala di Santa Petronilla**, named after Guercino's huge canvas *Seppellimento di Santa Petronilla* (The Burial of St Petronilla;

Galata morente (Dying Gaul), Palazzo Nuovo

1621–23). This airy hall also boasts two works by Caravaggio.

Tabularium

A tunnel links Palazzo dei Conservatori to Palazzo Nuovo via the Tabularium, ancient Rome's central archive, beneath **Palazzo Senatorio**.

Palazzo Nuovo

Palazzo Nuovo contains some unforgettable showstoppers. Chief among them is the *Galata morente* (Dying Gaul), a Roman

> ★ **Don't Miss**
> The Sala degli Orazi e Curiazi is where the 1957 Treaty of Rome was signed, establishing the European Economic Community, precursor of the European Union.

VIACHESLAV LOPATIN/SHUTTERSTOCK ©

copy of a 3rd-century-BC Greek original that movingly depicts the anguish of a dying Gaul warrior. Another superb figurative piece is the *Venere capitolina* (Capitoline Venus), a sensual yet demure portrayal of the nude goddess.

What's Nearby?

Vittoriano   Monument

(Victor Emanuel Monument; Map p246; Piazza Venezia; ◷9.30am-5.30pm summer, to 4.30pm winter; ☒Piazza Venezia) FREE You can't ignore the Vittoriano (aka the Altare della Patria, Altar of the Fatherland), the massive mountain of white marble that towers over Piazza Venezia. Begun in 1885 to honour Italy's first king, Vittorio Emanuele II – who's immortalised in its vast equestrian statue – it incorporates the **Museo Centrale del Risorgimento** (Map p246; ☏06 679 35 98; www.risorgimento.it; adult/reduced €5/2.50; ◷9.30am-6.30pm), a small museum documenting Italian unification, and the **Tomb of the Unknown Soldier**. For Rome's best 360-degree views, take the **Roma dal Cielo** (Map p246; adult/reduced €10/5; ◷9.30am-7.30pm, last admission 6.45pm) lift to the top.

Bocca della Verità   Monument

(Mouth of Truth; Map p254; Piazza Bocca della Verità 18; voluntary donation; ◷9.30am-5.50pm summer, to 4.50pm winter; ☒Piazza Bocca della Verità) A bearded face carved into a giant marble disc, the *Bocca della Verità* is one of Rome's most popular curiosities. Legend says if you put your hand in its mouth and tell a lie, the Bocca will slam shut and bite your hand off.

The mouth, which was originally part of a fountain, or possibly an ancient manhole cover, now lives in the portico of the **Chiesa di Santa Maria in Cosmedin**, a handsome medieval church.

> ✕ **Take a Break**
> Head up to the 2nd floor of Palazzo dei Conservatori for a coffee at the panoramic Terrazza Caffarelli (p124).

Via Appia Antica

Ancient Rome's regina viarum (queen of roads) is now one of Rome's most exclusive addresses, a beautiful cobbled thoroughfare flanked by grassy fields, ancient ruins and towering pine trees. But it has a dark history – it was here that Spartacus and 6000 of his slave rebels were crucified, and the early Christians buried their dead in the underground catacombs.

Great for...

ⓘ Need to Know

Appian Way; 📞06 513 53 16; www.parcoappia antica.it; ⊘main site 24hr, individual sites hours vary; 🚍Via Appia Antica

★ **Top Tip**

Rent bikes and pick up maps at **Service Center Appia Antica** (📞 06 513 53 16; www.parcoappiaantica.it; Via Appia Antica 58-60; 🕑 9.30am-1pm & 2pm-dusk Mon-Fri, 9.30am-sunset Sat & Sun; 🚌 Via Appia Antica).

Heading southeast from Porta San Sebastiano, Via Appia Antica was named after Appius Claudius Caecus, who laid the first 90km section in 312 BC. It was later extended in 190 BC to reach Brindisi, some 540km away on the southern Adriatic coast.

Catacombe di San Sebastiano

The **Catacombe di San Sebastiano** (☏06 785 03 50; www.catacombe.org; Via Appia Antica 136; adult/reduced €8/5; ⊙10am-5pm Mon-Sat Jan-Nov; ☐Via Appia Antica) were the first burial chambers to be called catacombs – the name was derived from the Greek *kata* (near) and *kymbas* (cavity), because they were located near a cave. During the persecution of Christians by the emperor Vespasian from AD 258,

some believe that the catacombs were used as a safe haven for the remains of St Peter and St Paul.

Within the catacombs there are three beautifully preserved and decorated mausoleums. Above the catacombs, the **Basilica di San Sebastiano** preserves one of the arrows allegedly used to kill St Sebastian, and the column to which he was tied.

Catacombe di San Callisto

Rome's most-visited catacombs, this tangle of tunnels was founded at the end of the 2nd century. Named after Pope Calixtus I, the **Catacombe di San Callisto** (☏06 513 01 51; www.catacombe.roma.it; Via Appia Antica 110-126; adult/reduced €8/5; ⊙9am-noon & 2-5pm Thu-Tue Mar-Jan; ☐Via

Roadside monument, Via Appia Antica

Appia Antica) became the official cemetery of the newly established Roman Church. In the 20km of tunnels that have been explored to date, archaeologists have found the tombs of 16 popes, dozens of martyrs and thousands upon thousands of Christians.

The patron saint of music, St Cecilia, was also buried here, though her body was later removed to the Basilica di Santa Cecilia in Trastevere. When her body was exhumed in 1599, more than a thousand years after her death, it was apparently perfectly preserved.

★ Don't Miss

The ruins of Villa di Massenzio, which litter the green fields by the side of the cobbled road.

ALESSANDROO770/GETTY IMAGES ©

Catacombe di Santa Domitilla

The **Catacombe di Santa Domitilla** (☎06 511 03 42; www.domitilla.info; Via delle Sette Chiese 282; adult/reduced €8/5; ☉9am-noon & 2-5pm Wed-Mon mid-Jan–mid-Dec; ☐Via Appia Antica) contains Christian wall paintings and the haunting underground **Chiesa di SS Nereus e Achilleus**, a 4th-century church dedicated to two Roman soldiers martyred by Diocletian.

What's Nearby?

Mausoleo di Cecilia Metella   Ruins

(☎06 3996 7700; www.coopculture.it; Via Appia Antica 161; adult/reduced €5/2.50, incl Villa dei Quintili & Complesso di Santa Maria Nova €10; ☉9am-1pm & 2-5pm Mon-Fri, 9am-2pm Sat; ☐Via Appia Antica) Dating to the 1st century BC, this great drum of a mausoleum encloses a burial chamber, now roofless. In the 14th century it was converted into a fort by the Caetani family, who were related to Pope Boniface VIII and used to frighten passing traffic into paying a toll.

Villa di Massenzio   Ruins

(☎06 06 08; www.villadimassenzio.it; Via Appia Antica 153; ☉10am-4pm Tue-Sun; ☐Via Appia Antica) **FREE** The outstanding feature of Maxentius' enormous 4th-century palace complex is the **Circo di Massenzio**, Rome's best-preserved ancient racetrack – you can still make out the starting stalls used for chariot races. The 10,000-seat arena was built by Maxentius around 309, but he died before ever seeing a race here. Above the arena are the ruins of Maxentius' imperial residence. Near the racetrack, the **Mausoleo di Romolo** (Tombo di Romolo) was built by Maxentius for his 17-year-old son Romulus.

✕ Take a Break

Enjoy a garden lunch beneath orange trees at Il Giardino di Giulia e Fratelli (p143), almost opposite the Mausoleo di Cecilia Metella.

Tempio di Saturno (p83)

Roman Forum

The Roman Forum was ancient Rome's showpiece centre, a grandiose district of temples, basilicas and vibrant public spaces. Nowadays, it's a collection of impressive, if sketchily labelled, ruins that can leave you drained and confused. But if you can get your imagination going, there's something wonderfully compelling about walking in the footsteps of Julius Caesar and other legendary figures of Roman history.

Great for...

ⓘ Need to Know

Foro Romano; Map p246; ☑06 3996 7700; www.parcocolosseo.it; Largo della Salara Vecchia, Piazza di Santa Maria Nova; adult/ reduced incl Colosseum & Palatino €12/7.50, SUPER ticket €18/13.50; ⏰8.30am-1hr before sunset, SUPER ticket sites Tue, Thu, Sat & afternoon Sun only; 🚌Via dei Fori Imperiali)

★ **Top Tip**

Orientate yourself by viewing the Forum from the balcony on the Palatino (p60).

Originally an Etruscan burial ground, the Forum was first developed in the 7th century BC, growing over time to become the social, political and commercial hub of the Roman Empire. But like many of ancient Rome's great urban developments, it fell into disrepair after the fall of the Roman Empire until eventually it was used as pastureland. In the Middle Ages it was known as the Campo Vaccino (Cow Field) and extensively plundered for its stone and marble. The area was systematically excavated in the 18th and 19th centuries, and excavations continue to this day.

Via Sacra to Campidoglio

Entering the Forum from Largo della Salara Vecchia, you'll see the **Tempio di Antonino e Faustina** ahead to your left. Erected in AD 141, this was transformed into a church

in the 8th century, the **Chiesa di San Lorenzo in Miranda**. To your right is the 179 BC **Basilica Fulvia Aemilia**.

At the end of the path, you'll come to **Via Sacra**, the Forum's main thoroughfare, and the **Tempio di Giulio Cesare**, which stands on the spot where Julius Caesar was cremated.

Heading right brings you to the **Curia**, the original seat of the Roman Senate, though what you see today is a reconstruction of how it looked in the reign of Diocletian (r 284–305).

At the end of Via Sacra, the **Arco di Settimio Severo** is dedicated to the eponymous emperor and his sons, Caracalla and Geta. Close by, the **Colonna di Foca** rises above what was once the Forum's main square, Piazza del Foro. The eight granite columns that rise behind the Colonna are

Mercati di Traiano (Trajan's Markets), Imperial Forums

all that survive of the **Tempio di Saturno**, an important temple that doubled as the state treasury.

Tempio di Castore e Polluce & Casa delle Vestali

From the path that runs parallel to Via Sacra, you'll pass the stubby ruins of the **Basilica Giulia**. At the end of the basilica, three columns remain from the 5th-century-BC **Tempio di Castore e Polluce.**

Nearby, the 6th-century **Chiesa di Santa Maria Antiqua** is the oldest church in the Forum, a veritable treasure trove of early Christian art. Accessible from in front of the church is the **Rampa di Domiziano**, a passageway that linked the Forum to the Palatine. Both require a SUPER ticket.

Back towards Via Sacra is **Casa delle Vestali**, home of the virgins who tended the flame in the adjoining **Tempio di Vesta**.

Via Sacra Towards the Colosseum

Heading up Via Sacra past the **Tempio di Romolo** (also only accessible with a SUPER ticket), you come to the **Basilica di Massenzio**, the forum's largest building. Beyond, the Arco di Tito was built in AD 81 to celebrate Vespasian and Titus' victories against rebels in Jerusalem.

What's Nearby?

Imperial Forums　　Archaeological Site
(Fori Imperiali; Map p246; ☑06 06 08; Piazza Santa Maria di Loreto; adult/reduced €4/3, free 1st Sun of month Oct-Mar; ☺by reservation; 🚌Via dei Fori Imperiali) Visible from Via dei Fori Imperiali and, when it's open, Via Alessandrina, the forums of Trajan, Augustus, Nerva and Caesar are known collectively as the Imperial Forums. These were largely buried when Mussolini bulldozed Via dei Fori Imperiali through the area in 1933, but excavations have since unearthed much of them. Minutely detailed reliefs on the landmark **Colonna Traiana** (Trajan's Column; Map p246) celebrate Trajan's military victories over the Dacians (from modern-day Romania).

> ## ✕ Take a Break
> Alongside its views of the Colonna Traiana, Terre e Domus (p124) offers regional dishes and Lazio wines.

PISAPHOTOGRAPHY/SHUTTERSTOCK ©

> ## ★ Don't Miss
> The Forum's oldest and most important Christian site, frescoed **Chiesa di Santa Maria Antiqua** (Map p246; SUPER ticket adult/reduced €18/13.50; ☺9am-6.30pm Tue, Thu & Sat, from 2pm Sun summer, 9am-3.30pm Tue, Thu & Sat, from 2pm Sun winter), requires a SUPER ticket.

Roman Forum

A HISTORICAL TOUR

In ancient times, a forum was a market place, civic centre and religious complex all rolled into one, and the greatest of all was the Roman Forum (Foro Romano). Situated between the Palatino (Palatine Hill), ancient Rome's most exclusive neighbourhood, and the Campidoglio (Capitoline Hill), it was the city's busy, bustling centre. On any given day it teemed with activity. Senators debated affairs of state in the ❶ Curia, shoppers thronged the squares and traffic-free streets and crowds gathered under the ❷ Colonna di Foca to listen to politicians holding forth from the ❷ Rostri. Elsewhere, lawyers worked the courts in basilicas including the ❸ Basilica di Massenzio, while the Vestal Virgins quietly went about their business in the ❹ Casa delle Vestali.

Special occasions were also celebrated in the Forum: religious holidays were marked with ceremonies at temples such as ❺ Tempio di Saturno and ❻ Tempio di Castore e Polluce, and military victories were honoured with dramatic processions up Via Sacra and the building of monumental arches like ❼ Arco di Settimio Severo and ❽ Arco di Tito.

The ruins you see today are impressive but they can be confusing without a clear picture of what the Forum once looked like. This spread shows the Forum in its heyday, complete with temples, civic buildings and towering monuments to heroes of the Roman Empire.

TOP TIPS

➡ Get grandstand views of the Forum from the Palatino and Campidoglio.

➡ Visit first thing in the morning or late afternoon; crowds are worst between 11am and 2pm.

➡ In summer it gets hot in the Forum and there's little shade, so take a hat and plenty of water.

Colonna di Foca & Rostri

Campidoglio (Capitoline Hill)

The free-standing, 13.5m-high Column of Phocus is the Forum's youngest monument, dating to AD 608. Behind it, the Rostri provided a suitably grandiose platform for pontificating public speakers.

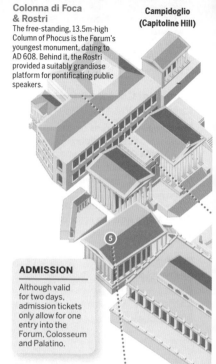

ADMISSION

Although valid for two days, admission tickets only allow for one entry into the Forum, Colosseum and Palatino.

Tempio di Saturno

Ancient Rome's Fort Knox, the Temple of Saturn was the city treasury. In Caesar's day it housed 13 tonnes of gold, 114 tonnes of silver and 30 million sestertii worth of silver coins.

JASCIC/SHUTTERSTOCK ©

VIACHESLAV LOPATIN/SHUTTERSTOCK ©

Tempio di Castore e Polluce

Only three columns of the Temple of Castor and Pollux remain. The temple was dedicated to the Heavenly Twins after they supposedly led the Romans to victory over the Latin League in 496 BC.

Arco di Settimio Severo

One of the Forum's signature monuments, this imposing triumphal arch commemorates the military victories of Septimius Severus. Relief panels depict his campaigns against the Parthians.

Curia

This big barn-like building was the official seat of the Roman Senate. Most of what you see is a reconstruction, but the interior marble floor dates to the 3rd-century reign of Diocletian.

Basilica di Massenzio

Marvel at the scale of this vast 4th-century basilica. In its original form the central hall was divided into enormous naves; now only part of the northern nave survives.

Via Sacra

Tempio di Giulio Cesare

JULIUS CAESAR

Julius Caesar was cremated on the site where the Tempio di Giulio Cesare now stands.

Arco di Tito

Said to be the inspiration for the Arc de Triomphe in Paris, the well-preserved Arch of Titus was built by the emperor Domitian to honour his elder brother Titus.

Casa delle Vestali

White statues line the grassy atrium of what was once the luxurious 50-room home of the Vestal Virgins. The virgins played an important role in Roman religion, serving the goddess Vesta.

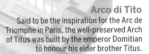

BELENOS/SHUTTERSTOCK ©

Trevi Fountain

The Fontana di Trevi is Rome's largest and most celebrated fountain. A foaming ensemble of mythical figures, wild horses and cascading rock falls, it takes up the entire side of the 17th-century Palazzo Poli.

Immortalised by Federico Fellini's film *La dolce vita* – apparently Anita Ekberg wore waders under her iconic black ballgown when she took her famous dip – the Trevi Fountain is one of Rome's must-see sights. It was completed in 1762 and named Trevi in reference to the *tre vie* (three roads) that converge on it.

The water comes from the Aqua Virgo, an underground aqueduct that was built 2000 years ago, during the reign of Augustus, to bring water in from the Salone springs around 19km away.

The Design

The fountain's design, conceived by Nicola Salvi in 1732, depicts Neptune, the god of the sea, in a shell-shaped chariot being led by Tritons and two sea horses, one wild, one docile, representing the moods of the

Great for...

Don't Miss

The contrasting horses – one tempestuous, one calm – which depict the moods of the sea.

Neptune

ℹ Need to Know

Fontana di Trevi; Map p245; Piazza di Trevi;
ⓂBarberini

✕ Take a Break

Recommended dining spots near the
fountain include Il Chianti (p133) and
Hostaria Romana (p130).

★ Top Tip

Come at dawn to avoid the crowds,
or in the evening when the fountain is
beautifully lit.

What's Nearby?
Palazzo del Quirinale   Palace

(Map p245; ☎06 3996 75 57; www.quirinale.
it; Piazza del Quirinale; tours from €1.50;
⊗9.30am-4pm Tue, Wed & Fri-Sun, closed Aug;
🚌Via Nazionale, ⓂRepubblica) Perched atop
the Quirinale Hill, one of Rome's seven
hills, this former papal summer residence
has been home to the Italian head of state
since 1948. Originally commissioned by
Pope Gregory XIII (r 1572–85) it was built
and added to over 150 years by architects
including Ottaviano Mascherino, Domenico
Fontana, Francesco Borromini, Gian Lorenzo Bernini and Carlo Maderno. Guided
tours of its grand reception rooms should
be booked at least five days ahead by telephone, or online at www.coopculture.it.

sea. In the niche to the left of Neptune, a
statue represents Abundance; to the right
is Salubrity.

On the eastern side is a strange conical
urn. Known as the *Asso di coppe* (Ace
of Cups), this was supposedly placed by
Nicola Salvi to block the view of a busybody
barber who had been a vocal critic of Salvi's
design during the fountain's construction.

Throw In Your Money

The famous tradition (since the 1954 film
Three Coins in the Fountain) is to toss a
coin into the water and thus ensure you'll
one day return to Rome. About €3000 is
thrown in on an average day. This money
is collected daily and goes to the Catholic
charity Caritas, with its yield increasing
significantly since the crackdown on people
extracting the money for themselves.

Basilica di Santa Maria del Popolo

A magnificent repository of art, this is one of Rome's earliest and richest Renaissance churches, with lavish chapels decorated by artists including Caravaggio, Bernini, Raphael and Pinturicchio.

Great for...

Don't Miss

As all eyes are turned on Caravaggio's canvases, don't miss Pinturicchio's wonderful frescoes in the Della Rovere Chapel.

The first chapel was built here in 1099 to exorcise the ghost of Nero, who was secretly buried here and whose malicious spirit was thought to haunt the area. There were subsequent overhauls, but the church's most important makeover came when Bramante renovated the presbytery and choir in the early 16th century and Pinturicchio added frescoes. Bernini further reworked the church in the 17th century.

Cerasi Chapel

The church's dazzling highlight is the Cappella Cerasi, with two works by Caravaggio: the *Conversion of Saul* (1601) and the *Crucifixion of St Peter* (1601), dramatically spotlit via the artist's use of light and shade. The central altarpiece painting is the *Assumption* (1590) by Annibale Carracci.

Bernini's *Habakkuk & the Angel*, Chigi Chapel

ZVONIMIR ATLETIC/SHUTTERSTOCK ©

ℹ Need to Know

Map p252; ☏ 392 3612243; www.smaria
delpopolo.com; Piazza del Popolo 12; ⏱7am-
noon & 4-7pm Mon-Sat, 8am-1.30pm & 4.30-
7.30pm Sun; Ⓜ Flaminio

✕ Take a Break

Enjoy a people-watching coffee break
on the spacious pavement terrace of
historic cafe Rosati (p172), on Piazza del
Popolo.

★ Top Tip

Admire the oldest stained-glass windows in Rome in the basilica's apse.

Chigi Chapel

Raphael designed the Cappella Chigi,
dedicated to his patron Agostino Chigi,
but never lived to see it completed. Bernini
finished the job more than 100 years
later, contributing statues of Daniel and
Habakkuk to the altarpiece. Only the floor
mosaics were retained from Raphael's
original design, including that of a kneeling
skeleton, placed there to remind the living
of the inevitable.

Delle Rovere Chapel

This 15th-century chapel features works by
Pinturicchio and his school. Frescoes in the
lunettes depict episodes from the life of St
Jerome, while the main altarpiece shows
the Nativity with St Jerome.

What's Nearby?

Piazza del Popolo Piazza

(Map p252; Ⓜ Flaminio) This dazzling piazza
was laid out in 1538 to provide a grandiose
entrance to what was then Rome's main
northern gateway and was remodelled by
Giuseppe Valadier in 1823. Guarding its
southern approach are Carlo Rainaldi's twin
17th-century churches, and a 36m-high
obelisk, brought by Augustus from ancient
Egypt, pierces its centre.

Via Margutta Street

(Map p252; Ⓜ Spagna) Antique shops, art galleries and boutiques pepper Via Margutta,
one of Rome's prettiest pedestrian cobbled
lanes, strung with ivy-laced *palazzi,* decorative potted plants, marble-engraved shop
plaques and the odd monumental fountain.
Picasso worked at a gallery at No 54 and
the Italian Futurists had their first meeting
here in 1917.

Walking Tour: Literary Footsteps

This walk through the Tridente district explores the literary haunts, both real and fictional, that litter the area. Discover the cafe where Casanova drank, the hotel that inspired Cocteau and the house where Keats breathed his last.

Start Pincio Hill Gardens

Distance 1km

Duration 2½ hours

2 Dan Brown's *Angels & Demons* made use of the art-rich **Basilica di Santa Maria del Popolo** (p88) in its convoluted plot.

3 Jean Cocteau stayed at the **Hotel de Russie** with Picasso, and wrote a letter home describing picking oranges from outside his window.

4 Cobbled **Via Margutta** (p89) is where Truman Capote wrote his short story *Lola*. Fellini, Picasso, Stravinsky and Puccini all lived here at some point.

0 500 m
0 0.25 miles

1 Begin your walk in the panoramic **Pincio Hill Gardens** (p58), where Henry James' Daisy Miller walked with Frederick Winterbourne.

Classic Photo Spanish Steps

6 Leaving the cafe, you're almost at the **Spanish Steps** (p94), which Dickens described in his *Pictures from Italy*. Byron stayed at 25 Piazza di Spagna in 1817.

VILLA BORGHESE

Viale dell' Obelisco

Viale delle Magnolie

① START

Galoppatoio

Viale del Muro Torto

Viale Trinità dei Monti

Via Margutta

Via Alibert

CAMPO MARZIO   Ⓜ Spagna

Piazza di Spagna

Via delle Carrozze

Via dei Condotti

⑤

⑥

⑦

FINISH   Piazza Mignanelli

Via Mario de' Fiori

Via Sistina

Via dei Due Macelli

Via di Porta Pinciana

Take a Break... Compose your own whimsical tale in the Hassler Hotel's romantic rooftop restaurant, **Imàgo** (p133).

7 Overlooking the Spanish Steps, the **Keats-Shelley House** (p95) is now a small museum devoted to the Romantic poets.

5 Head to Via dei Condotti, where William Thackeray stayed, and stop at **Antico Caffè Greco** (p130), a former haunt of Casanova, Goethe, Keats, Byron and Shelley.

Basilica di San Giovanni in Laterano

Dating to the 4th century, this monumental cathedral was the first Christian basilica built in the city, and until the late 14th century it was the pope's main place of worship.

The oldest of Rome's four papal basilicas was commissioned by Emperor Constantine and consecrated by Pope Sylvester I in 324. From then until 1309, when the papacy moved to Avignon, it was the principal pontifical church, and the adjacent Palazzo Laterano was the pope's official residence. Both buildings fell into disrepair during the papacy's French interlude, and when Pope Gregory XI returned to Rome in 1377 he preferred to decamp to the fortified Vatican rather than stay in the official papal digs.

The basilica was notably revamped by Borromini in the 17th century, and by Alessandro Galilei, who added the immense white facade in 1735.

Great for...

Don't Miss

The incomplete Giotto fresco on the first column in the right-hand nave.

The cloister

❶ Need to Know

Map p255; ☑06 6988 6493; Piazza di San Giovanni in Laterano 4; basilica free, cloister incl Museo del Tesoro €5; ⏲7am-6.30pm, cloister 9am-6pm; Ⓜ San Giovanni

✕ Take a Break

Head south of the basilica for fabulous pizza at Sbanco (p139).

★ Top Tip

Look down as well as up – the basilica has a beautiful inlaid marble floor.

The Facade

Surmounted by 15 7m-high statues – Christ with St John the Baptist, John the Evangelist and the 12 Apostles – Galilei's huge facade is an imposing work of late-baroque classicism. The **central bronze doors** were moved here from the Roman Forum; on the far right, the **Holy Door** is only opened in jubilee years.

The Interior

The cavernous interior owes much of its present look to Francesco Borromini, who styled it for the 1650 jubilee. It's a breathtaking sight with a golden gilt **ceiling**, a 15th-century **mosaic floor**, and a wide **nave** lined with 18th-century sculptures of the apostles, each 4.6m high and set in its own dramatic niche.

At the end of the nave, an elaborate Gothic **baldachin** stands over the papal altar. Dating to the 14th century, this is said to contain the relics of the heads of Sts Peter and Paul. In front, a double staircase leads down to the **confessio** and the Renaissance tomb of Pope Martin V.

Behind the altar, the massive **apse** is decorated with sparkling mosaics mainly added in the 1800s.

At the other end of the basilica, on the first pillar in the right-hand aisle, is an incomplete Giotto fresco.

The Cloister

To the left of the altar, the basilica's 13th-century cloister is a lovely, peaceful place with graceful twisted columns set around a central garden. Lining the ambulatories are marble fragments from the original church, including the remains of a 5th-century papal throne and inscriptions of two papal bulls.

S.BORISOV/SHUTTERSTOCK ©

Spanish Steps

Rising above Piazza di Spagna, the Spanish Steps provide a perfect people-watching perch, and you'll almost certainly find yourself taking stock here at some point in your visit to Rome. Just remember: no eating on the steps and good luck dodging the many newlyweds posing for official wedding portraits.

The area around the steps has long been a magnet for foreigners. In the late 1700s, it was much loved by English travellers on the Grand Tour, and was known locally as *'er ghetto de l'inglesi'* (the English ghetto). Poet John Keats lived for a short time in some rooms overlooking the Spanish Steps, and died here of tuberculosis at the age of 25.

The Steps

Piazza di Spagna was named after the Spanish Embassy to the Holy See, but the 135-step staircase – in Italian, *Scalinata della Trinità dei Monti* – was designed by an Italian, Francesco de Sanctis, and built in 1725 with money bequeathed by the French.

Great for...

Don't Miss

The sweeping rooftop views from the top of the steps.

ⓘ Need to Know

Map p245; Ⓜ Spagna

✕ Take a Break

Watch the sun set over the steps from the terrace of cocktail bar Il Palazzetto (p113).

★ Top Tip

No picnics on the steps, please – or risk a fine of up to €500.

Lorenzo. The bees and suns that decorate the structure, which is sunken to compensate for the low pressure of the feeder aqueduct, represent the Barberini family who commissioned the fountain.

Opposite the fountain, **Via dei Condotti** is Rome's most exclusive shopping strip.

Chiesa della Trinità dei Monti

The **Chiesa della Trinità dei Monti** (Map p245; ☏06 679 41 79; http://trinitadeimonti.net/it/chiesa/; Piazza Trinità dei Monti 3; ⊙10.15am-8pm Tue-Thu, noon-9pm Fri, 9.15am-8pm Sat, 9am-8pm Sun; Ⓜ Spagna) was commissioned by King Louis XII of France and consecrated in 1585. In addition to great rooftop views, it boasts some wonderful frescoes by Daniele da Volterra. His *Deposizione* (Deposition), in the second chapel on the left, is regarded as a masterpiece of mannerist painting.

Piazza di Spagna

At the foot of the steps, the fountain of a sinking boat, the **Barcaccia** (Map p245), dating from 1627, is believed to be by Pietro Bernini, father of the more famous Gian

What's Nearby?

Keats-Shelley House   Museum

(Map p245; ☏06 678 42 35; www.keats-shelley-house.org; Piazza di Spagna 26; adult/reduced €5/4; ⊙10am-1pm & 2-6pm Mon-Sat; Ⓜ Spagna) The Keats-Shelley House is where Romantic poet John Keats died of tuberculosis at the age of 25, in February 1821. Keats came to Rome in 1820 to try to improve his health in the Italian climate, and rented two rooms on the 3rd floor of a townhouse next to the Spanish Steps, with painter companion Joseph Severn (1793–1879).

Campo de' Fiori

GIULIO_DOR/GETTY IMAGES ©

Roman Market Meanders

Be it picnic-shopping for cheese, salami and seasonal zero-kilometre produce at a farmers' market or browsing racks of vintage fashion, market-going is a prime opportunity to mingle with locals and lap up the grassroots vibe of the capital's different neighbourhoods.

Great for...

☑ Don't Miss

The festive Christmas market that spills across showpiece Piazza Navona each December (until 6 January).

Campo de' Fiori   Piazza

(Map p250; 🚌Corso Vittorio Emanuele II) Colourful and always busy, Il Campo hosts one of the city's best-known markets; by night it heaves with tourists and young drinkers who spill out of its many bars and restaurants. For centuries the square was the site of public executions. The spot where philosopher Giordano Bruno was burned for heresy in 1600 is marked by a sinister statue of the hooded monk, created by Ettore Ferrari in 1889.

Mercado de Porta Portese   Market

(Map p254; Piazza Porta Portese; 🕑6am-2pm Sun; 🚌Viale di Trastevere, 🚋Trastevere/Min P Istruzione) Head to this mammoth flea market to see Rome bargain-hunting. Thousands of stalls sell everything from rare

Pasta stall, Campo de' Fiori

BELLENA/SHUTTERSTOCK ©

ⓘ Need to Know

Bring your own bag or basket, and know that haggling is not really the thing to do.

✕ Take a Break

For a market-inspired lunch, take your pick of food stalls at Mercato Centrale (p133) near Stazione Termini.

★ Top Tip

To get the most out of Rome's food markets, consider a guided tour with local foodies at Casa Mia (p198).

Mercato di Piazza San Cosimato   Market

(Map p254; Piazza San Cosimato; ⊗7am-2pm Mon-Sat; 🚊Viale di Trastevere, 🚊Trastevere/ Mastai) Trastevere's open-air neighbourhood market is a top spot to stock up on globe and violet artichokes, *broccolo romanesco* (Roman broccoli), dandelion greens and other seasonal foodstuffs, as has been the case for at least a century.

Nuovo Mercato di Testaccio   Market

(entrances Via Beniamino Franklin, Via Volta, Via Manuzio, Via Ghiberti; ⊗7am-3.30pm Mon-Sat; 🚊Via Marmorata) A trip to Testaccio's neighbourhood market is always fun. Occupying a modern, purpose-built site, it hums with activity as locals go about their daily shopping, picking, prodding and sniffing the brightly coloured produce and browsing displays of shoes, hats and clothes. Come lunchtime the focus shifts to the market's increasing number of street-food stalls.

Mercato Monti Urban Market   Market

(Map p246; www.mercatomonti.com; Via Leonina 46; ⊗10am-8pm Sat & Sun Sep-Jun; Ⓜ Cavour) Vintage clothes, accessories, one-off pieces by local designers: this market in the hip 'hood of Monti is well worth a weekend rummage.

books and fell-off-a-lorry bikes to Peruvian shawls and off-brand phones. It's crazily busy and a lot of fun.

Mercato Campagna Amica al Circo Massimo   Market

(Map p246; www.mercatocircomassimo.it; Via di San Teodoro 74; ⊗8am-3pm Sat & Sun; 🚊Via dei Cerchi) One of Rome's best loved farmers' markets, this weekly *mercato* provides a showcase for regional producers from Lazio and central Italy. Stalls sell all manner of edible fare, including potential take-home gifts: cheese, conserves, jars of honey, ready-made sauces, olive oils and wines.

Mosaic, Terme di Nettuno

BILL PERRY/SHUTTERSTOCK ©

Day Trip: Ostia Antica

Rome's answer to Pompeii, the Scavi Archeologici di Ostia Antica is one of Italy's most underappreciated archae-ological sites. The amazingly preserved ruins of Rome's main seaport provide a thrilling glimpse into the workings of an ancient town.

Great for...

Don't Miss

The views over the site from atop the Terme di Nettuno.

Founded in the 4th century BC, the city started life as a fortified military camp guarding the mouth of the Tiber – hence the name 'Ostia', which is a derivation of the Latin word *ostium* (mouth). It quickly grew, and by the 2nd century AD was a thriving port with a population of around 50,000.

Decline set in after the fall of the Roman Empire, and by the 9th century the city had largely been abandoned, its citizens driven off by barbarian raids and outbreaks of malaria. Over subsequent centuries, it was plundered of marble and building materials and its ruins were gradually buried in river silt, which actually preserved them.

Theatrical-mask statue

BENEDICTUS/SHUTTERSTOCK ©

The Ruins

Near the entrance, **Porta Romana** gives on to the **Decumanus Maximus**, the site's central strip, which runs over 1km to Porta Marina, the city's original sea-facing gate.

On the Decumanus, the **Terme di Nettuno** is a must-see. This baths complex, one of 20 that originally stood in town, dates to the 2nd century and boasts some superb mosaics, including one of Neptune driving his seahorse chariot. In the centre of the complex are the remains of an arcaded **palestra** (gym).

Next to the Terme is the 1st-century BC **Teatro**, an amphitheatre built by Agrippa and later enlarged to hold 4000 people.

The grassy area behind the amphitheatre is the **Piazzale delle Corporazioni** (Forum of the Corporations), home to the offices of Ostia's merchant guilds. The mosaics that line the perimeter – ships, dolphins, a lighthouse and an elephant – are thought to represent the businesses housed on the square: ships and dolphins indicated ship-ping agencies, while the elephant probably referred to a business involved in the ivory trade.

The **Forum**, Ostia's main square, is over-looked by what remains of the **Capitolium**, a temple built by Hadrian and dedicated to Jupiter, Juno and Minerva.

Nearby is another highlight: the **Ther-mopolium**, an ancient cafe complete with a bar, frescoed menu, kitchen and small courtyard where customers would have relaxed by a fountain.

Across the road are the remains of the 2nd-century **Terme del Foro**, originally the city's largest baths complex. Here, in the *forica* (public toilet), you can see 20 well-preserved latrines set sociably into a long stone bench.

From Rome, take the Roma–Lido train from Stazione Porta San Paolo (next to Piramide metro station) to Ostia Antica (every 15 minutes). The 25-minute trip is covered by a standard Rome public trans-port ticket (€1.50).

Basilica courtyard

STEFANO_VALERI/SHUTTERSTOCK ©

Basilica di San Clemente

Nowhere better illustrates the various stages of Rome's turbulent past than this fascinating, multilayered church near the Colosseum: a 12th-century basilica sits atop a 4th-century church, in turn atop a 2nd-century pagan temple and 1st-century Roman house.

Great for...

Don't Miss

The temple to Mithras, deep in the bowels of the basilica.

Basilica Superiore

The street-level *basilica superiore* contains some glorious works of medieval art. These include a golden 12th-century apse mosaic, the *Trionfo della Croce* (Triumph of the Cross), showing the Madonna and St John the Baptist standing by a cross on which Christ is represented by 12 white doves. Also impressive are Masolino's 15th-century frescoes in the **Cappella di Santa Caterina**, depicting a crucifixion scene and episodes from the life of St Catherine.

Basilica Inferiore

Steps lead down to the 4th-century *basilica inferiore*. This was mostly destroyed by Norman invaders in 1084, but some faded 11th-century frescoes remain, illustrating the life of San Clemente.

Altar of the *basilica superiore*

PARIS JEFFERSON/GETTY IMAGES ©

ⓘ Need to Know

Map p255; ☑06 774 00 21; www.basilicasan
clemente.com; Piazza di San Clemente; basilica free, excavations adult/reduced €10/5;
◷9am-12.30pm & 3-6pm Mon-Sat, 12.15-6pm
Sun; ◱Via Labicana

✗ Take a Break

Enjoy an expertly chosen glass of Italian
wine at nearby Wine Concept (p176).

★ Top Tip

Bring a sweater: the temperature drops
underground.

Follow the steps down another level
and you'll come to a 1st-century Roman
house and a dark, 2nd-century **temple
to Mithras**, with an altar showing the god
slaying a bull. Beneath it all, you can hear
the eerie sound of a subterranean river
flowing through a Republic-era drain.

What's Nearby?

Basilica dei
SS Quattro Coronati   Basilica

(Map p255; ☑335 495248; Via dei Santi Quattro
20; cloisters €2, Oratorio di San Silvestro €1;
◷basilica 6.30am-12.45pm & 3.30-8pm, cloisters
9.45am-11.45am & 3.45-5.45pm Mon-Sat; ◱Via
di San Giovanni in Laterano) This brooding
fortified church harbours some lovely
13th-century frescoes and a delightful hidden **cloister**, accessible from the left-hand

aisle. The frescoes, in the **Oratorio di San
Silvestro**, depict the story of Constantine
and Pope Sylvester I and the so-called
Donation of Constantine, a notorious
forged document with which the emperor
supposedly ceded control of Rome and the
Western Roman Empire to the papacy.

To access the oratorio, ring the bell in the
entrance courtyard.

Chiesa di Santo
Stefano Rotondo   Church

(Map p246; www.santo-stefano-rotondo.it; Via
di Santo Stefano Rotondo 7; ◷10am-1pm &
2-5pm Tue-Sun winter, 10am-1pm & 3.30-6.30pm
Tue-Sun summer; ◱Via Claudia) Set in its own
secluded grounds, this haunting church
boasts a porticoed facade and a round,
columned interior. But what really gets the
heart racing is the graphic wall decor – a
cycle of 16th-century frescoes depicting
the tortures suffered by many early Christian martyrs.

VIACHESLAV LOPATIN/SHUTTERSTOCK ©

Terme di Caracalla

The remains of the emperor Caracalla's vast baths complex are among Rome's most awe-inspiring ruins. Inaugurated in AD 216, the original 10-hectare complex comprised baths, gyms, libraries, shops and gardens.

The baths remained in continuous use until AD 537, when the invading Visigoths cut off Rome's water supply. Excavations in the 16th and 17th centuries unearthed important sculptures – many went into the Farnese family's art collection. In its heyday, the complex attracted up to 8000 people daily, while hundreds of slaves sweated in a 9.5km tunnel network, tending to the plumbing systems.

The Ruins

Most of the ruins are what's left of the central bathhouse. This was a huge rectangular edifice bookended by two **palestre** (gyms) and centred on a **frigidarium** (cold room), where bathers would stop after spells in the warmer **tepidarium** and dome-capped **caldarium** (hot room). As you traverse the ruins towards the *palestra*

Great for...

Don't Miss

The white marble slab that was once part of an ancient board game.

ℹ Need to Know

📞06 3996 7700; www.coopculture.it; Viale delle Terme di Caracalla 52; adult/reduced €8/4; ⏱9am-1hr before sunset Tue-Sun, 9am-2pm Mon; 🚍Viale delle Terme di Caracalla

✖ Take a Break

Push on to Testaccio for a taste of genuine Roman cooking at the ever-popular Flavio al Velavevodetto (p139).

★ Top Tip

The Terme's virtual reality video guide (€7) allows you to see how the original complex looked.

orientale, look out for a slab of white, pockmarked marble on your right. This is a board from an ancient game called *tropa* (the hole game).

In summer the ruins stage opera and ballet performances.

What's Nearby?

Villa Celimontana   Park

(Map p246; Via della Navicella 12; ⏱7am-sunset; 🚍Via della Navicella) With its grassy banks and flower beds, this park is a wonderful place to escape the crowds and picnic. At its centre is a 16th-century villa housing the Italian Geographical Society; south is a 12m-plus Egyptian obelisk.

Basilica di Santa Sabina   Basilica

(Map p254; 📞06 57 94 01; Piazza Pietro d'Illiria 1; ⏱6.30am-12.45pm & 3-8pm; 🚍Lungotevere Aventino) This solemn, early-Christian church was founded by Peter of Illyria around AD 422. It was enlarged in the 9th century and again in 1216, just before it was given to the newly founded Dominican order – note the tombstone of Muñoz de Zamora, one of the order's founding fathers, in the nave floor. A 20th-century restoration returned it to its original look.

Villa del Priorato
di Malta   Historic Building

(Villa Magistrale; Map p254; Piazza dei Cavalieri di Malta; 🚍Lungotevere Aventino) Fronting an ornate cypress-shaded piazza, the Roman headquarters of the Sovereign Order of Malta, aka the Cavalieri di Malta (Knights of Malta), boasts one of Rome's most celebrated views. Look through the keyhole in the villa's green door and you'll see the dome of St Peter's Basilica perfectly aligned at the end of a hedge-lined avenue.

Palazzo della Civiltà Italiana (p107)

Modern Architecture

Rome is best known for its classical architecture, but the city also boasts a string of striking modern buildings, many created and designed by the 21st-century's top 'starchitects'.

Great for...

ⓘ Need to Know

The Auditorium and MAXXI can be accessed by tram 2 from Piazzale Flaminio.

★ **Top Tip**

Take in a gig at the Auditorium Parco della Musica (p188) to experience its perfect acoustics.

Auditorium Parco della Musica
Cultural Centre

(📞06 8024 1281; www.auditorium.com; Viale Pietro de Coubertin; ⏰11am-8pm Mon-Sat, 10am-8pm Sun summer, to 6pm winter; 🚊Viale Tiziano) Designed by Renzo Piano and inaugurated in 2002, Rome's flagship cultural centre is an audacious work of architecture consisting of three silver pod-like concert halls set round a 3000-seat amphitheatre. There's a pleasant cafe in the central square and the grounds include a children's park. There's also a fabulous book and music shop.

Excavations during its construction revealed remains of an ancient Roman villa, some of which are now on show in the Auditorium's small **Museo Archeologico** (⏰10am-8pm summer, 11am-6pm Mon-Sat, 10am-6pm Sun winter) `FREE`.

Check online for occasional English-language tours of the complex.

Museo Nazionale delle Arti del XXI Secolo
Gallery

(MAXXI; 📞06 320 19 54; www.maxxi.art; Via Guido Reni 4a; adult/reduced €12/9; ⏰11am-7pm Tue-Fri & Sun, to 10pm Sat; 🚊Viale Tiziano) As much as the exhibitions, the highlight of Rome's leading contemporary art gallery is the Zaha Hadid–designed building it occupies. Formerly a barracks, the curved concrete structure is striking inside and out with a multilayered geometric facade and a cavernous light-filled interior full of snaking walkways and suspended staircases.

The gallery has a permanent collection of 20th- and 21st-century works, of which

Museo Nazionale delle Arti del XXI Secolo

a selection are on free display in Gallery 4, but more interesting are its international exhibitions.

Museo dell'Ara Pacis   Museum

(Map p250; ☑06 06 08; www.arapacis.it; Lungotevere in Augusta; adult/reduced €10.50/8.50; ☉9.30am-6.30pm; Ⓜ Flaminio) The first modern construction in Rome's historic centre since WWII, Richard Meier's controversial and widely detested glass-and-marble pavilion houses the *Ara Pacis Augustae* (Altar of Peace), Augustus' great monument to peace. One of the most important works of ancient Roman sculpture, the vast marble altar – measuring 11.6m by 10.6m by 3.6m – was completed in 13 BC.

Palazzo della Civiltà Italiana   Historic Building

(Palace of Italian Civilisation; ☑06 3345 0970; www.fendi.com; Quadrato della Concordia; ☉depends on exhibition; Ⓜ EUR Magliana) **FREE** Also known more prosaically as the Square Colosseum, this iconic building in the EUR district is a masterpiece of rationalist architecture with its symmetrical rows of 216 arches and gleaming white travertine marble. For much of its 72-year history – it was completed in 1943 – it has remained unoccupied, but in 2015 the Fendi fashion house transferred its global headquarters here. Watch for contemporary-art exhibitions hosted by the Italian fashion house on the ground floor for six months of each year.

Rome Convention Centre La Nuvola   Architecture

(☑06 5451 3710; www.romaconventiongroup.it; Viale Asia, entrance cnr Via Cristoforo Colombo; Ⓜ EUR Fermi) Contemporary architecture buffs will appreciate Rome's congress centre (2016) designed by Italian architects Massimiliano and Doriana Fuksas. The striking building comprises a transparent, glass-and-steel box (40m high, 70m wide and 175m long) called **Le Theca** (The Shrine), inside of which hangs organically shaped **La Nuvola** (The Cloud) containing an auditorium and conference rooms seating up to 8000 people. A separate black skyscraper called **La Luma** (The Blade), contains a hotel that closed shortly after it opened as the entire €270-million complex fell into fiscal trouble. Rumours are it will reopen as a Hilton.

To visit, check www.romaconventiongroup.it for special openings and guided tours.

★ **Don't Miss**

The outlying EUR district, which is home to some impressive rationalist architecture.

MAXXI NATIONAL MUSEUM OF XXI CENTURY ARTS, PHOTO M3STUDIO COURTESY FONDAZIONE MAXXI ©

✕ **Take a Break**

Tucked away behind MAXXI, Neve di Latte (p141) serves scoops of near-perfect gelato.

JULIE MAYFENG/SHUTTERSTOCK ©

Basilica di Santa Maria Maggiore

One of Rome's four patriarchal basilicas, this monumental church stands on the summit of the Esquilino Hill, on the site of a miraculous snowfall in the summer of AD 358. An architectural hybrid, it boasts a Romanesque belfry, an 18th-century baroque facade and interior, and glorious 5th-century mosaics.

Great for...

Don't Miss

The luminous 13th-century apse mosaics by Jacopo Torriti.

Exterior

The basilica's exterior is decorated with glimmering 13th-century mosaics, protected by Ferdinand Fuga's baroque porch (1741). Rising behind, the 75m-high belfry is Rome's highest.

In front of the church, the 18.78m-high column originally stood in the Basilica di Massenzio in the Roman Forum.

Interior

The vast interior retains its original structure, despite the basilica's many overhauls. Particularly spectacular are the **5th-century mosaics** in the triumphal arch and nave, depicting Old Testament scenes. The central image in the apse, signed by Jacopo Torriti, dates from the 13th century and represents the coronation of the Virgin Mary. Beneath

ℹ Need to Know

Map p245; ☑06 6988 6800; Piazza Santa Maria Maggiore; basilica free, adult/reduced museum €3/2, loggia €5; ⏱7am-6.45pm, loggia guided tours 9.30am-5.45pm; MTermini or Cavour

✕ Take a Break

Lunch on pastries, fruit tartlets, focaccia, *pizza al taglio* (pizza by the slice) and daily specials at Panella (p135).

★ Top Tip

Come during the Festa della Madonna della Neve (5 August) to revel in a magical recreation of the historic snowfall.

your feet, the nave floor is a fine example of 12th-century Cosmati paving.

The **baldachin** over the high altar is heavy with gilt cherubs; the altar itself is a porphyry sarcophagus, said to contain the relics of St Matthew.

A simple stone plaque embedded in the floor to the right of the altar marks the spot where Gian Lorenzo Bernini and his father Pietro are buried. Steps lead down to the **confessio** where a statue of Pope Pius IX kneels before a reliquary containing a fragment of Jesus' manger.

Through the souvenir shop on the right-hand side of the church is the **Museo del Tesoro** with a glittering collection of religious artefacts. Most interesting, however, is Ferdinando Fuga's **Loggia delle Benedizioni** (upper loggia; accessible only by guided tours). Here you can get a close look at the facade's iridescent 13th-century mosaics created by Filippo Rusuti and Bernini's magnificent helical staircase.

What's Nearby?

Basilica di San Pietro in Vincoli
Basilica

(Map p246; ☑06 9784 4950; Piazza di San Pietro in Vincoli 4a; ⏱8am-12.20pm & 3-6.50pm summer, to 5.50pm winter; MCavour) Pilgrims and art lovers flock to this 5th-century basilica for two reasons: to marvel at Michelangelo's colossal *Moses* (1505) sculpture and to see the chains that supposedly bound St Peter when he was imprisoned in the Carcere Mamertino (near the Roman Forum). Access to the church is via a flight of steps through a low arch that leads up from Via Cavour.

Piazza di Santa Maria in Trastevere

CATARINA BELOVA/SHUTTERSTOCK ©

Trastevere Treasures

On the left-bank of the Tiber, boho Trastevere is one of Rome's most vivacious neighbourhoods, its old-world medieval lanes studded with art-rich churches and villas, bars, cafes and atmospheric trattorias.

Great for...

Don't Miss

The golden mosaics in the Basilica di Santa Maria in Trastevere.

Basilica di Santa Maria in Trastevere

Basilica

(Map p254; ☏06 581 48 02; Piazza di Santa Maria in Trastevere; ⊗7.30am-9pm Sep-Jul, 8am-noon & 4-9pm Aug; ☒Viale di Trastevere, ☒Belli)
Nestled in a quiet corner of Trastevere's focal square, this is said to be the oldest church dedicated to the Virgin Mary in Rome. In its original form, it dates to the early 3rd century, but a major 12th-century makeover saw the addition of a Romanesque bell tower and glittering facade. The portico came later, added by Carlo Fontana in 1702. Inside, the 12th-century mosaics are the headline feature.

In the apse, look out for Christ and his mother flanked by various saints and, on the far left, Pope Innocent II holding a model of the church. Beneath this are six

Basilica di Santa Cecilia in Trastevere

STEFANO_VALERI/SHUTTERSTOCK ©

🛈 Need to Know

To get to Trastevere, take tram 8 from Largo di Torre Argentina.

✕ Take a Break

Eat at Trattoria Da Cesare al Casaletto (p135) – many reckon it's Rome's best trattoria.

★ Top Tip

Trendy pop-up summer bars, open until late, pepper Trastevere's riverside quays between Ponte Mazzini and Ponte Cestio.

mosaics by Pietro Cavallini illustrating the life of the Virgin (c 1291).

According to legend, the church stands on the spot where a fountain of oil miraculously sprang from the ground. It incorporates 21 ancient Roman columns, some plundered from the Terme di Caracalla, and boasts a 17th-century wooden ceiling.

Villa Farnesina   Historic Building

(Map p250; ☎06 6802 7268; www.villafarnesina. it; Via della Lungara 230; adult/reduced €6/5; ☺9am-2pm Mon-Sat, to 5pm 2nd Sun of the month; ☒Lungotevere della Farnesina) The interior of this gorgeous 16th-century villa is fantastically frescoed from top to bottom. Several paintings in the Loggia of Cupid and Psyche and the Loggia of Galatea, both on the ground floor, are attributed to Raphael.

On the 1st floor, Peruzzi's dazzling frescoes in the Salone delle Prospettive are a superb illusionary perspective of a colonnade and panorama of 16th-century Rome.

Basilica di Santa Cecilia in Trastevere   Basilica

(Map p254; ☎06 4549 2739; www.benedettine santacecilia.it; Piazza di Santa Cecilia 22; fresco & crypt each €2.50; ☺basilica & crypt 10am-12.30pm & 4-6pm Mon-Sat, 11.30am-12.30pm & 4.30-6.30pm Sun, fresco 10am-12.30pm Mon-Sat, 11.30am-12.30pm Sun; ☒Viale de Trastevere, ☒Belli) The last resting place of the patron saint of music features Pietro Cavallini's stunning 13th-century fresco, in the nuns' choir of the hushed convent adjoining the church. Inside the church itself, Stefano Maderno's mysterious sculpture depicts St Cecilia's miraculously preserved body, unearthed in the Catacombs of San Callisto in 1599. You can also visit the excavations of Roman houses, one of which was possibly that of Cecilia.

DZMITRY RYSHCHUK/SHUTTERSTOCK ©

Craft-Cocktail Culture

Rome's millennial love affair with craft cocktails shows no sign of waning as a sweet peppering of golden oldies and new openings keeps cocktail lovers in the capital on their toes. Expect expertly crafted drinks, with mixologists pairing unexpected seasonal flavours with homemade syrups and unusual bitters.

Great for...

☑ Don't Miss

A classic Aperol spritz (two parts Aperol, an amber-coloured bitter, to three parts prosecco and a dash of soda water).

Niji Roma
Cocktail Bar

(Map p254; ☑06 581 95 20; www.facebook. com/niji.cafe.roma; Via dei Vascellari 35; ⊙7pm-3am; ⏏Belli) A cosy, stylish, artistic bar in Trastevere that looks like a film set designed to portray just that. The range of cocktails continues the bar's themes. They are exquisitely poured and presented and are almost, *almost*, too good-looking to drink. The mood here is mellow but never slouchy.

Zuma Bar
Cocktail Bar

(Map p250; ☑06 9926 6622; www.zumares taurant.com; Via della Fontanella di Borghese 48, Palazzo Fendi; ⊙6pm-1am Sun-Thu, to 2am Fri & Sat; ☎; ⓂSpagna) Dress up for a drink on the rooftop terrace of Palazzo Fendi of fashion-house fame – few cocktail bars in

Aperol spritz

ELFLACO1982/SHUTTERSTOCK ©

Club Derrière
Cocktail Bar

(Map p250; ☎393 5661077; www.facebook.com/clubderriereroma; Vicolo delle Coppelle 59; ⏲10pm-4am; ☎; 🚌Corso del Rinascimento) Found in the back room of an unassuming trattoria (Osteria delle Coppelle) in Rome's historic centre, Club Derrière is an enigmatic speakeasy where a suit of armour serves as unofficial bouncer. Bartenders don ties and waistcoats and sling sleek cocktails (€12) often inspired by cultural figures, such as their Edgar Allan Poe, a heady mix of sherry, Knob Creek rye, chocolate and Angostura bitters.

Keyhole
Cocktail Bar

(Map p254; Via dell'Arco di San Calisto 17; ⏲midnight-5am; 🚌Viale di Trastevere, 🚊Belli) This achingly hip, underground speakeasy ticks all the boxes: no identifiable name or signage outside; a black door smothered in keyhole plates; and Prohibition-era decor including Chesterfield sofas, dim lighting and a craft cocktail menu. Not sure what to order? The mixologists will create your own bespoke cocktail (around €10).

No password is required to get into Keyhole, but you need to fill in a form to become a member (€5). No phones.

Rome are as sleek, hip or achingly sophisticated as this (shiso with juniper berries, elderflower and prosecco anyone?). City rooftop views are fabulous and DJs spin Zuma playlists at weekends.

Il Palazzetto
Cocktail Bar

(Map p245; ☎06 6993 4560; Vicolo del Bottino 8; ⏲noon-6pm winter, 4pm-midnight summer, closed in bad weather; Ⓜ Spagna) No terrace proffers such a fine view of the Spanish Steps over an expertly shaken cocktail. Ride the lift up from the discreet entrance on narrow Vicolo del Bottino or look for stairs leading to the bar from the top of the steps. Given everything is al fresco, the bar is only open in warm, dry weather.

PHANT/SHUTTERSTOCK ©

Galleria Nazionale d'Arte Antica – Palazzo Barberini

Palazzo Barberini, one of Rome's grandest palaces, provides the sumptuous setting for a riveting collection of Old Masters and baroque masterpieces.

Great for...

☑ Don't Miss

Hans Holbein's celebrated depiction of King Henry VIII.

The *palazzo*, commissioned to celebrate the Barberini family's rise to papal power, impresses even before you clap eyes on the breathtaking art inside. Many of the 17th century's top architects worked on it, including Bernini, who designed a large square-shafted staircase, and Borromini, his hated rival, who added a monumental helicoidal stairway.

Amid the artistic treasures on show, don't miss Pietro da Cortona's mind-blowing ceiling fresco, *Il Trionfo della Divina Provvidenza* (Triumph of Divine Providence; 1632–39), in the 1st-floor main salon. Other must-sees include Hans Holbein's famous portrait of a pugnacious Henry VIII (c 1540); Filippo Lippi's luminous *Annunciazione* (Annunciation); and Raphael's *La Fornarina* (The Baker's Girl), a portrait of his mistress, who worked in a bakery in Trastevere.

Cortona's Il Trionfo della Divina Provvidenza

RICHARD A. MCGUIRK/SHUTTERSTOCK ©

❶ Need to Know

Galleria Nazionale d'Arte Antica; Map p245; 🗹06 481 45 91; www.barberinicorsini.org; Via delle Quattro Fontane 13; adult/reduced €12/6; ⓢ8.30am-6pm Tue-Sun; Ⓜ Barberini

✕ Take a Break

Treat yourself to fabulous regional cuisine from Emilia-Romagna at nearby Colline Emiliane (p129).

★ Top Tip

Galleria Corsini (Palazzo Corsini; Map p250; 🗹06 6880 2323; Via della Lungara 10; adult/reduced incl Palazzo Barberini €12/6; ⓢ8.30am-7pm Wed-Mon; 🚊 Lungotevere della Farnesina) in Trastevere displays the rest of the Galleria Nazionale d'Arte Antica's collection.

Works by Caravaggio include *San Francesco d'Assisi in meditazione* (St Francis in Meditation), *Narciso* (Narcissus; 1571–1610) and the mesmerisingly horrific *Giuditta e Oloferne* (Judith Beheading Holophernes; c 1597–1600).

What's Nearby?

Chiesa di San Carlino alle Quattro Fontane   Church

(Map p245; 🗹06 488 32 61; Via del Quirinale 23; cloister €1; ⓢ10am-1pm Mon-Sat, from noon Sun; Ⓜ Repubblica) This tiny church is a masterpiece of Roman baroque. It was Borromini's first church, and the play of convex and concave surfaces and the dome illuminated by hidden windows cleverly transform the small space into a place of light and beauty. The church, completed in 1641, stands at the intersection known as the **Quattro Fontane**,

named after the late-16th-century fountains on its four corners, representing Fidelity, Strength and the Rivers Arno and Tiber.

Convento dei Cappuccini   Museum

(Map p245; 🗹06 8880 3695; www.cappucciniviaveneto.it; Via Vittorio Veneto 27; adult/reduced €8.50/5; ⓢ9am-6.30pm; Ⓜ Barberini) This church and convent complex safeguards what is possibly Rome's strangest sight: crypt chapels where everything from the picture frames to the light fittings is made of human bones. Between 1732 and 1775 resident Capuchin monks used the bones of 3700 of their departed brothers to create this macabre *memento mori* (reminder of death) – a 30m-long passageway ensnaring six crypts, each named after the type of bone used to decorate (skulls, shin bones, pelvises etc).

Villa d'Este

Day Trip: Tivoli

A summer retreat for ancient Romans and the Renaissance rich, the hilltop town of Tivoli is home to two Unesco World Heritage Sites: sprawling Villa Adriana and the 16th-century Villa d'Este.

Great for...

☑ Don't Miss

Admire the rich mannerist frescoes of Villa d'Este before heading into the gardens.

Villa d'Este

In Tivoli's hilltop centre, the steeply terraced grounds of **Villa d'Este** (☎0774 33 29 20; www.villadestetivoli.info; Piazza Trento 5; adult/reduced €10/5; ⊗8.30am-7.45pm Tue-Sun, from 2pm Mon, gardens close sunset, ticket office closes 6.45pm) are a superlative example of a Renaissance garden, complete with monumental fountains, elegant tree-lined avenues and landscaped grottoes. The villa, originally a Benedictine convent, was converted into a luxury retreat by Lucrezia Borgia's son, Cardinal Ippolito d'Este, in the late 16th century. It provided inspiration for composer Franz Liszt, who stayed here between 1865 and 1886 and immortalised it in his 1877 piano composition *The Fountains of the Villa d'Este*.

The canopo, Villa Adriana

PAOLO GALLO/SHUTTERSTOCK ©

ℹ️ Need to Know

Information is available from the **tourist information point** (☎0774 31 35 36; Piazzale delle Nazioni Unite; ⏱9.30am-5.30pm) near where the bus arrives.

🍴 Take a Break

Enjoy a meal with a view at **Sibilla** (☎0774 33 52 81; www.ristorantesibilla.com; Via della Sibilla 50; meals €40-50; ⏱12.30-3pm & 7.30-10.30pm Tue-Sun) in the hilltop centre.

★ Top Tip

Tivoli makes an excellent day trip from Rome, but to cover its two main sites you'll have to start early.

now open to the public. You'll need several hours to explore.

Must-see sights include the **canopo**, a landscaped canal overlooked by a *nymphaeum* (shrine to the water nymph), and the **Teatro Marittimo**, Hadrian's personal refuge. To the east, **Piazza d'Oro** makes for a memorable picture, particularly in spring when its grassy centre is cloaked in yellow wild flowers.

Getting There & Around

Tivoli lies 30km east of Rome. It's accessible by Cotral bus (€1.30, 50 minutes, at least twice hourly) from Ponte Mammolo metro station. By car, take Via Tiburtina or the quicker Rome–L'Aquila *autostrada* (A24). Trains run from Rome's Stazione Tiburtina to Tivoli (€2.60, one to 1¼ hour, at least hourly).

The best way to see both main sites is to visit Villa d'Este first, then have lunch up in the centre, before heading down to Villa Adriana. To get to the villa from the centre, take local CAT bus 4 or 4X (€1.30, 10 minutes, half-hourly) from Piazza Garibaldi. After you've visited Villa Adriana, pick up the Cotral bus back to Rome.

In the gardens, look out for the Bernini-designed **Fountain of the Organ**, which uses water pressure to play music through a concealed organ, and the 130m-long **Avenue of the Hundred Fountains**.

Villa Adriana

The ruins of Emperor Hadrian's vast country **villa** (☎0774 38 27 33; www.villaadriana.beniculturali.it; Largo Marguerite Yourcenar 1; adult/reduced €10/5; ⏱8.30am-1hr before sunset), 5km outside Tivoli proper, are quite magnificent, easily on a par with anything you'll see in Rome. Built between AD 118 and 138, the villa was one of the largest in the ancient world, encompassing more than 120 hectares – of which about 40 are

DINING OUT

Pizza, pasta and delicious gelato

Dining Out

This city lives to eat – food feeds the Roman soul. The restaurant scene is increasingly sophisticated, but traditional no-frills trattorias still provide some of Rome's most memorable gastronomic experiences. Cooking with local, seasonal ingredients remains the norm – fresh, often sun-ripened ingredients zing with flavour, and the best food is deliciously zero-kilometri. Think big round artichokes from Cerveteri between March and June, courgette flowers and grass-green fave (broad beans) in May, hare and wild boar from the Lazio hills in autumn.

In This Section

Price Ranges & Tipping

The pricing here refers to the average cost of a meal that includes an antipasto or *primo* (first course), a *secondo* (second course), a glass of house wine and *coperto* (cover charge). Don't be surprised to see *pane e coperto* (bread and cover charge; €1 to €5 per person) added to your bill.

€ less than €25

€€ €25–€45

€€€ more than €45

Although service is almost always included, leave a tip: anything from 5% in a pizzeria to 10% in a more upmarket place. Or at least round up the bill.

Previous page: Classic Italian dishes including salad, pasta and pizza

Vatican City, Borgo & Prati
Sophisticated restaurants, delicious takeaways, heavenly gelaterie (p128)

Villa Borghese & Northern Rome
Park cafes and smart, fashionable restaurants (p141)

Tridente, Trevi & the Quirinale
Classy neighbourhood eateries, great gelaterie and upmarket cafes (p129)

Centro Storico
Romantic hideaways, old-school trattorias, top pizzerias (p124)

Monti, Esquilino & San Lorenzo
Ethnic eats, cool bars, boho restaurants (p133)

Ancient Rome
Hidden gems among the tourist traps (p124)

Trastevere & Gianicolo
Touristy but terrific trattorias, gelaterie, bars and pizzerias (p135)

San Giovanni & Testaccio
Traditional Roman cuisine, good cheap eats (p139)

Southern Rome
Trend-setting foodie venues in ex-industrial Ostiense district (p142)

Useful Phrases

I'd like to reserve a table for...
Vorrei prenotare un tavolo per...
(Vo.ray pre. no.ta.re oon ta.vo.lo per...)

...two people
...due persone
(...doo.e per. so.ne)

...eight o'clock
...le otto
(...le o.to)

What would you recommend?
Cosa mi consiglia?
(ko.za mee kon.see.lya)

Can I have the bill please?
Mi porta il conto, per favore?
(mee por.taeel kon.to per fa.vo.re)

Must Try

Spaghetti alla carbonara Hailing from Rome, the genuine article mixes spaghetti with *pecorino romano* cheese, *guanciale* (cured pig's cheek) and a silky egg sauce.

Bucatini all'amatriciana Thick spaghetti with a tomato-pancetta sauce spiked with chilli.

Carciofo alla romana Roman-style artichokes, stuffed with parsley, mint and garlic, and braised until soft.

Pizza bianca Sliced pizza with no tomato topping, just salt and olive oil.

The Best...

Experience Rome's top restaurants and cafes

Pizzerias

Sbanco (p139) Creative pizzas and craft beer.

Alle Carrette (p134) *Baccalà* (salted cod) and super-thin pizza.

Giulietta (p139) Trendy pizzeria set in a former car showroom.

Traditional Roman

Flavio al Velavevodetto (p139) Classic *cucina romana* (Roman cooking).

La Tavernaccia (p136) Family-run trattoria with classic *cucina*.

Trattoria Da Cesare al Casaletto (p135) Trattoria beloved by locals.

Da Enzo (p135) Hugely popular Trastevere address.

Modern Roman

L'Arcangelo (p129) Updated takes on classic Roman dishes.

Pianostrada (p125) Modern Roman dining with lots of veg.

Metamorfosi (p141) Playful updates of Roman classics.

La Ciambella (p124) Unabashedly modern cuisine amid ancient ruins.

Great Wine Lists

La Barrique (p134) Interesting wines from small producers.

Salumeria Roscioli (p124) Sensational wines by the glass and bottle.

Litro (p137) Vintage-styled bistro-bar with natural and organic wines.

Trattoria Da Cesare al Casaletto (p135) Offers one of the best house wines in Rome.

Cafes

Sciascia Caffè (p128) Old-school elegance.
La Bottega del Caffè (p133) Set on Monti's prettiest piazza.
Antico Caffè Greco (p130) Rome's oldest cafe.

Gelaterie

Fatamorgana Corso (p131) Rome's finest artisanal flavours.
Gelateria del Teatro (p126) Forty flavours made on site.
Otaleg (p138) Classic and experimental flavours.
Gelateria dei Gracchi (p129) A taste of heaven in several locations across Rome.

Fast Food

Trapizzino (p140) Temple to the *trapizzino* (a cone of focaccia stuffed with tasty fillings).
Supplì (p137; pictured above) Fried-risotto-ball snacks and pizza by the slice.
Fa-Bìo (p128) Popular organic takeaway near the Vatican.

Lonely Planet's Top Choices

La Ciambella (p124) Modern Roman cuisine.
Colline Emiliane (p129) Regional cuisine from Emilia-Romagna.
La Tavernaccia (p136) One of the city's most sought-after trattorias.
Flavio al Velavevodetto (p139) Model Roman trattoria in Testaccio.
Trattoria Da Cesare al Casaletto (p135) Possibly Rome's best trattoria.
Salumeria Roscioli (p124) Deli-restaurant with top-notch food and wine.

✪ Ancient Rome

Terre e Domus
Lazio €€

(Map p246; ☑06 6994 0273; Via Foro Traiano 82-4; meals €30-40; ⊗9am-midnight Mon & Wed-Sat, from 10am Sun; 🚇Via dei Fori Imperiali) Staffed by young graduates from a local *scuola alberghiera* (catering college), this luminous modern restaurant is the best option in the touristy Forum area. With minimal decor and large windows overlooking the Colonna Traiana (p83), it's a relaxed spot to sit down to rustic local staples, all made with locally sourced ingredients, and a glass or two of regional wine.

Prices are quite high for the style of food, but that's largely down to the location.

Terrazza Caffarelli
Cafe €

(Caffetteria dei Musei Capitolini; Map p246; ☑06 6919 0564; Piazzale Caffarelli 4; ⊗9.30am-7pm; 🚇Piazza Venezia) The terrace cafe of the Capitoline Museums (p72) is a memorable place to relax over a sunset drink and swoon over magical views of the city's domes and rooftops. It also does snacks and simple meals but it's the panoramas that you'll remember here.

You don't need a museum ticket to reach the 2nd-floor cafe, which can be accessed from Piazzale Caffarelli.

✪ Centro Storico

La Ciambella
Italian €€

(Map p250; ☑06 683 29 30; www.la-ciambella. it; Via dell'Arco della Ciambella 20; meals €35-45; ⊗noon-11pm Tue-Sun; 🚇Largo di Torre Argentina) Near the Pantheon but as yet largely undiscovered by the tourist hordes, this friendly restaurant beats much of the neighbourhood competition. Its handsome, light-filled interior is set over the ruins of the Terme di Agrippa, visible through transparent floor panels, setting an attractive stage for interesting, imaginative food.

Salumeria Roscioli
Ristorante €€€

(Map p250; ☑06 687 52 87; www.salumeria roscioli.com; Via dei Giubbonari 21; meals €55; ⊗12.30-4pm & 7pm-midnight Mon-Sat; 🚇Via Arenula) The name Roscioli has long been

Pizza al taglio (pizza by the slice), Antico Forno Urbani (p127)

ALEXANDRA BRUZZESE/LONELY PLANET ©

a byword for foodie excellence in Rome, and this deli-restaurant is the place to experience it. Tables are set alongside the counter, laden with mouthwatering Italian and foreign delicacies, and in a small bottle-lined space behind. The food, including traditional Roman pastas, is top-notch and there are some truly outstanding wines. Reservations essential.

Pianostrada   Ristorante €€

(Map p250; ☑06 8957 2296; www.facebook. com/pianostrada; Via delle Zoccolette 22; meals €40-45; ⊗1-4pm & 7pm-midnight Tue-Fri, 10am-midnight Sat & Sun; ☑Via Arenula) This uberhip bistro-restaurant, in a white space with vintage furnishings and a glorious summer courtyard, is a must. Reserve ahead, or settle for a stool at the bar and enjoy views of the kitchen at work. The cuisine is creative, seasonal and veg-packed, including gourmet open sandwiches and sensational focaccia, as well as full-blown mains.

Barnum Cafe   Cafe €

(Map p250; ☑06 6476 0483; www.barnumcafe. com; Via del Pellegrino 87; ⊗9am-10pm Mon, 8.30am-2am Tue-Sat; 🛜; ☑Corso Vittorio Emanuele II) A laid-back *Friends*-style cafe, evergreen Barnum is the sort of place you could quickly get used to. With its shabby-chic furniture and white bare-brick walls, it's a relaxed spot for a breakfast cappuccino, a light lunch or a late-afternoon drink. Come evening, a coolly dressed-down crowd sips expertly mixed craft cocktails.

Forno Roscioli   Bakery €

(Map p250; ☑06 686 40 45; www.anticoforno roscioli.it; Via dei Chiavari 34; pizza slices from €2, snacks €2.50; ⊗7am-8pm Mon-Sat, 8.30am-7pm Sun; ☑Via Arenula) This is one of Rome's top bakeries, much loved by lunching locals who crowd here for luscious sliced pizza, prize pastries and hunger-sating *supplì* (risotto balls). The pizza margherita is superb, if messy to eat, and there's also a counter serving hot pastas and vegetable side dishes.

🍽 Picnic in Ancient Rome

Trawling through ancient Rome's ruins can be hungry work. But rather than stopping off for an overpriced bite in a touristy restaurant, search out **Alimentari Pannella Carmela** (Map p246; Via dei Fienili 61; panini €3.50-4.80; ⊗8.30am-2.30pm Mon-Sat & 5-8pm Mon-Fri; ☑Via Petroselli) for a fresh, cheap *panino*. A small, workaday food store concealed behind a curtain of creeping ivy, this spot is a lunchtime favourite, supplying hungry workers with fresh, made-to-order *panini*, sliced pizza and salads.

Caffè Sant'Eustachio   Coffee €

(Map p250; ☑06 6880 2048; www.santeustach ioilcaffe.it; Piazza Sant'Eustachio 82; ⊗7.30am-1am Sun-Thu, to 1.30am Fri, to 2am Sat; ☑Corso del Rinascimento) Always busy, this workaday cafe near the Pantheon is reckoned by many to serve the best coffee in town. To make it, the bartenders sneakily beat the first drops of an espresso with several teaspoons of sugar to create a frothy paste to which they add the rest of the coffee. The result is superbly smooth.

Il Pagliaccio   Gastronomy €€€

(Map p250; ☑06 6880 9595; www.ristorante ilpagliaccio.com; Via dei Banchi Vecchi 129a; meals €85, lunch/8-/10-course tasting menus €75/150/170; ⊗7.30-10pm Tue, 12.30-2pm & 7.30-10pm Wed-Sat; 🛜🍴; ☑Corso Vittorio Emanuele II) Rome's only two-Michelin-starred restaurant, Il Pagliaccio is Italian fine dining at its best. Chef Anthony Genovese – who was born in France to Italian parents and honed his craft in Asia – draws vivid inspiration from his eclectic background, creating dishes such as lobster with passion fruit and *stracchino* (soft cheese), oyster and green-apple granita, and a memorable take on green curry.

Diners can go à la carte or order a tasting menu: a three-course option at lunchtime and eight- or 10-course menus at dinner.

Rome Food Blogs

Katie Parla (http://katieparla.com) Finger-on-the-pulse restaurant reviews by food-and-beverage journalist Katie, a Rome-based New Jersey native and author of the highly recommended *Tasting Rome* (2017).

Eizabeth Minchilli in Rome (www.elizabethminchilliinrome.com) Reliable dining recommendations by the author of *Eating Rome*, an American food writer at home in Italy.

Heart Rome (www.heartrome.com) Food and lifestyle in the eternal city seen through the smart eyes of Australian Maria Pasquale.

An American in Rome (http://anamericaninrome.com) Bar and restaurant reviews by freelance writer Natalie Kennedy who arrived in Rome, fresh from California, in 2010.

Romeing Guide (www.romeing.it) Guide to Rome's cultural life, events and food hotspots written for tourists and expats visiting or living in Rome.

Casa Coppelle   Ristorante €€€

(Map p250; ☎06 6889 1707; www.casacoppelle.com; Piazza delle Coppelle 49; meals from €65, lunch/dinner tasting menu €55/80; ⊗noon-3.30pm & 6.30-11.30pm; ☐Corso del Rinascimento) Boasting an enviable setting near the Pantheon and a plush, theatrical look – think velvet drapes, black-lacquer tables and bookshelves – Casa Coppelle sets a romantic stage for high-end Italian-French cuisine. Gallic trademarks like foie gras and *vichyssoise* feature alongside updated Roman favourites such as *cacio e pepe*, here deconstructed as a cheese and pepper risotto with sautéed prawns. Book ahead. Cheaper lunch menus are available.

Casa Bleve   Ristorante €€€

(Map p250; ☎06 686 59 70; www.casableve.it; Via del Teatro Valle 48-49; meals €55-70;

⊗12.30-3pm & 7.30-11pm Mon-Sat; ☐Largo di Torre Argentina) Ideal for a special-occasion dinner, this palatial restaurant dazzles with its column-lined dining hall and stained-glass roof. Its wine list, one of the best in town, accompanies a refined menu of classic Italian starters, seasonal pastas and sumptuous mains such as slow-cooked beef in Nebbiolo wine.

I Dolci di Nonna Vincenza   Pastries €

(Map p250; ☎06 9259 4322; www.dolcinonnavincenza.it; Via Arco del Monte 98a; pastries from €2.50; ⊗7.30am-8.30pm Mon-Sat, to 8am Sun; ☐Via Arenula) Bringing the sweet flavours of Sicily to Rome, this pastry shop is a delight. Browse the traditional cakes and tempting *dolci* (sweet pastries) arrayed in the old wooden dressers, before adjourning to the adjacent bar to tear into creamy, flaky, puffy pastries and ricotta-stuffed *cannoli*.

Tiramisù Zum   Desserts €

(Map p250; ☎06 6830 7836; www.zumroma.it; Piazza del Teatro di Pompeo 20; tiramisu €4.50-6.50; ⊗11am-11pm Sun-Thu, to 1am Fri & Sat; ☐Corso Vittorio Emanuele II) The ideal spot for a midafternoon pick-me-up, this fab dessert bar specialises in tiramisu, that magnificent marriage of mascarpone and liqueur-soaked biscuits. Choose between the classic version with its cocoa powdering or one of several tempting variations, flavoured with rum, forest fruits or Sicilian pistachio nuts.

Gelateria del Teatro   Gelato €

(Map p250; ☎06 4547 4880; www.gelateriadelteatro.it; Via dei Coronari 65; gelato from €3; ⊗11am-8pm winter, 10am-10.30pm summer; ☐Via Zanardelli) All of the gelato served at this excellent gelateria is prepared on-site – look through the window and you'll see how they do it. There are numerous flavours, all made from premium seasonal ingredients, ranging from evergreen favourites such as pistachio and hazelnut to inventive creations like rosemary, honey and lemon.

La Casa del Caffè Tazza d'Oro
Coffee €

(Map p250; ☎06 678 97 92; www.tazzadoro coffeeshop.com; Via degli Orfani 84-86; ⊙7am-8pm Mon-Sat, 10.30am-7.30pm Sun; ⊠Via del Corso) A busy cafe with burnished 1940s fittings, this is one of Rome's best coffee houses. Its position near the Pantheon makes it touristy but its coffees are brilliant – the espresso hits the mark every time and there's a range of delicious *caffè* concoctions, including *granita di caffè,* a crushed-ice coffee served with whipped cream.

Antico Forno Urbani
Bakery €

(Map p250; ☎06 689 32 35; Piazza Costaguti 31; pizza slices from €1.50; ⊙7.40am-2.30pm & 5-7.45pm Mon-Fri, 8.30am-1.30pm Sat, 9.30am-1pm Sun; ⊠Via Arenula) This Ghetto kosher bakery makes some of the best *pizza al taglio* (sliced pizza) in town. It can get extremely busy but once you catch a whiff of the yeasty smell it's impossible to resist a quick stop. Everything's good, including its fabulous pizza *con patate* (pizza topped with thin slices of potato).

Renato e Luisa
Roman €€

(Map p250; ☎06 686 96 60; www.renato eluisa.it; Via dei Barbieri 25; meals €35-45; ⊙8pm-midnight Tue-Sun; ⊠Largo di Torre Argentina) A Roman favourite, this much-lauded backstreet trattoria is often packed. Chef Renato's menu features updated Roman classics that while modern and seasonal are also undeniably local, such as his signature *cacio e pepe e fiori di zucca* (pasta with *pecorino* cheese, black pepper and courgette flowers). Bookings advised.

Osteria dell'Ingegno
Italian €€

(Map p250; ☎06 678 06 62; www.osteria dellingegno.com; Piazza di Pietra 45; meals €35-45; ⊙noon-midnight; ⊠Via del Corso) This fashionably casual restaurant wine-bar is an enticing spot with its colourful, art-filled interior and prime location on a charming central piazza. The daily menu hits all the right notes with a selection of seasonal pastas, inventive mains and homemade desserts, while the 200-strong wine list boasts some interesting Italian labels.

Vivi Bistrot (p128)

 ### Kosher Rome

To eat kosher in Rome head to Via del Portico d'Ottavia, the main strip through the **Jewish Ghetto** (Map p254; 🚇Lungotevere de' Cenci). Lined with trattorias and restaurants specialising in Roman-Jewish cuisine, it's a lively hang-out, especially on hot summer nights when diners crowd the many pavement tables. On Piazza Costaguti, a queue invariably marks the entrance to Antico Forno Urbani (p127), a kosher bakery known for cooking up some of the finest *pizza al taglio* (pizza by the slice) in town.

Deep-frying is a staple of *cucina ebraico-romanesca* (Roman Jewish cooking), which developed between the 16th and 19th centuries when the Jews were confined to the city's ghetto. To add flavour to their limited ingredients they fried everything, from mozzarella to *baccalà* (salted cod). Particularly addictive are the locally grown artichokes, flattened to form a flower shape, deep-fried to a golden crisp and salted to become *carciofi alla giudia* (Jewish-style artichokes).

For a taste of typical ghetto cooking, try long-standing neighbourhood favourite Ba'Ghetto. Further down the road, the unmarked **Cremeria Romana** (Map p250; 📞06 8898 3229; Via del Portico d'Ottavia 1b; gelato from €2.50; ⏱9am-9.30pm Mon-Thu & Sun, to 4pm Fri, 9pm-midnight Sat; 🚇Via Arenula) has a small selection of tasty kosher gelato.

Carciofi alla giudia (Jewish-style artichokes)
FABRIZIO ESPOSITO/SHUTTERSTOCK ©

Vivi Bistrot
Bistro €€

(Map p250; 📞06 683 37 79; www.vivibistrot. com; Palazzo Braschi, Piazza Navona 2; meals €25-35; ⏱10am-midnight Tue-Sun; 🍴; 🚇Corso del Rinascimento) Rustic decor goes hand in hand with baroque elegance at this handsome bistro on the ground floor of Palazzo Braschi. With its country wood tables, dried flowers and a menu that ranges from bruschetta starters to burgers, curries and vegan salads, it's a great spot to escape the hurly-burly outside.

Ba'Ghetto
Jewish €€

(Map p254; 📞06 6889 2868; www.baghetto. com; Via del Portico d'Ottavia 57; meals €30-35; ⏱noon-11.30pm Mon-Thu & Sun, to 3pm Fri, 6-11.30pm Sat; 🚇Via Arenula) This historic kosher restaurant whips up Roman Jewish fare such as *amatriciana* with beef instead of the classic pork, braised oxtail, and Middle Eastern offerings. Down the street at number 2a, **Ba'Ghetto Milky** specialises in fish- and dairy-based dishes. Both feature the restaurant's famous *carciofi alla giudia*: whole artichokes trimmed and deep-fried twice until they look like golden flowers.

Restaurants are separate in accordance with Jewish dietary laws.

⊗ Vatican City, Borgo & Prati

Sciascia Caffè
Cafe €

(Map p253; 📞06 321 15 80; http://sciascia caffe1919.it; Via Fabio Massimo 80/a; ⏱7am-9pm; 🚇Ottaviano-San Pietro) There are several contenders for the best coffee in town, but in our opinion nothing tops the *caffè eccellente* served at this polished old-school cafe. A velvety smooth espresso served in a delicate cup lined with melted chocolate, it's nothing short of magnificent, and has been since 1919.

Fa-Bìo
Sandwiches €

(Map p253; 📞06 3974 6510; Via Germanico 71; meals €5-7; ⏱10.30am-5.30pm Mon-Fri, to 4pm Sat; 🚇Piazza del Risorgimento, 🚇Ottaviano-San

Pietro) 🍴 Sandwiches, wraps, salads and fresh juices are all prepared with speed, skill and fresh organic ingredients at this busy takeaway. Locals, Vatican tour guides and in-the-know visitors come here to grab a quick lunchtime bite. If you can't find room in the small interior, there are stools along the pavement.

Panificio Bonci
Bakery €

(☏06 3973 4457; www.bonci.it; Via Trionfale 36; snacks €2-6; ☺8.30am-3pm & 5-8.30pm Mon-Thu, 8.30am-8.30pm Fri & Sat; ✍; ☐Largo Trionfale) From Gabriele Bonci of the vaunted Bonci Pizzarium, this mellow bakery and deli offers a wide range of splendid takeaway fare, starting with the signature thin and crispy pizza slices. There are sandwiches, wholegrain breads and superb pastries. Your main challenge will be seating (there is none). Enjoy *panini* stuffed with slow-roasted porchetta (pork) and tangy Gorgonzola.

Gelateria dei Gracchi
Gelato €

(☏06 321 66 68; www.gelateriadeigracchi.it; Via dei Gracchi 272; gelato from €2.50; ☺noon-12.30am; ☐Piazza Cola Di Rienzo) The original location of the small chain of gelato shops that has taken Rome by storm. The proprietors here only use fresh fruit in season — no fruit concentrate, no peach gelato in January etc. The flavours vary by day and season, but you're always assured of a top treat. Try one of the chocolate-covered gelato bars.

Tordomatto
Lazio €€€

(☏06 6935 2895; www.tordomattoroma. com; Via Pietro Giannone 24; meals €65-125; ☺1-2.30pm Fri-Sun, 7.30-10.45pm Thu-Tue; ☐Trionfale/Telesio) The dining room is elegant simplicity itself at this Michelin-starred restaurant, which puts the food ahead of fuss. With a corner spot on genteel streets, Tordomatto promises a relaxed evening of fine cuisine. See the chefs in action by booking the kitchen tablé well in advance. Look for Roman classics, exquisitely imagined and prepared.

🍽 Vatican Snack Attack

When hunger bites in the Vatican, make a beeline for **Bonci Pizzarium** (Map p253; ☏06 3974 5416; www.bonci.it; Via della Meloria 43; pizza slices €5; ☺11am-10pm Mon-Sat, from noon Sun; Ⓜ Cipro). The takeaway of Gabriele Bonci, Rome's acclaimed pizza emperor, it serves Rome's best sliced pizza, bar none. Scissor-cut squares of soft, springy base are topped with original combinations of seasonal ingredients and served for immediate consumption. Often jammed, there are only a couple of benches and stools for the tourist hordes; head across to the plaza at the metro station for a seat.

L'Arcangelo
Lazio €€€

(Map p250; ☏06 321 09 92; www.larcangelo. com; Via Giuseppe Gioachino Belli 59; meals €45-80, lunch set menu €30; ☺1-2.30pm Mon-Fri, 8-11pm Mon-Sat; ☐Piazza Cavour) Styled as an informal bistro with wood panelling, leather banquettes and casual table settings, L'Arcangelo enjoys a stellar local reputation. Dishes are modern and creative yet still undeniably Roman in their use of traditional ingredients such as sweetbreads and *baccalà* (cod). A further plus is the well-curated wine list. Whimsical touches include toy cars on tables.

⊗ Tridente, Trevi & the Quirinale

Colline Emiliane
Italian €€

(Map p245; ☏06 481 75 38; www.collineemil iane.com; Via degli Avignonesi 22; meals €45; ☺12.45-2.45pm & 7.30-10.45pm Tue-Sat, 12.45-2.45pm Sun; Ⓜ Barberini) Serving sensational regional cuisine from Emilia-Romagna, this restaurant has been operated by the Latini family since 1931; the current owners are Paola (dessert queen) and Anna (watch her making pasta each morning in the

From left: La Casa del Caffè Tazza d'Oro (p127); Pastries, Andreotti (p143); Antico Caffè Greco

glassed-off lab). Our three recommendations when eating here: start with the *antipasti della casa* (€26 for two persons), progress to pasta and don't scrimp on dessert.

The kitchen flies the flag for Emilia-Romagna, the well-fed Italian province that has blessed the world with Parmesan, balsamic vinegar, bolognese sauce and Parma ham. Seasonal delights include white truffles in winter and fresh porcini mushrooms in spring, but the menu is delectable whatever the season. Service can be uneven; we find it most friendly at lunch.

Hostaria Romana   Trattoria €€

(Map p245; ☏06 474 52 84; www.hostaria romana.it; Via del Boccaccio 1; meals €45; ⏰12.30-3pm & 7.15-11pm Mon-Sat; Ⓜ Barberini) Beloved of locals and tourists alike, this bustling place in Trevi is everything an Italian trattoria should be. Order an antipasto or pasta (excellent) and then move on to a main – traditional Roman dishes including *saltimbocca* and tripe are on offer, as are lots of grilled meats. If you're lucky, your meal may be rounded off with

complimentary *biscotti*. Bookings highly recommended.

Antico Caffè Greco   Cafe €

(Map p250; ☏06 679 17 00; www.facebook.com/ AnticoCaffeGreco; Via dei Condotti 86; ⏰9am-9pm; Ⓜ Spagna) Rome's oldest cafe, open since 1760, is still working the look with the utmost elegance: waiters in black tails and bow tie or frilly white pinnies, scarlet flock walls and age-spotted gilt mirrors. Prices reflect this amazing heritage: pay €9 for a cappuccino sitting down or join locals for the same standing at the bar (€2.50).

Casanova, Goethe, Wagner, Keats, Byron, Shelley and Baudelaire were all regulars, and you can even flop down on Hans Christian Andersen's ginger-coloured canapé – from the entrance on Via dei Condotti, walk through the series of eight rooms to the final drawing room with grand piano. Count on paying €12 for a cup of tea, €21 for a cocktail.

Piccolo Arancio   Trattoria €€

(Map p245; ☏06 678 61 39; www.piccoloarancio. it; Vicolo Scanderbeg 112; meals €38; ⏰noon-3pm & 7pm-midnight Tue-Sun; Ⓜ Barberini) In a

'hood riddled with tourist traps, this back-street eatery – tucked inside a little house next to grandiose Palazzo Scanderberg – stands out. The kitchen mixes Roman classics with more contemporary options and, unusually, includes a hefty number of seafood choices – the *linguini alla pescatora* (handmade pasta with shellfish and baby tomatoes) is sensational. Bookings essential.

Tables spill on to the quaint cobbled street in summer. Service can be abrupt but the food is so good that we tend to overlook this.

Il Margutta   Vegetarian €€

(Map p252; ☑06 3265 0577; www.ilmargutta. bio; Via Margutta 118; lunch buffet weekdays/ weekends €15/25, meals €35; ☺8.30am-11.30pm; ☑; Ⓜ Spagna) This chic art-gallery-bar-restaurant is packed at lunchtime with Romans feasting on its good-value, eat-as-much-as-you-can buffet deal. Everything on its menu is organic, and the evening menu is particularly creative – vegetables and pulses combined and presented with

care and flair. Among the various tasting menus is a vegan option.

Fatamorgana Corso   Gelato €

(Map p252; ☑06 3265 22 38; www.gelateria fatamorgana.com; Via Laurina 10; cups & cones €2.50-5; ☺noon-11pm; Ⓜ Flaminio) The wonderful all-natural, gluten-free gelato served at Fatamorgana is arguably Rome's best artisanal ice cream. Innovative and classic ambrosial flavours abound, all made from the finest seasonal ingredients. There are several branches around town.

Caffè Ciampini   Cafe €

(Map p252; ☑06 678 56 78; Viale Trinità dei Monti; ☺8am-11pm Mar-Oct; Ⓜ Spagna) Hidden away a short walk from the top of the Spanish Steps towards the Pincio Hill Gardens (p58), this cafe has a vintage garden-party vibe, with green wooden latticework and orange trees framing its white-clothed tables. There are lovely views over the backstreets behind Spagna, and the gelato – particularly the *tartufo al cioccolato* (chocolate truffle) – is renowned. Serves food too. Note that it may close earlier in the shoulder season.

Rome on a Plate

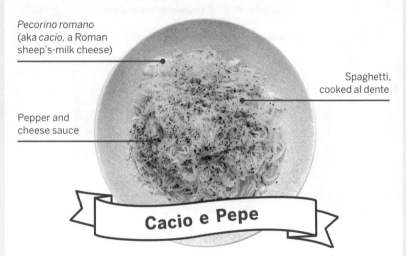

Pecorino romano
(aka *cacio*, a Roman
sheep's-milk cheese)

Spaghetti,
cooked al dente

Pepper and
cheese sauce

ROBYNMAC/GETTY IMAGES ©

Cacio e Pepe

The Art of Simplicity

In theory there could not be a simpler
dish to serve – a sassy bowl of spaghetti
in a silky pepper and cheese sauce. Yet
combining the grated *pecorino romano*
with freshly ground black pepper and a
few tablespoons of boiling-hot cooking
water (from the spaghetti pan) is a fine
art that requires patience, practice and
a zillion repeated attempts to perfect.

● Traditional *cacio e pepe* mixes
spaghetti with *cacio* (Roman dialect
for *pecorino romano* cheese) and *pepe*
(pepper).

● Forget Parmesan – the only cheese to
use is *pecorino romano* (a sheep's-milk
cheese made in the region forever).

● Cream is never used in this staple
Roman dish.

● There is only one way to cook the
pasta – al dente, with a subtle crunch.

Top Five For Cacio e Pepe

Trattoria Da Cesare al Casaletto
(p135) *Cacio e pepe* perfection at
Rome's finest trattoria.

Da Enzo (p135) Trastevere top choice.

Salumeria Roscioli (p124) Celebrated
deli-restaurant serving sublime pasta.

Casa Coppelle (p126) The dish is given
a contemporary deconstruction.

Renato e Luisa (p127) Paired with courgette flowers to become *cacio e pepe e
fiori di zucca*.

Da Enzo (p135)
BOAZ ROTTEM/ALAMY STOCK PHOTO ©

VyTA Enoteca Regionale del Lazio
Italian €€

(Map p250; ☑06 8771 60 18; www.vytaenoteca
lazio.it/en; Via Frattina 94; cicheti from €3,
platters €15, restaurant meals €55; ⊙9am-11pm
Sun-Thu, to midnight Fri & Sat; MSpagna) Showcasing food and wine of the Lazio region,
this mega-stylish address owes its design
to fashionable Roman architect Daniela
Colli and its contemporary menu to chef
Dino De Bellis. The burnished copper bar is
a perfect perch for enjoying *panini*, *cicheti*
(snacks) and *taglieri* (cheese and meat
plates) – it also offers a tempting *aperitivo*
spread. Upstairs, a glam restaurant awaits.

Il Chianti
Tuscan €€

(Map p245; ☑06 679 24 70; www.vineriailchianti.
com; Via del Lavatore 81-82a; pizzas €8-12,
taglieri €14, meals €50; ⊙noon-11.30pm; MBarberini) The name says it all: this pretty ivy-
clad place specialises in Tuscan-style wine
and food. Cosy up inside its bottle-lined
interior or grab a table on the lovely street
terrace and dig into Tuscan favourites
including crostini (toasts with toppings),
taglieri, hearty soups, handmade pasta and
Florence's iconic T-bone steak. Pizzas are
available, too.

Pompi
Desserts €

(Map p250; ☑06 6994 17 52; www.barpompi.it;
Via della Croce 82; tiramisu €4; ⊙11am-9.30pm
Mon-Thu, to 10.30pm Fri-Sun; MSpagna) Now
a chain operation, Rome's most famous
vendor of tiramisu (which literally means
'pick me up') sells takeaway cartons of the
deliciously rich yet light-as-air dessert. As
well as classic, flavours include strawberry,
pistachio and banana-chocolate. Eat on the
spot (standing) or buy frozen portions that
will keep for a few hours until you're ready
to tuck in at home.

Imàgo
Italian €€€

(Map p245; ☑06 6993 4726; www.imagorestau
rant.com; Piazza della Trinità dei Monti 6, Roma
Hassler; tasting menus €130-170; ⊙7-10.30pm
Feb-Dec; 🅿; MSpagna) Even in a city of great
views, the panoramas from Roma Hassler's

Mercato Centrale

A gourmet oasis for hungry travellers
at Stazione Termini, **Mercato Centrale**
(Map p255; www.mercatocentrale.it/roma;
Stazione Termini, Via Giolitti 36; snacks/
meals from €3/10; ⊙8am-midnight; 🛜;
MTermini) is a dazzling three-storey
food hall beneath a vaulted 1930s
ceiling. Its many tempting stalls sell
good-quality fast food and fresh
produce, munched on the move or
enjoyed around shared tables in situ.
Woo taste buds with a *panino* filled with
artisanal cheese from Beppe Giovali; a
slice of focaccia or pizza from Gabriele
Bonci; or a Chianina burger from Enrico
Lagorio – all washed down with a craft
beer from the on-site *birreria* (beer
house). Or head upstairs to 1st-floor
Il Ristorante di Oliver Glowig (meals
€45; ⊙noon-3pm & 7-11pm), which offers
a menu signed off by the Rome-based
Michelin-starred chef.

Michelin-starred romantic rooftop restaurant are special, extending over a sea of
roofs to the great dome of St Peter's Basilica; request the corner table. Complementing the views are the bold, modern-Italian
creations.

✪ Monti, Esquilino & San Lorenzo

La Bottega del Caffè
Cafe €

(Map p246; ☑06 474 15 78; Piazza Madonna dei
Monti 5; ⊙8am-2am; 🛜; MCavour) On one
of Rome's prettiest squares in Monti, La
Bottega del Caffè – named after a comedy
by Carlo Goldoni – is the hotspot in Monti
for lingering over excellent coffee, drinks,
snacks and lunch or dinner. Heaters in
winter ensure balmy al fresco action
year-round.

Ba'Ghetto Milky (p128)

Alle Carrette   Pizza €

(Map p246; 06 679 27 70; www.facebook.com/allecarrette; Via della Madonna dei Monti 95; pizza €5.50-9; 11.30am-4pm & 7pm-midnight; Cavour) Authentic pizza, super-thin and swiftly cooked in a wood-burning oven, is what this traditional Roman pizzeria on one of Monti's prettiest streets has done well for decades. Romans pile in here at weekends for good reason – it's cheap, friendly and delicious. All of the classic toppings are available, as well as gourmet choices such as anchovy and courgette flower (yum!).

Consider beginning your local feast with some fried *supplì* (risotto balls) or *baccalà* (salted cod). And note that if you order the Pizza Amnesty (tomato, mozzarella, ricotta and aubergine), €1 is donated to Amnesty International. The rear laneway seating is popular in summer.

Said   Desserts €

(Map p255; 06 446 92 04; www.said.it; Via Tiburtina 135; praline assortment €8, desserts €8-10; 10am-12.30am Tue-Thu, to 1.30am Fri, noon-1.30am Sat, noon-midnight Sun;

Reti) Housed in a 1920s chocolate factory, this hybrid cafe-bar, restaurant and boutique is San Lorenzo's most fashionable address. Its top-quality chocolate can be indulged in here or purchased to take home. Enjoying a coffee, dessert or meal in the urban chic interior will give you lots of opportunities to people-watch as the place literally heaves at night, particularly on weekends. For a wickedly decadent treat, order a chocolate cocktail (€10) or hot chocolate (€4 to €6).

La Barrique   Italian €€

(Map p245; 06 4782 5953; www.facebook.com/la.barrique.94/; Via del Boschetto 41b; meals €40; 1-2.30pm & 7.30-11pm Mon-Fri, 7.30-11.30pm Sat; Cavour) This traditional *enoteca* is a classy yet casual place to linger over a meal. There's a large wine list, mostly sourced from small producers, with lots of natural wines to choose from. A small menu of creative pastas and mains provide a great accompaniment – this is one of the best places to eat in Monti. Bookings recommended.

Panella
Bakery €

(Map p255; ☑06 487 24 35; www.panellaroma.
com; Via Merulana 54; meals €7-15; ⊘7am-11pm
Mon-Thu & Sun, to midnight Fri & Sat; Ⓜ️Vittorio
Emanuele) Freshly baked pastries, fruit tartlets, *pizza al taglio* (pizza by the slice) and
focaccia fill display cases in this famous
bakery, and there's also a *tavola calda* (hot
table) where an array of hot dishes are on
offer. Order at the counter and eat at bar
stools between shelves of gourmet groceries, or sit on the terrace for waiter service.

Necci dal 1924
Cafe €

(☑06 9760 1552; www.necci1924.com; Via
Fanfulla da Lodi 68; ⊘8am-1am Sun-Thu, to 2am
Fri & Sat; 🛜�️; 🚋Prenestina/Officine Atac) An
all-round hybrid in Pigneto, iconic Necci
opened as a gelateria in 1924 and later
became a favourite drinking destination
of film director Pier Paolo Pasolini. These
days it caters to a buoyant hipster crowd,
offering a laid-back vibe, retro interior and
all-day food. Huge kudos for the fabulous
summertime terrace, which is very family
friendly.

❌ Trastevere & Gianicolo

Trattoria Da Cesare
al Casaletto
Trattoria €€

(☑06 53 60 15; www.trattoriadacesare.it; Via
del Casaletto 45; meals €25-50; ⊘12.45-3pm
& 8-11pm Thu-Tue; 🚋Casaletto) Rome's best
trattoria? Many think so and you will too
after an amazing meal of Roman standards
where virtually every dish is prepared just
so. The restaurant is simplicity itself: dozens of tables in a plain setting – in summer
outside under a vine-covered arbour on a
vast terrace. The food is rightfully the star.
The service is efficient and relaxed.

First courses are exquisite, especially the
various versions of freshly fried fish and
the meatballs – which could be called little
balls of joy. Mains include silky fettuccine
and gnocchi that defines the dish. Don't
bother reading the wine list, just ask for
the superb house wines priced incredibly
cheap (€2.50 for a ¼L of red).

 **Roman
Cuisine**

Like most Italian cuisines, the *cucina
romana* (Roman cooking) was born of
careful use of local ingredients – making
use of the cheaper cuts of meat, like
guanciale (pig's cheek), and greens that
could be gathered wild from the fields.

There are a few classic Roman pasta
dishes that almost every trattoria and
restaurant in Rome serves. These
carb-laden comfort foods are seemingly
simple, yet notoriously difficult to prepare well. Iconic Roman dishes include
carbonara (pasta with *guanciale*, egg
and salty *pecorino romano;* sheep's milk
cheese), *alla gricia* (with *guanciale* and
onions), *amatriciana* (invented when
a chef from Amatrice added tomatoes
to *alla gricia*) and *cacio e pepe* (with
pecorino romano and black pepper).

Other Roman specialities include
baccalà con i ceci (salted cod with chick-
peas), *trippa alla romana* (tripe stewed
in tomato sauce and topped with *pecorino* cheese), *saltimbocca alla Romana*
(pan-fried veal escalopes wrapped
with prosciutto and sage and finished
in white wine) and *coda alla vaccinara*
(oxtail stew, cooked with tomato sauce,
celery, clove and bitter chocolate).

Saltimbocca alla Romana (pan-fried veal escalopes)

SUSAN WRIGHT/LONELY PLANET ©

Da Enzo
Trattoria €€

(Map p254; ☑06 581 22 60; www.daenzo
al29.com; Via dei Vascellari 29; meals €30-
35; ⊘12.30-3pm & 7.30-11pm Mon-Sat;
🚋Lungotevere Ripa, 🚋Belli) Vintage ochre
walls, yellow-checked tablecloths and a

The Culinary Calendar

According to the culinary calendar (initiated by the Catholic Church to vary the nutrition of its flock), fish is eaten on Friday. This translates as a fillet of *baccalà* (salted cod), typically left to soak from Wednesday onward in fresh water in order to rehydrate it – century-old groceries such as Antica Caciara Trasteverina (p160) in Trastevere still do this, as do many Romans in their own homes. Thursday is gnocchi (dumplings) day. The traditional, heavy Roman recipe uses semolina flour, but you can also find the typical gnocchi with potatoes. Many traditional Roman restaurants still offer dishes according to this calendar.

traditional menu featuring all the Roman classics: what makes this tiny and staunchly traditional trattoria exceptional is its careful sourcing of local, quality products, many from nearby farms in Lazio. The seasonal, deep-fried Jewish artichokes and the *pasta cacio e pepe* (cheese-and-black-pepper pasta) are among the best in Rome.

Your waiter will likely pull up a chair and tell you what to order. Let him. There are 12 seats outside.

La Tavernaccia   Trattoria €€

(☑06 581 27 92; www.latavernacciaroma.com; Via Giovanni da Castel Bolognese 63; meals €30-45; ☺12.45-3pm & 7.30-11pm Thu-Tue; ⊞Stazione Trastevere) This family-run trattoria bustles every minute it's open. Book in advance to get one of Rome's most sought after tables. The setting is simplicity itself, and the food is sensational. Roman classics get stellar treatment here. First courses include various preserved meats and hams that melt away. Besides pastas there are many roasts. Staff are cheery and helpful.

Dining here easily becomes an event as dishes emerge from the kitchen in waves, offering a seemingly never-ending

evening of eating joy. Among the don't-miss classics is a sprightly rendition of the often humdrum eggplant parmigiana. If possible, save room for the creative desserts.

Fior di Luna   Gelato €

(Map p254; ☑06 6456 1314; http://fiordiluna. com; Via della Lungaretta 96; gelato from €2.50; ☺1-8pm Sun & Mon, 1-11pm Tue-Sat; ⊞Belli, ⊞Viale di Trastevere) For many Romans this busy little hub makes the best hand-made gelato and sorbet in the world. It's produced in small batches using natural, seasonal ingredients. Seasonal favourites include pear and banana, blueberry yogurt, strawberry and pistachio (the nuts are ground by hand). Get a kick with a cup of *cafe bio* (organic coffee, €1). Note the 'no franchising' sign.

Bar San Calisto   Cafe €

(Map p254; Piazza San Calisto 3-5; ☺6am-2am Mon-Sat; ⊞Viale di Trastevere, ⊞Viale di Trastevere) Head to 'Sanca' for its basic, stuck-in-time atmosphere, cheap prices and large terrace. It attracts everyone from intellectuals to people-watching idlers and foreign students. It's famous for its chocolate – come for hot chocolate with cream in winter, and chocolate gelato in summer. Try the *sambuca con la mosca* ('with flies' – raw coffee beans). Expect occasional late-night jam sessions.

Trattoria Da Teo   Trattoria €€

(Map p254; ☑06 581 83 55; www.facebook.com/ Trattoria.da.teo; Piazza dei Ponziani 7; meals €35-45; ☺12.30-3pm & 7.30-11.30pm Mon-Sat; ⊞Viale di Trastevere, ⊞Belli) One of Rome's classic trattorias, Da Teo buzzes with locals digging into steaming platefuls of Roman standards, such as carbonara, *pasta cacio e pepe* and the most fabulous seasonal artichokes – both Jewish (deep-fried) and Roman-style (stuffed with parsley and garlic, and boiled). In keeping with hard-core trattoria tradition, Teo's homemade gnocchi is only served on Thursday. In warm weather dine al fresco at one of the much-coveted tables on the low-key piazza. The wise-cracking servers are a delight as

Antica Norcineria Iacozzilli

are the cookies served at the end of the meal. Reservations essential.

Litro — Italian €€

(☑06 4544 7639; www.facebook.com/litrovineria; Via Fratelli Bonnet 5; meals €30-35; ☺12.30-3.30pm & 6pm-midnight Mon-Fri, 12.30pm-1am Sat; ☎; ☑Via Fratelli Bonnet) ✪ Crunchy bread comes in a paper bag and the 1950s clocks on the wall – all three dozen of them – say a different time at this understated vintage-styled bistro-bar in wonderfully off-the-beaten-tourist-track Monteverde. The creative Roman kitchen is predominantly organic, with ingredients sourced from small local producers, and the choice of natural and organic wines is among the best in Rome.

Antica Norcineria Iacozzilli — Deli €

(Map p254; ☑06 581 27 34; Via Natale del Grande 15; sandwich €4.50; ☺9am-1pm & 4.30-8.30pm Mon-Sat; ☑✚☎; ☑Trastevere/Mastai) Three generations of the Iacozzilli family work in this old-school deli that dates to 1924. It's hailed for its *porchetta*: seasoned with salt and rosemary, this slow-roasted pork is

juicy in the middle and exquisitely crispy on top. Ask for a *porchetta panino*, find a wall outside to lean on and relish the savoury goodness.

Pizzeria Ai Marmi — Pizza €

(Panattoni; Map p254; ☑06 580 09 19; http://facebook.com/aimarmi; Viale di Trastevere 53; meals €10-20; ☺6.30pm-2am Thu-Tue; ☑Viale di Trastevere, ☑Trastevere/Mastai) Also called *l'obitorio* (the morgue) because of its vintage marble-slab tabletops, this is Trastevere's most popular pizzeria. Think super-thin pizzas, a clattering buzz, testy waiters, a huge street terrace and some fantastic fried starters – the *supplì* (risotto balls), *baccalà* (salted cod) and courgette flowers are all heavenly. Skip the pastas. They're serious here: the menu notes the few toppings that are frozen.

Supplì — Italian €

(Map p254; ☑06 589 71 10; www.suppliroma.it; Via di San Francesco a Ripa 137; pizza & fritti €2.50-6; ☺9am-10pm Mon-Sat; ☑Viale di Trastevere) This blink-and-you-miss-it Trastevere *tavola calda* (hot table) has Roman street

Top Spots for Vegetarians

Pianostrada (p125)

Verde Pistacchio (p142)

Il Margutta (p131)

Il Pagliaccio (p125)

From left: Il Pagliaccio (p125); Pesto *trapizzino*, Trapizzino (p140); Il Margutta (p131)

food down to an art. Locals queue for its namesake *supplì:* fried risotto balls spiked with *ragù* (meat and tomato sauce) and mozzarella. The family-run eatery also gets top marks for pizza by the slice. Daily specials include gnocchi (Thursday) and fried fish and calamari (Tuesday and Friday).

Otaleg
Gelato €

(Map p254; ☑338 6515450; www.otaleg.com; Via di San Cosimato 14a; gelato from €2; ☺noon-midnight; ☑; ☐Trastevere/Mastai) Revered *gelataio* Marco Radicioni skilfully churns some of the capital's best gelato at this slick little shop off Piazza San Cosimato. Otaleg (gelato spelled backwards) has a soft spot for the classics – think pistachio, lemon and dark chocolate – but proves delightfully experimental with seasonal combinations such as prickly pear and acacia honey.

Spirito DiVino
Italian €€

(Map p254; ☑06 589 66 89; www.ristorante spiritodivino.com; Via dei Genovesi 31; meals €35-45; ☺7pm-midnight Mon-Sat; ☐Belli) Chef and Slow Food aficionado Eliana Catalani buys ingredients directly from local producers.

The restaurant's trademark dish is *maiale alla mazio,* an ancient pork and red-wine stew said to have been a favourite of Caesar. Between courses diners can visit the wine cellar, which dates to 80 BC. Note the ancient columns on the side facade with old Hebrew inscriptions.

C'è pasta... E pasta!
Italian €

(☑06 5832 0125; Via Ettore Rolli 29; meals €15-25; ☺8.30am-3pm Sun-Fri, 5-9.30pm Sun-Thu, meals served from noon; ☐Stazione Trastevere) Fresh pasta is sold here ready for you to prepare and eat at home, ready to eat and wrapped for takeaway, or ready to eat at one of the simple tables here, inside or out. Everything is superb (and kosher), especially the artichoke ravioli and the traditional Roman-style lasagne. Browse the cases filled with edible joy and assemble a great-value meal.

La Renella
Bakery €

(Map p254; ☑06 581 72 65; http://larenella. com; Via del Moro 15; pizza slices from €2.50; ☺7am-midnight Sun-Thu, to 3am Fri & Sat; ☐Piazza Trilussa) Watch pizza masters at work at this historic Trastevere bakery. Savour

ALEXANDRA BRUZZESE/LONELY PLANET ©

the wood-fired ovens, bar-stool seating and heavenly aromas of pizza, bread (get the *casareccia*, crusty Roman-style bread) and biscuits. Piled-high toppings (and fillings) vary seasonally, to the joy of everyone from punks with big dogs to old ladies with little dogs. It's been in the biz since 1870.

⊗ San Giovanni & Testaccio

Flavio al Velavevodetto   Roman €€

(🕿06 574 41 94; www.ristorantevelavevodetto. it; Via di Monte Testaccio 97-99; meals €30-35; ⏰12.30-3pm & 7.45-11pm; 🚇Via Galvani) The pick of Testaccio's trattorias, this casual spot is celebrated locally for its earthy, no-nonsense *cucina romana* (Roman cuisine). For a taste, start with *carciofo alla giudia* (deep-fried artichoke) before moving on to *rigatoni alla carbonara* (pasta tubes wrapped in a silky egg sauce spiked with morsels of cured pig's cheek) and finishing up with tiramisu.

The trattoria is housed in a Pompeian-red villa set into the side of

Monte Testaccio (🕿06 06 08; Via Nicolo Zabaglia 24, cnr Via Galvani; adult/reduced €4/3, plus cost of tour; ⏰group visits only, reservation necessary; 🚇Via Marmorata), a hill made of smashed amphorae.

Giulietta   Pizza €

(Map p254; 🕿06 4522 9022; https://giulietta pizzeria.it; Piazza dell'Emporio 28; pizzas €6.50-13; ⏰7.30pm-11.30pm; 🚇Via Marmorata) Occupying a former car showroom, this trendy pizzeria is part of a multispace food hub part-owned by top Roman chef Cristina Bowerman. Its cavernous dining area, decorated in abstract contemporary style, sets the stage for sensational wood-fired pizzas topped with prime Italian ingredients.

Next door, and part of the same complex, is Romeo Chef & Baker, a designer deli, cocktail bar and restaurant serving modern Italian and international fare.

Sbanco   Pizza €

(🕿06 78 93 18; https://sbanco.eatbu.com; Via Siria 1; pizzas €7-13; ⏰7.30pm-midnight Mon-Sat, from 1pm Sun; 🚇Piazza Zama) With

¶◎¶ Fine Dining & Michelin Stars

Special-occasion, fine-dining restaurants are forever on the rise in foodie Rome. Two chefs in the city to recently gain their first Michelin star include Adriano Baldassare at Tordomatto (p129), located near the Vatican, and Riccardo Di Giacinto at All'Oro, whose modern, innovative kitchen, cocooned within a five-star boutique hotel – think contemporary club vibe (dark-wood ceilings, brass lamps and fireplace) – thrills diners.

At Palazzo Manfredi across the street from the Colosseum, Giuseppe Di Iorio continues to create a buzz at Michelin-starred Aroma, sensationally located on the rooftop of the luxury Palazzo Manfredi hotel. Views at Francesco Apreda's Imàgo (p133) are equally sensational. A lush garden pavilion is the enviable setting for one of Rome's youngest Michelin-starred chefs, Marco Martini, at home in an art nouveau villa-turned-luxury-boutique-hotel.

Favouring modern Roman cuisine, all these top chefs look to traditional Roman dishes or ingredients for inspiration, and play with unexpected flavours and combinations to create a creative, gastronomic dining experience.

Il Pagliaccio (p125)

its informal warehouse vibe and buzzing atmosphere, Sbanco is one of the capital's best modern pizzerias. Since opening in 2016, it's made a name for itself with its sumptuous fried starters and inventive, wood-fired pizzas, including a *cacio e pepe* (*pecorino* and black pepper) pizza baked with ice. To top things off, you can quaff delicious craft beer.

Trapizzino   Fast Food €

(☏06 4341 9624; www.trapizzino.it; Via Branca 88; trapizzini from €3.50; ⊙noon-1am Tue-Sun; ☐Via Marmorata) The original of what is now a growing countrywide chain, this is the birthplace of the *trapizzino,* a kind of hybrid sandwich made by stuffing a cone of doughy focaccia with fillers like *polpette al sugo* (meatballs in tomato sauce) or *pollo alla cacciatore* (stewed chicken). They're messy to eat but quite delicious.

Aroma   Gastronomy €€€

(Map p246; ☏06 9761 5109; www.aromares taurant.it; Via Labicana 125; meals €120-180; ⊙12.30-3pm & 7.30-11.30pm; ☐Via Labicana) One for a special occasion, the rooftop restaurant of the luxury Palazzo Manfredi hotel offers once-in-a-lifetime views of the Colosseum and Michelin-starred food that rises to the occasion. Overseeing the kitchen is chef Giuseppe Di Iorio, whose seasonal menus reflect his passion for inventive, forward-thinking Mediterranean cuisine.

Marco Martini Restaurant   Gastronomy €€€

(☏06 4559 7350; http://marcomartinichef.com; Viale Aventino 121; meals from €65, tasting menus from €100; ⊙12.30-2.30pm & 7-10pm, closed Sat lunch & Sun; ☞; ☐Viale Aventino, ☐Viale Aventino) A lush garden pavilion at the **Corner Townhouse** (https://thecornerrome.com) provides the lovely setting for this casual fine-dining restaurant. The man with his name on the menu is one of Rome's youngest Michelin-starred chefs, whose inventive dishes often riff on Italian culinary traditions. Order à la carte or opt for one of several tasting menus, including one for vegetarians.

✪ Villa Borghese & Northern Rome

All'Oro   Ristorante €€€
(📞06 9799 6907; www.ristorantealloro.it; Via Giuseppe Pisanelli 23-25; tasting menus €88-150; ⏱7-11pm daily, 1-2.45pm Sat & Sun; Ⓜ️Flaminio) This Michelin-starred restaurant, in the five-star H'All Tailor Suite hotel, is one of Rome's top fine-dining tickets. At the helm is chef Riccardo Di Giacinto, whose artfully presented food is modern and innovative while still being recognisably Italian. Complementing the cuisine, the decor strikes a contemporary club look with dark-wood ceilings, brass lamps and a fireplace.

Metamorfosi   Ristorante €€€
(📞06 807 68 39; www.metamorfosiroma.it; Via Giovanni Antonelli 30; tasting menus €100-130; ⏱12.30-2.30pm & 8-10.30pm, closed Sat lunch & Sun; 🚌Via Giovanni Antonelli) This Michelin-starred Parioli restaurant provides one of Rome's best dining experiences, offering international fusion cuisine and a contemporary look that marries linear clean-cut lines with warm earthy tones. Chef Roy Carceres' cooking is eclectic, often featuring playful updates of traditional Roman dishes, such as his signature Uovo 65° carbonara antipasto, a deconstruction of Rome's classic pasta dish.

Neve di Latte   Gelato €
(📞06 320 84 85; www.facebook.com/Nevedilatte RomaFlaminio; Via Poletti 6; gelato €2.50-5; ⏱noon-11pm Sun-Thu, to midnight Fri & Sat summer, noon-10pm winter; 🚌Viale Tiziano) Behind the MAXXI gallery (p106), this out-of-the-way gelateria is one of Rome's best. There are few exotic flavours, rather the onus is on the classics, all prepared with high-quality seasonal ingredients. The pistachio, made with nuts from the Sicilian town of Bronte, is excellent, as is the crème caramel.

Caffè delle Arti   Ristorante €€
(Map p252; 📞06 3265 1236; www.caffedelle artiroma.com; Via Gramsci 73; meals €40-45; ⏱8am-5pm Mon, to midnight Tue-Sun; 🚌Piazza Thorvaldsen) The cafe-restaurant of La Galleria Nazionale (p59) sits in neoclassical

Eataly (p143)

splendour in a tranquil corner of Villa Borghese. An elegant venue, it's at its best on warm sunny days when you can sit on the terrace and enjoy the romantic setting over a lunch salad, cocktail or dinner of classic Italian cuisine.

❌ Southern Rome

Caffè Palombini   Italian €

(☑06 591 17 00; www.palombini.com; Piazzale Konrad Adenauer 12; meals €10-20; ☺7am-10pm Sun-Thu, to 1am Fri & Sat) EUR's best option for a meal, a snack or a cocktail is this large, buzzing, bustling cafe and restaurant. Sit on the sunny terrace for a drink, browse the line-up of offerings in the cafeteria, nab a table in the dining room – the options are many. The food is excellent, from the pastries in the bar area to the various daily specials.

Trattoria Pennestri   Lazio €€

(☑06 574 24 18; www.facebook.com/Trattoria Pennestri; Via Giovanni da Empoli 5; meals €25-35; ☺noon-3pm Fri-Sun, 7-11pm Tue-Sun; ✐;

Ⓜ Piramide) Headed by Danish-Italian chef Tommaso Pennestri, this mellow trattoria pays its respects to staunch Roman classics (think carbonara and tripe) but is at its best when dishing out bright, bold comfort food, such as gnocchi tumbled with prawns and *stracciatella* cheese or suckling pig glazed in juniper with apple chutney. Save room for the heavenly chocolate and rosemary mousse.

Giolitti   Gelato €

(☑06 592 45 07; https://giolittieur.it; Viale Oceania 90; gelato from €2; ☺7am-midnight; ☏) Locals needn't make the long trek to the Pantheon for some of Rome's best gelato. Legendary Giolitti has a cafe right beside Lago dell'EUR. Get a cone or a dish of the impossibly creamy gelato. Consider a seasonal flavour such as peach. Or just get the addictive white chocolate. There are shady tables where you can enjoy waiter service.

Verde Pistacchio   Vegetarian, Vegan €

(☑06 4547 5965; www.facebook.com/verde pistacchioroma; Via Ostiense 181; meals €12-25;

Coda alla vaccinara (oxtail cooked butcher's style)

SUSAN WRIGHT/LONELY PLANET ©

⊙11am-4pm & 6pm-midnight Mon-Thu, 11am-4pm & 6pm-2am Fri, 5.30pm-2am Sat & Sun; 🛜🍴; 🚇Via Ostiense, Ⓜ️Garbatella) Camilla, Raffaele and Francesco are the friends behind Green Pistachio, a stylish bistro-cafe with a minimalist, vintage interior and pavement tables among a little strip of good eateries and cafes. The kitchen cooks up fantastic vegetarian and vegan cuisine, and the lunchtime deal is a steal. Lunch here before or after visiting Rome's second-largest church just over the road.

Andreotti   Pastries €

(☎06 575 07 73; www.andreottiroma.it; Via Ostiense 54; treats from €1.50; ⊙7.30am-10pm; 🛜; 🚇Via Ostiense, Ⓜ️Piramide) Try not to drool on the cases full of luscious pastry and gelato displays crafted at this 1934 *pasticceria*. Treats range from buttery *crostate* (tarts) to piles of golden *sfogliatelle romane* (ricotta-filled pastries). Hanging out with a coffee on the sunny pavement terrace is a warm-weather delight. Andreotti cooks up simple meals; pasta dishes ring in at around €6.

Film director and Ostiense local Ferzan Ozpetek (*Loose Cannons/Mine Vaganti*, 2010) is such a fan of the pastries that he's known to cast them in his films.

Il Giardino di
Giulia e Fratelli   Italian €

(☎347 5092772; Via Appia Antica 176; meals €10-30; ⊙noon-3pm & 7-11.30pm Tue-Sat; 👶; 🚇Via Appia Antica) Just north of the tomb of Cecilia Metella, this garden restaurant is a bucolic delight. Book one of the well-spaced tables beneath the orange trees and feast on standard Italian fare or *panini* amid flowery green views. On Sundays, locals in their finery gather for family lunches. There's even a playground.

Qui Nun Se More Mai   Lazio €€

(☎06 780 39 22; www.facebook.com/qvinun semoremai; Via Appia Antica 198; meals €35-45; ⊙noon-3pm & 7.30-11.45pm Tue-Sat, 12.30-3pm

🍽️ Offal Eating

For the heart (and liver and brains) of the *cucina romana*, head to Testaccio, a traditional working-class district clustered around the city's former slaughterhouse. In the past, butchers who worked in the city abattoir were often paid in cheap cuts of meat as well as money. The Roman staple *coda alla vaccinara* translates as 'oxtail cooked butcher's style'. It is cooked for hours to create a rich sauce with tender slivers of meat. A famous Roman dish that's not for the faint hearted is pasta with *pajata*, made with the entrails of young veal calves, considered a delicacy since they contain the mother's congealed milk. If you see the word *coratella* in a dish, it means you'll be eating lights (lungs), kidneys and hearts.

Sun; 🚇Via Appia Antica) This small, charismatic restaurant in an old stone house has an open fire for grilling, plus a small terrace. The menu offers Roman classics such as pasta amatriciana, carbonara, *alla gricia* (cured pork and *pecorino* cheese) and *cacio e pepe* (cheese and pepper) – just the thing to set you up for the road ahead.

Eataly   Italian €

(☎06 9027 9201; www.eataly.net; Piazzale XII Ottobre 1492; meals €10-50; ⊙shops 9am-midnight, restaurants typically noon-3.30pm & 7-11pm; 🛜; Ⓜ️Piramide, 🚉Ostiense) Be prepared for some serious taste-bud titillation in this flash food emporium of gargantuan proportions built in the former terminal for airport buses. Four shop floors showcase every conceivable Italian food product (dried and fresh), while multiple themed food stalls and restaurants offer plenty of opportunity to taste or feast on Italian cuisine.

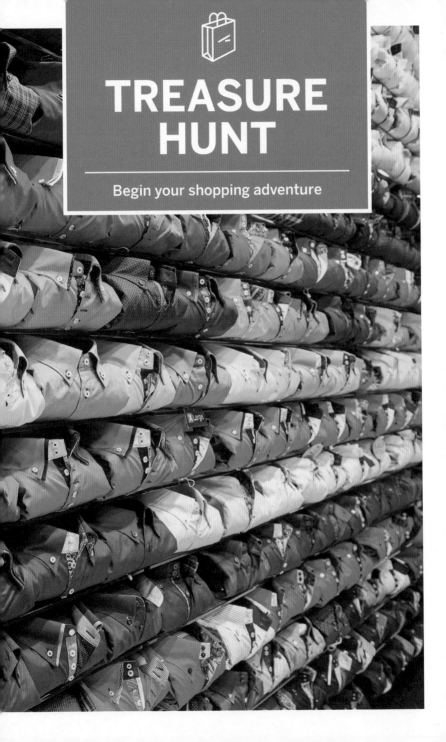

TREASURE HUNT

Begin your shopping adventure

Treasure Hunt

Rome has a huge and diverse array of specialist shops, fashion boutiques and artisans' workshops, with a particularly impressive portfolio of food, clothing and accessory boutiques. Many of these businesses are family owned, having been passed down through the generations. Others have grown from their modest origins into global brands known for their classic designs and quality workmanship.

In This Section

Useful Phrases

I'd like to buy...
Vorrei comprare...
(vo.ray kom.pra.re)

I'm just looking.
Sto solo guardando.
(sto so.lo gwar.dan.do)

Can I look at it?
Posso dare un'occhia- ta?
(po.so da.re oo.no.kya.ta)

How much is this?
Quanto costa ques- to?
(kwan.to. kos.ta. kwe.sto)

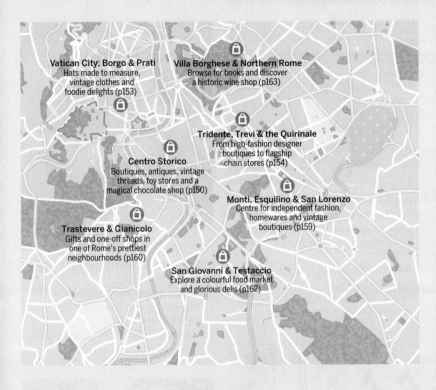

Vatican City, Borgo & Prati
Hats made to measure,
vintage clothes and
foodie delights (p153)

Villa Borghese & Northern Rome
Browse for books and discover
a historic wine shop (p163)

Tridente, Trevi & the Quirinale
From high-fashion designer
boutiques to flagship
chain stores (p154)

Centro Storico
Boutiques, antiques, vintage
threads, toy stores and a
magical chocolate shop (p150)

Monti, Esquilino & San Lorenzo
Centre for independent fashion,
homewares and vintage
boutiques (p159)

Trastevere & Gianicolo
Gifts and one-off shops in
one of Rome's prettiest
neighbourhoods (p160)

San Giovanni & Testaccio
Explore a colourful food market
and glorious delis (p162)

Opening Hours

- Most city-centre shops: 9am to
7.30pm (or 10am to 8pm) Monday to
Saturday; some close Monday morning

- Smaller shops: 9am to 1pm and
3.30pm to 7.30pm (or 4pm to 8pm)
Monday to Saturday

Sales Seasons

Winter sales *(saldi)* run from early
January – usually the first Saturday of
the month – to mid-February. Summer sales in Rome begin on the first
Saturday of July and continue to entice
bargain hunters until early September.

The Best...

Experience Rome's best shopping

Fashion

Bomba (p155) Gorgeous women's and men's clothing.

Chiara Baschieri (p154) Beautifully tailored womenswear by a young Roman designer.

Gente (p155) Emporium-style, multilabel boutique.

Tina Sondergaard (p159) Retro-inspired dresses, adjusted to fit.

Homewares

Bialetti (p163) The place to go for cool Italian kitchenware.

Mercato Monti Urban Market (p97) Vintage homeware finds cram this weekend market.

c.u.c.i.n.a. (p158) Gastronomic gadgets to enhance your culinary life.

Shoes

Calzoleria Petrocchi (p151) Bespoke and ready-to-wear shoes since 1946.

Fausto Santini (p155) Rome's best-known shoe designer; simple, architectural designs.

Marta Ray (p150) Ballerina flats in a rainbow of colours.

Artisanal Goods

Ibiz – Artigianato in Cuoio (p150) Leather accessories in a father-daughter workshop.

Artisanal Cornucopia (p156) Handmade pieces by Italian designers.

Flumen Profumi (p156) 'Made in Rome' couture fragrances.

Perlei (p159) Jewellery with a modernist aesthetic.

Bookshops

Almost Corner Bookshop (p161)
English-language bookshop.
Feltrinelli International (p159) Books
in several European languages.
Anglo American Bookshop (p156;
pictured above) As the name suggests.

Gourmet Delis

Antica Caciara Trasteverina (p160)
Century-old deli in Trastevere.
Paciotti Salumeria (p153) Family-run
deli stocking a cornucopia of Italian
edibles.
Salumeria Roscioli (p150) Byword for
foodie excellence.

Lonely Planet's Top Choices

Calzoleria Petrocchi (p151) Historic
store handcrafting shoes from the finest
leather.
Chez Dede (p151) Ultrachic boutique
selling handcrafted accessories, fashions, homewares and books.
Confetteria Moriondo & Gariglio
(p150) Historic chocolate shop selling
handmade chocolates made from
19th-century recipes.
Marta Ray (p150) A Roman-born brand
specialising in women's ballerina flats.
Mercado de Porta Portese (p96)
Mammoth Sunday-morning flea market.

Sweet Gifts

Biscottificio Innocenti (p160) Vintage
shop selling old-world biscuits.
Confetteria Moriondo & Gariglio
(p150; pictured above) Handmade
chocolates.
La Bottega del Marmoraro (p156)
Decorative marble plaques.

Centro Storico

Salumeria Roscioli Food & Drinks
(Map p250; 06 687 52 87; www.salumeriaroscioli.com; Via dei Giubbonari 21; 8.30am-8.30pm Mon-Sat; Via Arenula) Rome's most celebrated deli showcases a spectacular smorgasbord of prize products ranging from cured hams and cheeses to conserves, dried pastas, olive oils, aged balsamic vinegars and wines. Alongside celebrated Italian fare you'll also find top international foodstuffs such as French cheese, Iberian ham and Scottish salmon.

Confetteria Moriondo & Gariglio Chocolate
(Map p250; 06 699 08 56; Via del Piè di Marmo 21-22; 9am-7.30pm Mon-Sat; Via del Corso) Roman poet Trilussa was so smitten with this chocolate shop – established by the Torinese confectioners to the royal house of Savoy – that he was moved to mention it in verse. And we agree: it's a gem. Decorated like an elegant tearoom, it specialises in handmade chocolates and confections such as marrons glacés, many prepared according to original 19th-century recipes.

Ibiz – Artigianato in Cuoio Fashion & Accessories
(Map p250; 06 6830 7297; www.ibizroma.it; Via dei Chiavari 39; 10am-7.30pm Mon-Sat; Corso Vittorio Emanuele II) In her diminutive family workshop, Elisa Nepi and her team craft beautiful butter-soft leather wallets, bags, belts, key rings and sandals, in elegant designs and myriad colours. You can pick up a belt for about €35, while for a shoulder bag you should bank on around €145.

Marta Ray Shoes
(Map p250; 06 6880 2641; www.martaray.it; Via dei Coronari 121; 10am-8pm; Via Zanardelli) Women's ballet flats and elegant, everyday bags in rainbow colours and supersoft leather are the hallmarks of the Rome-born Marta Ray brand. At this shop, one of three in town, you'll find a selection of trademark ballerinas as well as ankle

Galleria Alberto Sordi (p153)

F8 STUDIO/SHUTTERSTOCK ©

boots and an attractive line in modern, beautifully designed handbags.

You'll find branch stores at Via della Reginella 4 in the Jewish Ghetto and Via del Moro 6 in Trastevere.

Calzoleria Petrocchi   Shoes

(Map p250; ☎06 687 62 89; www.calzoleria petrocchi.it; Vicolo Sugarelli 2; ⊙7am-1pm & 2-5.30pm Mon-Fri, 8am-1pm Sat, by appointment Sun; 🚌Corso Vittorio Emanuele II) This historic shoemaker has been handcrafting leather shoes for well-heeled Romans and film icons such as Audrey Hepburn and Robert De Niro since 1946. Choose from the ready-to-wear collection or design a bespoke pair of your own: head artisan Marco Cecchi personally takes clients' measurements and customises shoes based on their selection of leather and style.

Chez Dede   Concept Store

(Map p250; ☎06 8377 2934; www.chezdede.com; Via di Monserrato 35; ⊙3.30-7.30pm Mon, from 10.30am Tue-Sat; 🚌Lungotevere dei Tebaldi) This ultrachic boutique offers a curated selection of handcrafted accessories, fashions, homewares and books. Particularly sought after are its signature canvas and leather tote bags, but you'll also find original artworks, hand-painted ceramics and limited edition perfumes, all displayed with effortless cool in the belle-époque-styled interior.

namasTèy   Tea

(Map p250; ☎06 6813 5660; www.namastey. it; Via della Palombella 26; ⊙10.30am-7.30pm Mon-Sat, from 3pm Sun, closed Aug; 🚌Largo di Torre Argentina) After a visit to this charming shop, you'll be reminded of it every time you have a cup of tea. Set up like an apothecary with ceiling-high shelves and rows of jars, it stocks an encyclopedic range of blends from across the globe, as well as everything you could ever need for your home tea ritual – teapots, cups, infusers, filters.

Bartolucci   Toys

(Map p250; ☎06 6919 0894; www.bartolucci. com; Via dei Pastini 98; ⊙10am-10pm; 🚌Via

Ecclesiastical Threads

Even if you're not in the market for a bishop's mitre or a ceremonial cassock, Rome's religious outfitters offer some good deals. South of the Pantheon a string of ecclesiastical shops such as **Ghezzi** (Map p250; ☎06 686 97 44; www.ghezziluciano.it; Via dei Cestari 32-33; ⊙9am-6.30pm Mon-Fri, to noon Sat; 🚌Largo di Torre Argentina) and **Ditta Annibale Gammarelli** (Map p250; ☎06 6880 1314; www.gammarelli.com; Via di Santa Chiara 34; ⊙8.30am-7pm Mon-Fri; 🚌Largo di Torre Argentina) serve clerics from all over the world, supplying them with elaborate capes and classic dog collars. That might not be you, but if you're after a sober V-neck sweater, a decorative icon, or a pair of snappy socks in poppy red or cardinal purple, these places offer quality and value for money. Head to Via dei Cestari and environs.

Ecclesiastical garments, Ditta Annibale Gammarelli
WENN RIGHTS LTD/ALAMY STOCK PHOTO ©

del Corso) It's difficult to resist going into this magical toyshop where everything is carved out of wood. By the main entrance, a Pinocchio pedals his bike robotically, perhaps dreaming of the full-sized motorbike parked nearby, while inside there are all manner of ticking clocks, rocking horses, planes and more Pinocchios than you're likely to see in your whole life.

Materie   Jewellery

(Map p250; ☎06 679 31 99; www.materieshop. com; Via del Gesù 73; ⊙10.30-7.30pm Mon-Sat; 🚌Via del Corso) Materie is a lovely showcase

Top Five Rome Souvenirs

Shoes

Nothing screams quality or glamour more than a pair of Italian shoes. Get the latest fashions at Marta Ray (p150) or Fausto Santini (p155).

A Leather Bag

For a butter-soft, hand-stitched leather bag, head to a workshop such as Ibiz – Artigianato in Cuoio (p150) or Il Sellaio.

Jewellery

Linger in Rome's romantic jewellery shops: try Patrizia Corvaglia Gioielli, Materie (p151) and Re(f)use (p162) for unique pieces.

Deli Treats

Volpetti (p162) and Salumeria Roscioli (p150) are laden with the finest gourmet treats money can buy.

Marble

Choose your favourite Italian saying and set it in stone at La Bottega del Marmoraro (p156; pictured above).

for unique handcrafted jewellery. Each year owner Viviana Violo travels to source new pieces from designers and artisans working in materials as diverse as silver, silicone, rubber, metal, plastic and stone. As well as jewellery, you'll also find a small choice of bags, scarves and accessories.

Jerry Thomas Emporium   Drinks
(Map p250; ☑06 8697 0138; Vicolo Cellini 16; ⊙2-8pm Mon-Sat; ☐Corso Vittorio Emanuele II) An offshoot of the cult Jerry Thomas Project speakeasy (p170), this shop stocks a collector's dream of vermouth, spirits and liqueurs. Among the Italian and international labels, including their own *del Professore* brand, you'll find limited editions and artisanal blends made from historical recipes.

Patrizia Corvaglia Gioielli   Jewellery
(Map p250; ☑06 4555 1441; www.patriziacor vaglia.it; Via dei Banchi Nuovi 45; ⊙11am-7.30pm Mon-Sat; ☐Corso Vittorio Emanuele II) At her boutique in the former workshop of Renaissance goldsmith Benvenuti Cellini, Patrizia Corvaglia crafts her own line of jewellery. Her abstract, sometimes baroque, creations feature precious metals set with raw gemstones, often in geometric designs or patterns inspired by nature.

Aldo Fefè   Arts & Crafts
(Map p250; ☑06 6880 3585; Via della Stelletta 20b; ⊙8am-7.30pm Mon-Sat; ☐Corso del Rinascimento) In his small, cluttered workshop, master craftsman Aldo Fefè patiently binds books and produces beautifully hand-painted notebooks, boxes, picture frames and albums (from €15). You can also buy Florentine wrapping paper and calligraphic pens.

Casali   Art
(Map p250; ☑06 687 37 05; Via dei Coronari 115; ⊙10am-1pm & 3-7pm Mon-Fri, 10am-1pm Sat; ☐Via Zanardelli) On Via dei Coronari, a street renowned for its antique shops, Casali deals in original and reproduction etchings and prints, many delicately hand coloured. The shop is small but the choice isn't, ranging from 16th-century botanical

High-Street Shopping in Style

Galleria Alberto Sordi (Map p250; ☑06 6919 0769; www.galleriaalbertosordi.it; Galleria di Piazza Colonna, Piazza Colonna; ⊙8.30am-9pm Mon-Fri, to 10pm Sat, 9.30am-9pm Sun; ☐Via del Corso) is the elegant stained-glass arcade that starred in Alberto Sordi's 1973 classic film, *Polvere di stelle* (Stardust). It has since been renamed in his honour and is a great spot to shop at high-street stores such as Zara and Feltrinelli.

manuscripts to 18th-century maps of Rome and postcard prints.

There's a second branch near the Pantheon at Piazza della Rotonda 81a.

⊛ Vatican City, Borgo & Prati

Il Sellaio   Fashion & Accessories
(Map p253; ☑06 321 17 19; www.serafini pelletteria.it; Via Caio Mario 14; ⊙9.30am-7.30pm Mon-Fri, 9.30am-1pm & 3.30-7.30pm Sat; ⓂOttaviano-San Pietro) During the 1960s Ferruccio Serafini was one of Rome's most sought-after artisans, making handmade leather shoes and bags for the likes of Liz Taylor and Marlon Brando. Nowadays, his daughter Francesca runs the family shop where you can pick up beautiful hand-stitched bags, belts and accessories. Have designs made to order or get your leather handbags and luggage reconditioned.

Paciotti Salumeria   Food & Drinks
(☑06 3973 3646; www.paciottisalumeria.it; Via Marcantonio Bragadin 51/53; ⊙7.30am-8.30pm Mon-Wed, Fri & Sat, 12.30-8.30pm Thu; ⓂCipro) This family-run deli is a fantasyland of Italian edibles. Whole prosciutto hams hang in profusion. Cheeses, olive oil, dried pasta, balsamic vinegar, wine and truffle pâtés crowd the shelves, and can be

bubbled-wrapped and vacuum-sealed for travel. Patriarch Antonio Paciotti and his three affable sons merrily advise customers in both Italian and English.

Antica Manifattura Cappelli   Hats

(Map p253; ☑06 3972 5679; www.antica-cappelleria.it; Via degli Scipioni 46; ⊙9am-7pm Mon-Sat; ⓂOttaviano-San Pietro) A throwback to a more elegant age, the prim, hat-sized atelier-boutique of milliner Patrizia Fabri offers a wide range of beautifully crafted hats. Choose from the off-the-peg line of straw panamas, vintage cloches, felt berets and tweed deerstalkers, or have one made to measure. Prices range from about €70 to €300. Ordered hats can be delivered within the day.

There's also a second branch at Via dell'Oca 34 near Piazza del Popolo.

> *To shop 'local', go for the country's most famous Roman global brands...*

Enoteca Costantini   Wine

(Map p250; ☑06 320 35 75; https://enoteca costantinipiero.it; Piazza Cavour 16; ⊙9am-1pm Tue-Sat, 4.30-8pm Mon-Sat; ⓇPiazza Cavour) If you're after a hard-to-find grappa or a special wine, this excellent *enoteca* is the place. Piero Costantini's superbly stocked shop is a point of reference for aficionados, with its 800-sq-metre basement cellar and a colossal collection of Italian and international wines, champagnes and more than 1000 spirits. Note the beautiful wrought-iron grape vines on the facade.

🄶 Tridente, Trevi & the Quirinale

Chiara Baschieri   Clothing

(Map p252; ☑333 6364851; www.chiara baschieri.it; Via Margutta, cnr Vicolo Orto di Napoli; ⊙11am-7pm Tue-Sat; ⓂSpagna) One of Rome's most impressive independent designers, Chiara Baschieri produces classic, meticulously tailored clothing featuring exquisite fabrics. Her style has echoes of 1960s Givenchy – if Audrey

Tod's (p158)

Hepburn had ever stopped by, Chiara would no doubt have gained another fan.

Bomba
Clothing

(Map p252; ☑06 361 28 81; www.cristinabomba. com; Via dell'Oca 39; ⊙11am-7.30pm Tue-Sat, from 3.30pm Mon; Ⓜ Flaminia) Opened by designer Cristina Bomba over four decades ago, this gorgeous boutique is now operated by her fashion-designing children Caterina (womenswear) and Michele (menswear). Using the highest-quality fabrics, their creations are tailored in the next-door atelier (peek through the front window); woollens are produced at a factory just outside the city. Pricey but oh-so-worth-it.

Gente
Fashion & Accessories

(Map p252; ☑06 320 76 71; www.genteroma.com; Via del Babuino 77; ⊙10.30am-7.30pm Mon-Fri, to 8pm Sat, 11.30am-7.30pm Sun; Ⓜ Spagna) This multilabel boutique was the first in Rome to bring all the big-name luxury designers – Italian, French and otherwise – under one roof and its vast emporium-styled space remains an essential stop for every serious fashionista. Labels include Dolce & Gabbana, Prada, Alexander McQueen, Sergio Rossi and Missoni.

Its men's store is across the road, at Via Babuino 185. A second **women's store** (Map p250; ☑06 678 91 32; Via Frattina 92; ⊙10.30am-7.30pm Mon-Fri, to 8pm Sat, 11.30am-7.30pm Sun; ☐ Via del Corso) focuses on accessories.

Fausto Santini
Shoes

(Map p250; ☑06 678 41 14; www.faustosantini. com; Via Frattina 120; ⊙10am-7.30pm Mon-Sat, 11am-7pm Sun; Ⓜ Spagna) Rome's best-known shoe designer, Fausto Santini is famous for his beguilingly simple, architectural shoe designs, with beautiful boots and shoes made from butter-soft leather. Colours are beautiful, and the quality is impeccable. Seek out the end-of-line discount shop (p159) in Monti to source a bargain – its stock is regularly refreshed.

Designer Fashion

Big-name designer boutiques hawk their covetable wares in the grid of streets between Piazza di Spagna and Via del Corso in Tridente. All the great Italian and international names are here – Gucci, Salvatore Ferragamo, Armani, Prada, Dior, Versace and Bulgari included – as well as many lesser-known designers, selling fashionable clothes, shoes and accessories for men, women and children.

To shop 'local', go for the country's most famous Roman global brands: rubber-studded loafers from Tod's (p158), something chic from 1960s designer **Valentino** (Map p245; ☑06 9451 57 10; www.valentino.com; Piazza di Spagna 38; ⊙10am-7.30pm Mon-Sat, to 7pm Sun; Ⓜ Spagna), top-quality leather from Fendi (p156), or a handbag, wallet or suitcase with a distinctive contemporary look from affordable Mandarina Duck (p156).

Via dei Condotti is Rome's immaculately clad designer-fashion spine, but plenty more haute-couture boutiques pepper Via Borgognona, Via Frattina, Via della Borghese, Via della Vite and Via del Babuino.

For independent boutiques stocking chic pieces by lesser-known or rising designers, mooch **Via dell'Oca** and **Via della Penna** near Piazza del Popolo, or head to **Via del Boschetto** in Monti and **Via del Governo Vecchio** in the *centro storico*.

Gucci handbags

Artisan Workshops & Studios

Rome's shopping scene has a surprising number of artists and artisans who create their goods on the spot in hidden workshops. There are a number of good options in Tridente (try Via Margutta, Via dell'Oca and Via della Penna) and in Monti (try Via del Boschetto and Via Panisperna).

Artisanal Cornucopia   Design

(Map p252; ☑342 8714597; www.artisanal cornucopia.com; Via dell'Oca 38a; ⊙10.30am-7.30pm Tue-Sat, from 3.30pm Mon, from 4.30pm Sun; Ⓜ Flaminio) One of several stylish independent boutiques on Via dell'Oca, this chic concept store showcases exclusive handmade pieces by Italian designers: the delicate gold necklaces and other jewellery crafted by Giulia Barela are a highlight, but there are loads of bags, shoes, candles, homewares and other objects to covet.

Flumen Profumi   Perfume

(Map p250; ☑06 6830 7635; www.flumen profumi.com; Via della Fontanella di Borghese 41; ⊙11am-2pm & 3.30-7.30pm; ☑Via del Corso) Unique 'made in Rome' scents are what this artisan perfumery is all about. Natural perfumes are oil-based, contain four to eight base notes and evoke *la dolce vita* – Incantro fuses pomegranate with white flower, while Ritrovarsi Ancora is a nostalgic fragrance evocative of long, lazy, family meals around a countryside table (smell the fig!).

Federico Buccellati   Jewellery

(Map p250; ☑06 679 03 29; Via dei Condotti 31; ⊙10am-1.30pm & 3-7pm Tue-Fri, 10am-1.30pm & 2-6pm Sat, 3-7pm Mon; Ⓜ Spagna) Run today by the third generation of one of Italy's most prestigious silver- and goldsmiths, this historical shop opened in 1926. Everything is handcrafted and often delicately engraved with decorative flowers, leaves and nature-inspired motifs. Don't miss the Silver Salon on the 1st floor showcasing some original silverware and jewellery pieces by grandfather Mario.

Fendi   Fashion & Accessories

(Map p250; ☑06 3345 0890; www.fendi.com; Largo Carlo Goldoni 420, Palazzo Fendi; ⊙10am-7.30pm Mon-Sat, from 10.30am Sun; Ⓜ Spagna) With travertine walls, stunning contemporary art and sweeping red-marble staircase, the flagship store of Rome's iconic fashion house inside 18th-century Palazzo Fendi is dazzling. Born in Rome in 1925 as a leather and fur workshop on Via del Plebiscit, this luxurious temple to Roman fashion is as much a concept store as maison selling ready-to-wear clothing for men and women.

The clothing range includes Fendi's signature leather and fur pieces. Redesigned in 2016, the flagship store includes a sumptuous apartment to receive VIPs on the 2nd floor, a **boutique hotel** (www. fendiprivatesuites.com) on the 3rd, and a glittering Japanese restaurant and cocktail terrace bar (p112) on the top floor.

Anglo American Bookshop   Books

(Map p245; ☑06 679 52 22; www.aab.it; Via della Vite 102; ⊙10.30am-7.30pm Tue-Sat, from 3.30pm Mon; Ⓜ Spagna) Particularly good for university reference books, the Anglo American Bookshop is well stocked and well known. It has an excellent range of literature, travel guides, children's books and maps, and if it hasn't got the book you want, staff will order it in.

La Bottega del Marmoraro   Art

(Map p252; ☑06 320 76 60; Via Margutta 53b; ⊙8am-7.30pm Mon-Sat; Ⓜ Flaminio) Watch *marmoraro* (marble artist) Sandro Fiorentini chip away in this atelier filled with his decorative marble plaques engraved with various inscriptions: *la dolce vita, la vita e bella* (life is beautiful) etc. Plaques start at €10 and Sandro will engrave any inscription you like (from €15).

Top Five Markets

Mercado de Porta Portese (p96)

Mercato Campagna Amica al Circo Massimo (p97)

Nuovo Mercato di Testaccio (p97)

Mercato di Piazza San Cosimato (p97)

Mercato Monti Urban Market (p97)

Clockwise from left: Mercado de Porta Portese (p96); Mercato di Piazza San Cosimato (p97); Mercato Monti Urban Market (p97)

JUMPING ROCKS/UIG VIA GETTY IMAGES ©; PETER PTSCHELINZEW/GETTY IMAGES © ALEXANDRA BRUZZESE/LONELY PLANET ©

Pifebo

> *...racks brim with sunglasses, boots, clothing, bags and an impressive sports jersey collection...*

Mandarina Duck
Fashion & Accessories

(Map p245; 📞06 678 64 14; www.mandarina duck.com; Via dei Due Macelli; ◷10am-7.30pm Mon-Sat, from 10.30am Sun; Ⓜ Spagna) Now a global brand, this Italian company produces handbags, wallets and suitcases with a distinctive contemporary design. Prices are extremely reasonable considering the quality.

Borsalino
Hats

(Map p252; 📞06 323 33 53; www.borsalino. com; Piazza del Popolo 20; Ⓜ Flaminia) Humphrey Bogart, Ingrid Bergman, Marcello Mastroianni and Jean Paul Belmondo all wore them, and now you can too. Borsalino has been producing quality men's and women's hats since 1857 and still does so – the must-buy numbers are the classic straw and felt models (including rollable panamas), but there are many other styles to choose from.

Tod's
Shoes

(Map p250; 📞06 6821 0066; www.tods.com; Via della Fontanella di Borghese 56a; ◷10.30am-7.30pm Mon-Sat, 10am-2pm & 3-7.30pm Sun; 🚌 Via del Corso) The trademark of this luxury Italian brand is its rubber-studded loafers – perfect weekend footwear for kicking back at your country estate. There's a second store nearby, at Via Condotti 53a. Tod's is known more recently as the generous benefactor behind the much-needed cleanup of the northern and southern facades of the Colosseum.

c.u.c.i.n.a.
Homewares

(Map p250; 📞06 679 12 75; www.cucinastore. com; Via Mario de' Fiori 65; ◷10am-7.30pm Tue-Fri, from 10.30am Sat, from 3.30pm Mon; Ⓜ Spagna) Make your own *cucina* (kitchen) look the part with the designer goods from this famous kitchenware shop, which stocks everything from classic *caffettiere* (Italian coffee makers) to cutlery and myriad devices you'll decide you simply must have.

Monti, Esquilino & San Lorenzo

Perlei · Jewellery

(Map p245; ☑06 4891 3862; www.perlei.com;
Via del Boschetto 35; ⊙10am-8pm Mon-Sat,
11am-2pm & 3-7pm Sun; Ⓜ Cavour) Pieces of
avant-garde body jewellery catch the eye
in the window of this tiny artisan jeweller
on Monti's best shopping street. Inside,
handmade pieces by Tammar Edelman
and Elinor Avni will appeal to those with
a modernist aesthetic – their graceful
arcs, sinuous strands and architectural arrangements are elegant and
eye-catching. There's a second store at
Via di Ripetta 10, located near Piazza del
Popolo.

Tina Sondergaard · Fashion & Accessories

(Map p245; ☑06 8365 57 61; www.facebook.
com/tina.sondergaard.rome; Via del Boschetto
1d; ⊙10.30am-7.30pm Mon-Sat, closed Aug;
Ⓜ Cavour) Sublimely cut and whimsically
retro-esque, Tina Sondergaard's handmade creations for women are a hit with
the local fashion cognoscenti. Styles
change by the week rather than the
season, femininity is the leitmotif, and you
can have adjustments made (included in
the price). Everything is remarkably well
priced considering the quality of the fabrics and workmanship. There's a second
shop at Via del Pellegrino 83, near the
Campo de' Fiori.

Feltrinelli International · Books

(Map p245; ☑06 482 78 78; www.lafeltrinelli.
it; Via VE Orlando 84-86; ⊙9am-8pm Mon-Sat,
10.30am-1.30pm & 4-8pm Sun; Ⓜ Repubblica)
The international branch of Italy's ubiquitous bookseller has a splendid collection of books in English, Italian, Spanish,
French, German and Portuguese. You'll
find everything from recent bestsellers to
dictionaries, travel guides, DVDs and an
excellent assortment of maps.

🛍 One-Off Boutiques & Vintage

One of the best strips for cutting-edge
designer boutiques and vintage clothes
is bohemian Via del Governo Vecchio,
running from a small square just off
Piazza Navona towards the river. Other
places for one-off boutiques are Via
del Pellegrino and around Campo de'
Fiori. Via del Boschetto, Via Urbana
and Via dei Serpenti in the Monti area
feature unique clothing boutiques,
including a couple where you can get
your clothes adjusted to fit, as well as
jewellery makers. Monti is also a centre
for vintage-clothes shops, as well as a
weekend vintage market, Mercato Monti
Urban Market (p97).

PAOLO CORDELLI/GETTY IMAGES ©

Pifebo · Vintage

(Map p246; ☑06 8901 5204; www.pifebo.com;
Via dei Serpenti 141; ⊙11am-3pm & 4-8pm Mon-
Sat, noon-8pm Sun; 🐾; Ⓜ Cavour) Seek out a
secondhand steal at Pifebo, the city's top
vintage boutique. Shelves and racks brim
with sunglasses, boots, clothing, bags and
an impressive sports jersey collection, all
hailing from the '70s, '80s and '90s. The
shop also specialises in rehabbing and
restoring leather items, handily returning
them to their original splendour. There's
another branch in San Giovanni (p162).

Giacomo Santini · Shoes

(Map p245; ☑06 488 09 34; Via Cavour 106;
⊙10am-1pm & 3.30-7.30pm Mon-Fri, 10am-
1.30pm & 3-7.30pm Sat; Ⓜ Cavour) This Fausto
Santini outlet, named after the Roman

accessory designer's father Giacomo, sells last season's and discounted Fausto Santini boots, shoes and bags. Expect to pay a snip of the regular retail price for a pair of his exquisite designs in soft leather. Sizes can be limited. Look for the 'Calzaturo' sign above the boutique.

🄳 Trastevere & Gianicolo

Biscottificio Innocenti   Food

(Map p254; 📞06 580 39 26; www.facebook. com/biscottificioInnocenti; Via della Luce 21; ⊙8am-8pm Mon-Sat, 9.30am-2pm Sun; 🚊Viale di Trastevere, 🚊Belli) For homemade biscuits, bite-sized meringues and fruit tarts large and small, there is no finer address in Rome than this vintage *biscottificio* with ceramic-tiled interior, fly-net door curtain and a set of old-fashioned scales on the counter to weigh biscuits (€17 to €25 per kilo). The shop has been run with much love and passion for several decades by the ever-dedicated Stefania.

The enormous yellow, 1960s oven filling half her shop is an astonishing 16m long –

biscuits are slowly baked as they pass from one end to the other on a conveyor belt. She sells 50-odd different types in all, including her famous *brutti ma buoni* (ugly but good).

Antica Caciara
Trasteverina   Food & Drinks

(Map p254; 📞06 581 28 15; www.facebook. com/anticacaciaratrasteverina; Via di San Francesco a Ripa 140; ⊙7.30am-8pm Mon-Sat; 🚊Viale di Trastevere, 🚊Trastevere/Mastai) The fresh ricotta is a prized possession at this century-old deli, and it's usually gone by lunchtime. If you're too late, take solace in the luscious *ricotta infornata* (oven-baked ricotta), wheels of famous, black-waxed *pecorino romano*, and garlands of *guanciale* (pig's jowl) ready for the perfect carbonara. The lovely, caring staff answer questions and plastic-wrap cheese and hams for transport home.

Owner Roberto, at home behind the counter since he was 13, will happily share his cooking tips. Wednesday sees fillets of *baccalà* (salted cod) thrown in a bowl of fresh water to soak, in preparation for

From left: Les Vignerons; Volpetti (p162); Confetteria Moriondo & Gariglio (p150)

Friday's traditional fish meal. Homemade bread, Sicilian anchovies, gourmet pasta and local wines too.

Atelier Livia Risi
Clothing

(Map p254; ☑06 5830 1667; www.liviarisi.it; Via dei Vascellari 37; ⏰10.30am-8pm Mon-Sat; 🚊Belli) Livia Risi designs women's clothes for that elusive sweet spot: elegant daily wear that's super-comfortable to wear while being both stylish and adaptable. Her wares hang on simple racks in her shop. Buy something ready-made or work with her on a creation just for you.

Les Vignerons
Wine

(Map p254; ☑06 6477 1439; www.lesvignerons. it; Via Mameli 61; ⏰4-9pm Mon, 11am-9pm Tue-Thu, to 9.30pm Fri & Sat; 🚊Viale di Trastevere, 🚊Trastevere/Min P Istruzione) If you're looking for interesting vintages, search out this lovely Trastevere wine shop. It boasts one of the capital's best collections of natural wines, mainly from small Italian and French producers, as well as a comprehensive selection of spirits and international craft beers. Staff offer great advice.

Almost Corner Bookshop
Books

(Map p254; ☑06 583 69 42; www.facebook. com/almostcornerbookshop; Via del Moro 45; ⏰11am-7pm Mon-Fri, to 8pm Sat-Sun; 🚊Piazza Trilussa) A crammed haven full of reads – every millimetre of wall space contains English-language fiction and nonfiction (including children's) books as well as travel guides. It's heaven to browse these shelves.

Acid Drop
Fashion & Accessories

(Map p254; ☑06 9603 5643; www.acidrop.com; Via del Moro 14, Trastevere; ⏰11am-8.30pm Tue-Thu, to 10pm Fri & Sat, noon-8.30pm Sun; 🚊Piazza Trilussa) Mother-daughter duo Ileana and Eleonora Ottini prove creativity is inherited at their quirky boutique. Unconventional statement pieces include punchy silk-screened T-shirts, steampunk-inspired accessories, hand-painted bags, and jewellery inspired by everything from *The Little Prince* to Frida Kahlo to the moon phases. All is made from scratch.

PAOLO CORDELLI/GETTY IMAGES ©

Almost Corner Bookshop (p161)

Re(f)use
Design

(Map p250; ☎06 6813 6975; www.carmina campus.com; Via della Fontanelle di Borghese 40; ⊙10.30am-7.30pm Tue-Sat, from 3pm Mon; 🚇Via del Corso) Fascinating to browse, this clever boutique showcases unique Carmina Campus pieces – primarily bags and jewellery – made from upcycled objects and recycled fabrics. The brand is the love child of Rome-born designer Ilaria Venturini Fendi (of the Fendi family), a passionate advocate of ethical fashion.

Upstairs, upcycled street signs become armchairs, computer keyboards become dining-room chairs, and the large petrol signs found at gas stations are turned into fabulous tabletops.

⑥ San Giovanni & Testaccio

Volpetti
Food & Drinks

(☎06 574 23 52; www.volpetti.com; Via Marmorata 47; ⊙8.30am-2pm & 4.30-8.15pm Mon-Fri, 8.30am-8.30pm Sat; 🚇Via Marmorata)

This super-stocked deli, one of the best in town, is a treasure trove of gourmet delicacies. Helpful staff will guide you through its extensive selection of Italian cheeses, homemade pastas, olive oils, vinegars, cured meats, wines and grappas. It also serves excellent, though pricey, sliced pizza.

Soul Food
Music

(Map p255; ☎06 7045 2025; www.haterecords. com; Via di San Giovanni in Laterano 192; ⊙10.30am-1.30pm & 3.30-7.30pm Tue-Sat; 🚇Via di San Giovanni in Laterano) Run by Hate Records, Soul Food is a laid-back record store with an encyclopedic collection of vinyl that runs the musical gamut, from '60s garage and rockabilly to punk, indie, new wave, folk, funk and soul. You'll also find retro T-shirts, posters, fanzines, even vintage toys.

Pifebo
Vintage

(☎06 9818 5845; https://pifebo.com; Via dei Valeri 10; ⊙noon-8pm Mon-Sat; 🚇Via dell'Ambra Aradam) One of Rome's best-stocked secondhand and vintage clothes stores. There's a definite rocker theme to the stock which includes endless racks of leather jackets, denims, cut-off shorts and cowboy boots. Dig further through the red-painted rooms and you'll discover plenty more to pimp up your wardrobe. There's another branch in Monti (p159).

⊙ Villa Borghese & Northern Rome

Bialetti
Homewares

(☎06 8778 4222; www.bialettistore.it; Via Salaria 52; ⊙10am-8pm Mon-Sat, 10am-1.30pm & 4-8pm Sun; ☐Via Salaria) In 1933 Alfonso Bialetti revolutionised domestic coffee-making by creating his classic *moka caffettiera*. His design has by now become a household staple, as ubiquitous in Italian kitchens as kettles in British homes. Here at this gleaming shop you'll find a full range as well as all manner of cool kitchenware.

 Tax-Free Shopping

Non-EU residents who spend over €155 on any one given day in a shop offering 'Tax Free for Tourists' shopping (www. taxrefund.it) are entitled to a tax refund of up to 22%. You'll need to show your passport, get a form and have it stamped by customs as you leave Italy.

Enoteca Bulzoni
Wine

(☎06 807 04 94; www.enotecabulzoni.it; Viale dei Parioli 36; ⊙8.30am-2pm & 4.30-8.30pm Mon-Sat; ☐Viale Parioli) This historic *enoteca* has been supplying Parioli's wine buffs since 1929. It has a formidable collection of Italian regional wines, as well as European and New World labels, and a carefully curated selection of champagnes, liqueurs, craft beers, olive oils and gourmet delicacies.

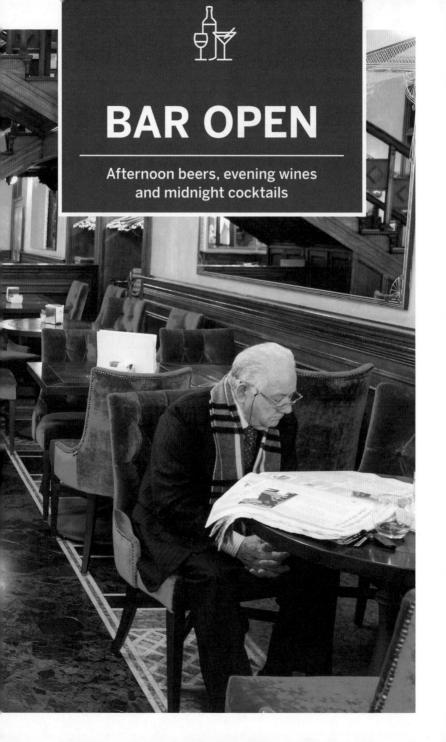

BAR OPEN

Afternoon beers, evening wines
and midnight cocktails

Bar Open

There's simply no city with better drinking and dancing backdrops than Rome: lounge on a piazza over an aperitivo (predinner drink) or wander from wine bar to restaurant to late-night drinking den, happily losing yourself in picturesque cobbled streets along the way. Night-owl Romans tend to eat late then drink at bars before heading off to a club at around 1am. The centro storico (historic centre) and Trastevere pull in a mix of locals and tourists after dark; Ostiense and Testaccio are the grittier clubbing districts.

In This Section

Opening Hours

- Cafe bars: 7.30am to 11pm, midnight or 1am

- Traditional bars: 7.30am to 1am or 2am

- Most bars, pubs and *enoteche* (wine bars): lunchtime or 6pm to 2am

- Nightclubs: 10pm to 4am

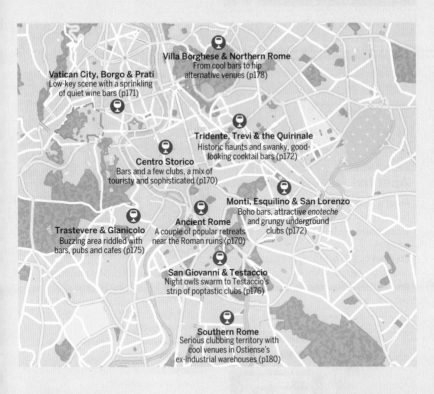

Villa Borghese & Northern Rome
From cool bars to hip
alternative venues (p178)

Vatican City, Borgo & Prati
Low-key scene with a sprinkling
of quiet wine bars (p171)

Tridente, Trevi & the Quirinale
Historic haunts and swanky, good-
looking cocktail bars (p172)

Centro Storico
Bars and a few clubs, a mix of
touristy and sophisticated (p170)

Monti, Esquilino & San Lorenzo
Boho bars, attractive *enoteche*
and grungy underground
clubs (p172)

Ancient Rome
A couple of popular retreats
near the Roman ruins (p170)

Trastevere & Gianicolo
Buzzing area riddled with
bars, pubs and cafes (p175)

San Giovanni & Testaccio
Night owls swarm to Testaccio's
strip of poptastic clubs (p176)

Southern Rome
Serious clubbing territory with
cool venues in Ostiense's
ex-industrial warehouses (p180)

Costs & Tipping

To save a few cents or euros, look out
for early-evening happy hours and
aperitivo specials.

Glass of wine From €3

Medium beer About €5

Cocktail From €10

Tipping in bars is not necessary, although many people leave small change
(perhaps €0.20) when ordering a coffee
at a bar.

Useful Phrases

Aperitivo A food buffet to accompany
evening drinks, usually served from
around 6pm till 9pm and included with
the price of one drink.

Apericena An abundant *aperitivo*
spread, sufficiently copious to double as
cena (dinner).

Enoteca (plural: *enoteche*) A wine bar;
anything from a cosy neighbourhood
hang-out to a hip, trendy bar.

Centri sociali Grungy venues staging
club nights and gigs.

The Best...

Experience Rome's finest drinking establishments

Aperitivi

Freni e Frizioni (p176) Perennially cool bar with lavish buffet.

Doppiozeroo (p180) Popular Ostiense address.

Momart (p178) Much loved by students and local professionals.

Rec 23 (p177) Hip New York–inspired venue in Testaccio.

Enoteche

Rimessa Roscioli (p170) Gourmet paradise; tastings and fine food.

Wine Concept (p176) Run by expert sommeliers; Italian regional labels and European vintages.

Ai Tre Scalini (p172) Buzzing *enoteca* with convivial pub vibe.

Cavour 313 (p170) This historic choice is near the Colosseum.

Craft Beer

Ma Che Siete Venuti a Fà (p175; pictured above) Pint-sized bar crammed with real-ale choices.

Open Baladin (p170) More than 40 beers on tap and up to 100 bottled brews.

Artisan (p173) Hipster San Lorenzo address.

Gay Venues

Coming Out (p178; pictured above) Gay bar with gigs, drag shows, karaoke.

L'Alibi (p178) Kitsch shows and music; mixed gay and straight crowd.

Lettere Caffè (p176) Trastevere bar hosting gay nights.

Terraces & Gardens

Stravinskij Bar (p172; pictured above) Luxurious bar with elegant courtyard.

Il Palazzetto (p113) Five-star Spanish Steps view.

Pimm's Good (p175) Small terrace amid the Trastevere action.

Speakeasies

Blackmarket Hall (p173) Cosy Monti hang-out; live jazz.

Jerry Thomas Project (p170) Master mixologists and retro decor.

Club Derrière (p113) Top-notch cocktails in the historic centre.

Keyhole (p113) Prohibition-era decor and craft cocktails.

Clubs

Azienda Cucineria & Circolo Degli Illuminati (p180) International DJs in Ostiense.

Vinile (p180) Food, music, dancing and party happenings.

Goa (p180) Serious clubbing in industrial-styled Ostiense.

Lonely Planet's Top Choices

Ai Tre Scalini (p172) Monti stalwart, with a lively student vibe, reasonable prices and good food.

Zuma Bar (p112) After-dark glamour and hobnobbing on a *palazzo* (mansion) rooftop.

Goa (p180) Motorbike-repair-workshop-turned-Rome-super-club.

Terra Satis (p175) Trastevere favourite serving quality tipples.

Open Baladin (p170) Leading light in Rome's craft-beer scene.

Ancient Rome

Cavour 313   Wine Bar

(Map p246; ☑06 678 54 96; www.cavour313.
it; Via Cavour 313; ☺12.30-2.45pm daily &
6-11.30pm Mon-Thu, to midnight Fri & Sat, 7-11pm
Sun, closed Aug; Ⓜ Cavour) Cavour 313 is a
historic wine bar, a snug, wood-panelled
retreat frequented by everyone from
tourists to actors and politicians. It serves
a selection of cold cuts and cheeses, as
well as daily specials, but the headline act
is the wine – with over 1000 mainly Italian
labels to choose from, you're sure to find
something to tickle your palate.

Centro Storico

Rimessa Roscioli   Wine Bar

(Map p250; ☑06 6880 3914; www.winetasting
rome.com; Via del Conservatorio 58; ☺6.30-
11.30pm Mon-Fri, noon-3pm & 6.30-11.30pm
Sat & Sun; ☏; ☒Lungotevere dei Tebaldi) An
offshoot of the popular Roscioli empire,
Rimessa is for wine lovers: labels from
all over Italy and further afield crowd
the shelves, while exquisite wine-tasting
dinners (€33 to €65) unfold in both
English and Italian. Also available is a
Tasting Bar option, where a sommelier
crafts a tasting tailored to your budget
and preferences.

Open Baladin   Craft Beer

(Map p250; ☑06 683 89 89; www.openbaladin
roma.it; Via degli Specchi 6; ☺noon-2am; ☏;
☒Via Arenula) This modern pub near Campo
de' Fiori has long been a leading light in
Rome's craft-beer scene, and with more
than 40 beers on tap and up to 100 bottled
brews (many from Italian artisanal micro-
breweries) it's a top place for a pint. As well
as great beer, expect a laid-back vibe and a
young, international crowd.

Jerry Thomas Project   Cocktail Bar

(Map p250; ☑06 9684 5937, 370 1146287;
www.thejerrythomasproject.it; Vicolo Cellini 30;
☺10pm-4am Tue-Sat; ☒Corso Vittorio Emanuele
II) A smoky speakeasy with a 1920s look
and a password to get in – check the website and call to book – this cult trendsetter

Be.re

ALEXANDRA BRUZZESE/LONELY PLANET ©

has led the way in Rome's recent love affair with craft cocktails. Its master mixologists know their stuff and the retro decor gives it a real Prohibition-era feel. Note there's a €5 'membership' fee. Also be warned: smoking is allowed inside.

Etablì Bar

(Map p250; ☑06 9761 6694; www.etabli.it; Vicolo delle Vacche 9a; ⏰7.30am-1am Mon-Wed, to 2am Thu-Sat, from 9am Sun; 🛜; 🚌Corso del Rinascimento) Housed in a 16th-century *palazzo*, Etablì is a rustic-chic lounge bar-restaurant where you can drop by for a morning coffee, have lunch or chat over an *aperitivo*. It's laid-back and good-looking, with Provence-inspired country decor – leather armchairs, rough wooden tables and a crackling fireplace.

It also has a bakery and serves full restaurant dinners (€40 to €45).

⊖ Vatican City, Borgo & Prati

L'Osteria di Birra del Borgo Roma Craft Beer

(Map p253; ☑06 8376 2316; http://osteria. birradelborgo.it; Via Silla 26; ⏰noon-2am; Ⓜ Ottaviano-San Pietro) Italy is no longer just about wine – for years a generation of brewers has been developing great craft beers. Try some of the best at this chic, contemporary bar with a soaring ceiling and stylish vats of brewing beer. It has a short menu of Italian standards at night and fine antipasto choices all day.

Passaguai Wine Bar

(Map p253; ☑06 8745 1358; www.passaguai.it; Via Leto 1; ⏰10am-2am Mon-Fri, 6pm-2am Sat & Sun; 🛜; 🚌Piazza del Risorgimento) A basement bar with tables in a cosy stone-clad interior and on a quiet side street, Passaguai feels pleasingly off the radar. It's a great spot for a post-sightseeing cocktail or glass of wine – there's an excellent choice of both – accompanied by cheese

ⓘ Politics & the Bella Figura

As with most cities, Rome's differing neighbourhoods morph into other characters after dark. For edgy clubs, live music and craft beer, wander off the beaten track into the grungy student 'hood of San Lorenzo or further east into boho Pigneto, a gritty district known for its alternative nightlife.

There are also subtle political divisions. San Lorenzo and Pigneto, to the east of central Rome, are popular with a left-leaning, alternative crowd, while areas to the north (such as Ponte Milvio and Parioli) attract a more right-wing, bourgeois milieu.

The *bella figura* (loosely translated as 'looking good') is important. The majority of locals spend evenings checking each other out, partaking in gelato, and not drinking too much. However, this is changing and certain areas – those popular with a younger crowd – can get rowdy with drunk teens and tourists (for example, Campo de' Fiori, San Lorenzo and parts of Trastevere).

Enoteca in Trastevere (p175)

and cold cuts, or even a full meal from the small menu.

Be.re Craft Beer

(Map p253; ☑06 9442 1854; www.be-re.eu; Piazza del Risorgimento, cnr Via Vespasiano; ⏰11am-2am; 🚌Piazza del Risorgimento) With its exposed-brick decor, high vaulted ceilings and narrow pavement tables, this

Top Five Cafes After Dark

Barnum Cafe (p125)

Caffè Sant'Eustachio (p125)

Bar San Calisto (p136)

La Bottega del Caffè (p133)

Necci dal 1924 (p135)

From left: Necci dal 1924 (p135); Bar San Calisto (p136); Caffè Sant'Eustachio (p125)

is a good spot for Italian craft beers. And should hunger strike, there's a branch of hit takeaway Trapizzino right next door that offers table service at Be.re. Picky coffee drinkers will enjoy the attached Pergamino as it includes concoctions made with soy milk.

❸ Tridente, Trevi & the Quirinale

Stravinskij Bar   Bar

(Map p252; ☎06 3288 88 74; www.roccoforte hotels.com/hotels-and-resorts/hotel-de-russie/; Via del Babuino 9, Hotel de Russie; ⊗9am-1am; MⒻlaminio) Can't afford to stay at the celeb-magnet Hotel de Russie? Then splash out on a drink at its swish bar. There are sofas inside, but the sunny courtyard is the fashionable choice, with sun-shaded tables overlooked by terraced gardens. Impossibly romantic in the best *dolce-vita* style, it's perfect for a pricey cocktail or beer accompanied by appropriately posh snacks.

Rosati   Cafe

(Map p252; ☎06 322 58 59; www.barrosati. com; Piazza del Popolo 5; ⊗7.30am-11.30pm; MⒻlaminio) Overlooking the vast disc of Piazza del Popolo, this historic 1922 cafe was once the hang-out of the left-wing chattering classes. Authors Italo Calvino and Alberto Moravia drank here while their right-wing counterparts went to the Canova across the square. Today tourists are the main clientele, but the views are as good as ever.

Drinking standing up at the bar will get you a reasonably priced coffee, but you'll pay a premium for a seat.

❸ Monti, Esquilino & San Lorenzo

Ai Tre Scalini   Wine Bar

(Map p246; ☎06 4890 7495; www.facebook. com/aitrescalini; Via Panisperna 251; ⊗12.30pm-1am; MⒸavour) A firm favourite since 1895, the 'Three Steps' is always packed, with predominantly young patrons spilling out of

CHRISTINE WEHRMEIER/ALAMY STOCK PHOTO ©

its bar area and into the street. Its a perfect spot to enjoy an afternoon drink or a simple meal of cheese, salami and dishes such as *polpette al sugo* (meatballs with sauce), washed down with superb choices of wine or beer.

Blackmarket Hall — Cocktail Bar

(Map p245; ☑339 7351926; www.facebook.com/ blackmarkethall/; Via de Ciancaleoni 31; ☺6pm-3am; MCavour) One of Monti's best bars, this multiroomed speakeasy in a former monastery has an eclectic vintage-style decor and plenty of cosy corners where you can enjoy a leisurely, convivial drink. It serves food up till midnight (burgers €12 to €15) and hosts live music – often jazz – on weekends. There's a second venue nearby on Via Panisperna 101.

Gatsby Café — Bar

(Map p255; ☑06 6933 9626; www.facebook. com/gatsbycafe; Piazza Vittorio Emanuele II 106; ☺8am-midnight Sun-Wed, to 1am Thu, to 2am Fri & Sat; MVittorio Emanuele) There's a good reason why the friendly bartenders here all wear flat caps, feather-trimmed trilbys and other traditional gents' hats: this fabulous 1950s-styled space with vintage furniture and flashes of geometric wallpaper was originally a milliner's shop called Galleria Venturini. Delicious *spritz*, craft cocktails, gourmet *panini* and *taglieri* (salami and cheese platters) make it a top *aperitivo* spot.

Artisan — Craft Beer

(Map p255; ☑327 9105709; www.facebook.com/ art.isan.90/; Via degli Arunci 9; ☺6pm-1am Sun & Mon, to 2am Tue-Thu, to 3am Fri & Sat; ☒Reti) A mecca for those who enjoy drinking craft beer, this hipster bar stocks artisanal tipples from around the globe and serves simple but tasty global food, too.

Bar Celestino — Bar

(Map p255; ☑06 4547 2483; www.facebook. com/bar-celestino; Via degli Ausoni 62-64; ☺7.30am-2am Mon-Sat; ☒Reti) Few places evoke the San Lorenzo student vibe quite like this grungy drinking den near Piazza dei Sanniti. A die-hard icon of this working-class neighbourhood, Celestino first opened in 1904 and is still going strong

Rome in a Glass

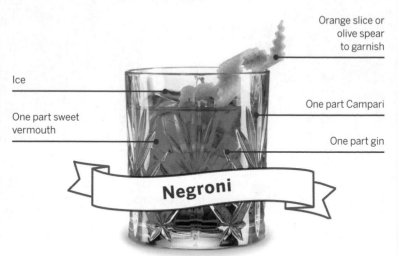

Orange slice or olive spear to garnish

Ice

One part sweet vermouth

One part Campari

One part gin

Negroni

SERHIY SHULLYE/SHUTTERSTOCK ©

How to Make a Negroni

• Take your pick between tumbler or highball glass and fill with ice cubes.

• Pour over equal parts of bitter orange-red Campari, gin and sweet vermouth (Carpano Antica Formula is the Italian Vermouth par excellence).

• Stir and garnish with a twist of orange or speared olive.

The Negroni Back Story

Consumed with passion by Romans it might be, but it's the Tuscan city of Florence that takes credit for creating the Negroni – in 1920 when a certain Count Camillo Negroni asked his bar man at historic Caffè Giacosa on Via del' Tornabuoni to add a shot of gin to his Americano (equal parts of bittersweet Campari and vermouth, with soda water).

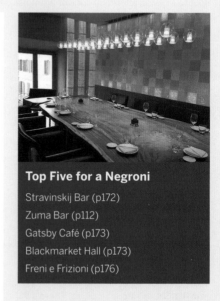

Top Five for a Negroni

Stravinskij Bar (p172)

Zuma Bar (p112)

Gatsby Café (p173)

Blackmarket Hall (p173)

Freni e Frizioni (p176)

Zuma Bar (p112)
MOREGALLERY/SHUTTERSTOCK ©

thanks to its simple, unpretentious vibe. Grab a seat or standing spot on the pavement or head inside. Find party updates on its Facebook page.

Trastevere & Gianicolo

Terra Satis
Cafe, Wine Bar

(Map p254; ☑06 9893 6909; Piazza dei Ponziani 1a; ☺7am-1am Mon-Thu, to 2am Fri & Sat; ☎; ☐Viale di Trastevere, ☐Belli) This hip neighbourhood cafe and wine bar in Trastevere has it all: newspapers, great coffee and charming bar staff, not to mention vintage furniture, comfy banquette seating and really good snacks. On warm days the laid-back action spills out on to its bijou, vine-covered terrace on cobbled Piazza di Ponziani. Good wine and beer selection.

Pimm's Good
Bar

(Map p254; ☑06 9727 7979; www.pimmsgood. it; Via di Santa Dorotea 8; ☺10am-2am; ☎; ☐Piazza Trilussa) 'Anyone for Pimm's?' is the catchphrase of both the namesake fruity English liqueur and this eternally popular bar. It has a part red-brick ceiling and does indeed serve Pimm's – the classic way or in a variety of cocktails. The lively bartenders are serious mixologists and well-crafted cocktails are their thing. Look for the buzzing street-corner pavement terrace.

Ma Che Siete Venuti a Fà
Pub

(Map p254; ☑06 6456 2046; www.football-pub.com; Via Benedetta 25; ☺11am-2am; ☐Piazza Trilussa) Named after a football chant, which translates politely as 'What did you come here for?', this pint-sized Trastevere pub is a beer-buff's paradise, packing in around 15 international craft beers on tap and even more by the bottle. Although it could easily be a cliché, the vibe here is real, and every surface is covered in beer labels.

Il Baretto
Bar

(Map p254; ☑06 589 60 55; Via Garibaldi 27; ☺7am-2am; ☐Via Garibaldi) Venture up a steep flight of steps from Trastevere – go

 Clubbing in Rome

Summer in the City

From around mid-June to mid-September, many nightclubs and live-music venues close, some moving to EUR or the beaches at Fregene or Ostia. The area around the Isola Tiberina throngs with life nightly during the **Lungo Il Tevere** (www.lungoiltevereroma. it; ☺mid-Jun–Aug), a summer festival along the riverbank, which sprouts bars, stalls and an open-air cinema. Pop-up bars stretch the length of the riverside footpaths between Ponte Palatino and Ponte Mazzini, and open nightly from around 5pm to 2am. Attempts are made to limit excessive alcohol consumption – water-edge bars are not allowed to serve double shots for example.

Be aware that in winter, bars often close earlier in the evening, particularly in areas where the norm is to drink outside. This said, an increasing number of bars have heated pavement terraces in winter, ensuring year-round al fresco drinking.

Club Talk

Rome has a range of nightclubs, mostly in Ostiense and Testaccio, with music policies ranging from lounge and jazz to dancehall and hip-hop. Clubs tend to get busy after midnight, or even after 2am. Often admission is free, but drinks are expensive. Cocktails usually cost between €10 and €20, but you can drink much more cheaply in the study clubs of San Lorenzo, Pigneto and the *centri sociali* (social centres).

on, it's worth it. Because here you'll discover this good-looking cocktail bar where the bass lines are meaty, the bar staff hip, and the interior a mix of vintage and

⊕ LGBT+ Rome

There is only a smattering of dedicated gay and lesbian clubs and bars in Rome, but the Colosseum end of Via di San Giovanni is a favourite hang-out and many clubs host regular gay and lesbian nights. The **Circolo Mario Mieli di Cultura Omosessuale** (📞06 541 39 85, Rainbow Help Line 800 110611; www.mariomieli.org; Via Efeso 2a; ⊙11am-6pm Mon-Fri; Ⓜ Basilica San Paolo) organises social functions. Its website has info and listings of forthcoming events.

Most gay venues (bars, clubs and saunas) require you to have an **Arcigay** (📞06 6450 1102; www.arcigayroma.it; Via Nicola Zabaglia 14; ⊙4-8pm Mon-Sat) membership card. These cost €10 and are available from the Arcigay headquarters in Testaccio or at any venue that requires one.

The biggest LGBT+ event of the year is **Gay Village** (📞350 0723346; www.gayvillage.it; Lungotevere Testacci; €3-20; ⊙7.30pm-3.30am Thu-Sat Jun–early Sep; Ⓜ Piramide). It attracts crowds of partygoers and an exuberant cast of DJs, musicians and entertainers to Testaccio's bars, cafes and clubs.

Gay Village flag
ANGELO CORDESCHI/SHUTTERSTOCK ©

pop art. Better yet, stop here on your way *down* from Gianicolo and have something cold on the tree-shaded terrace.

Lettere Caffè — Live Music

(Map p254; 📞340 0044154; www.lettere caffe.org; Via di San Francesco a Ripa 100/101; ⊙6pm-2am, closed mid-Aug–mid-Sep; 🚊 Viale di Trastevere, 🚊 Trastevere/Mastai) Like books? Poetry? Blues and jazz? Then you'll love this place: a clutter of bar stools and books, where there are regular live gigs, poetry slams, comedy and gay nights, plus DJ sets playing electronic, indie and new wave. *Aperitivo*, with a tempting vegetarian buffet, is served between 7pm and 9pm. Enjoy one of the cheap cocktail specials under the whirling fans.

Freni e Frizioni — Bar

(Map p254; 📞06 4549 7499; www.frenie frizioni.com; Via del Politeama 4-6; ⊙6.30pm-2am; 🚊 Piazza Trilussa) This perennially cool Trastevere bar is housed in an old mechanic's workshop – hence its name ('brakes and clutches') and shabby facade. It draws a young *spritz*-loving crowd that swells on to the piazza outside to sip well-mixed cocktails and seasonal punches, and fill up on its lavish *aperitivo* buffet (7pm to 10pm). Reservations are essential if you want a table on Friday and Saturday evenings.

⊙ San Giovanni & Testaccio

Wine Concept — Wine Bar

(Map p246; 📞06 7720 6673; www.wine concept.it; Via Capo d'Africa 21; ⊙noon-3pm & 6pm-midnight Mon-Thu, noon-3pm & 6pm-1am Fri, 6pm-1am Sat; 🚊 Via Labicana) Wine buffs looking to excite their palate should search out this smart *enoteca* (wine bar). Run by expert sommeliers, it has an extensive list of Italian regional labels and European vintages, as well as a small daily food menu. Wines are available to drink by the glass or buy by the bottle.

Blind Pig — Cocktail Bar

(Map p255; 📞06 8775 07 14; Via La Spezia 72; ⊙6.30pm-2am; Ⓜ Lodi) Cocktail bars have

Barnaba

been a growing trend in Rome for some time now but the trend shows no sign of waning and new places continue to open. Good-looking newcomer Blind Pig hits all the right notes with its dim lighting, green-and-black decor and professionally mixed cocktails. And that's without even mentioning its delicious focaccia.

Barnaba
Wine Bar

(📞06 2348 4415; www.facebook.com/barnaba winebarecucina; Via della Piramide Cestia 45-51; meals €38; ⏱12.30pm-12.30am; 📶; Ⓜ Piramide) Hands-down Testaccio's most sought-out spot after dark, wine bar Barnaba favours natural and independent producers spanning the *bel paese* (beautiful country). It also features an impressive champagne selection and more than 20 wines by the glass. Food depends on how hungry you are: choose upscale snacks like oysters and crostini with *burrata* cheese and sun-dried tomatoes or filling meat and pasta dishes.

> *Barnaba favours natural and independent producers spanning the bel paese (beautiful country).*

Rec 23
Bar

(📞06 8746 2147; www.rec23.com; Piazza dell'Emporio 2; ⏱6.30pm-2am daily, plus 12.30-3.30pm Sat & Sun; 🚌Via Marmorata) All exposed brick and mismatched furniture, this large, New York–inspired venue caters to all moods, serving *aperitivo* (drink plus buffet €10) and restaurant meals, as well as a weekend brunch (€18). Arrive thirsty to take on a 'Testaccio mule', one of Rec 23's original cocktails. Otherwise keep it simple with an Italian prosecco, Scottish whisky or Latin American rum.

L'Oasi della Birra
Bar

(📞06 574 61 22; Piazza Testaccio 41; ⏱4.30pm-1am Mon-Sat, from 6pm Sun; 🚌Via Marmorata) Housed in the Palombi Enoteca bottle shop, L'Oasi della Birra is

Lazio Wine

Local Lazio wines may not be household names, but they're worth trying. Whites dominate, but there are notable reds too.

Most Roman house white is from the Castelli Romani area, southeast of Rome, centred on Frascati and Marino. Frascati Superiore is an excellent tipple, Castel de Paolis' Vigna Adriana wins plaudits, while the emphatically named Est! Est!! Est!!!, produced by renowned wine house Falesco in Montefiascone on the volcanic banks of Lago Bolsena, is highly drinkable.

Falesco also produces the excellent Montiano, a red blended from merlot grapes. Colacicchi's world-class Torre Ercolana from Anagni is a velvety, complex and fruity red blending local Cesanese di Affile with cabernet sauvignon and merlot.

To sample Lazio wines, VyTA Enoteca Regionale del Lazio (p133) and Terre e Domus (p124) are top addresses. For biodynamic and natural vintages, try Litro (p137) in Monteverdi or La Barrique (p134) in Monti.

FRANCO VOLPATO/SHUTTERSTOCK ©

exactly what its name suggests – an oasis of beer. With hundreds of labels, from German heavyweights to British bitters and Belgian brews, plus wines, cheeses and cold cuts, it's ideally set up for an evening's quaffing, either in the cramped

cellar or on the piazza-side terrace. Good *aperitivo* buffet too (€10).

Coming Out   Bar

(Map p246; ☎06 700 98 71; www.comingout.it; Via di San Giovanni in Laterano 8; ⊗7am-5.30am; ⊋Via Labicana) On warm evenings, with lively crowds on the street and the Colosseum as a backdrop, there are few finer places to sip a drink than this friendly gay bar. It's open all day, but is at its best in the evening when the atmosphere hots up, the cocktails kick in and the karaoke and speed dating get under way.

L'Alibi   Club

(☎320 3541185; Via di Monte Testaccio 44; ⊗11pm-4am Thu, 11.30pm-5am Fri & Sat; ⊋Via Galvani) Gay-friendly L'Alibi is one of Rome's best known clubs, hosting regular parties and serving up a mash of house, hip-hop, Latino, pop and dance music to a young, mixed crowd. It can get pretty steamy inside, particularly on packed weekend nights, but you can grab a mouthful of air on the spacious summer terrace.

⊖ Villa Borghese & Northern Rome

Momart   Cafe

(☎06 8639 1656; www.momartcafe.it; Viale XXI Aprile 19; ⊗noon-2am Mon-Thu, to 3am Fri, 11.30am-3am Sat, to 2am Sun; ⊋Viale XXI Aprile) A modish restaurant-cafe in the university district near Via Nomentana, Momart serves one of Rome's most bountiful spreads of *apericena* (an informal evening meal involving *aperitivi* and tapas-style food). A mixed crowd of students and local professionals flocks here to fill up on the ample buffet (€12) and kick back over cocktails on the pavement terrace.

Enoteca Mostó   Wine Bar

(☎392 2579616; www.facebook.com/enoteca mosto; Viale Pinturicchio 32; ⊗6.30pm-2am Tue-Sun; ⊋Pinturicchio) Modern and busy, Enoteca Mostó is a popular local watering

JOHN CAREY © ONFOKUS/GETTY IMAGES © © MARCOMERRY/SHUTTERSTOCK ©

Top Five for Cocktails

Niji Roma (p112)

Zuma Bar (p112)

Il Palazzetto (p113)

Club Derrière (p113)

Keyhole (p113)

Clockwise from left: View of the Spanish Steps (p94) from Il Palazzetto (p113); Zuma Bar (p112); Aperol spritzes

Kiosk Bars

A recurring feature of Rome's streetscape are its green kiosks. Many of these are occupied by vendors selling newspapers, magazines and public transport tickets. Some of these kiosks, however, harbour long-standing and much-loved bars.

On the river, the **Chioschetto di Ponte Milvio** (☑347 6957141; www. facebook.com/ilchioschettodipontemilvio; Piazzale di Ponte Milvio; ⊙6pm-2am summer, 5pm-2am Thu-Sat, 8am-10.30pm Sun winter; ⓡPonte Milvio) is a classic case in point: it's a neighbourhood meeting point that buzzes on warm summer nights.

Another prime example is **Lemoncocco** (☑335 1618376; Piazza Buenos Aires; ⊙10am-2am; ⓡViale Regina Margherita), a local institution famous for its trademark lemon-and-coconut drink.

Roman kiosk

la) Enjoy showy cocktails and stylish bites at this lounge. It has a courtyard garden with potted plants and olive trees, which is a gorgeous space to kick-start the evening beneath the stars. Late in the night from Thursday to Saturday, it opens up into a club, Circolo Degli Illuminati. Tech house, hip-hop, chill music and top DJs rev up clubbers.

Goa   Club
(☑06 574 82 77; www.goaclub.com; Via Giuseppe Libetta 13; ⊙11.30pm-5am Thu-Sat; ⓜGarbatella) At home in a former motorbike-repair shop down a bamboo-lined dead-end alley in postindustrial-style Ostiense, Goa is Rome's serious superclub with exotic India-inspired decor and international DJs mixing house and techno. Expect a fashion-forward crowd, podium dancers, thumping dance floor, sofas to lounge on and heavies on the door.

Vinile   Club
(☑06 5728 8666; www.vinileroma.it; Via Giuseppe Libetta 19; ⊙8pm-2am Tue & Wed, to 3am Thu, to 4am Fri & Sat, 12.30-3.30pm & 8pm-2am Sun; ⓜGarbatella) On weekends a mixed bag of Romans hit the dance floor at Vinyl, a buzzing bar and club cooking up food, music and party happenings on the Via Giuseppe Libetta strip. Inside its cavernous interior – with part-vegetal, part-frescoed ceiling – the night starts with an *aperitivo* banquet from 8pm; DJ sets start at 11.30pm. On Sunday students pile in for the unbeatable-value brunch.

hole and eatery. Cram into the small space to sample from its selection of top-shelf wines, served by knowledgeable staff and accompanied by small tapas-style plates.

Southern Rome

Azienda Cucineria & Circolo Degli Illuminati   Lounge
(☑327 7615286; www.circolodegliilluminati.it; Via Giuseppe Libetta 3; ⊙kitchen 8pm-midnight Tue-Sat, club 10.30pm-late Thu-Sat; ⓜGarbatel-

Doppiozeroo   Italian $
(☑06 5730 1961; www.doppiozeroo.com; Via Ostiense 68; meals €12-35; ⊙7am-2am; ⓡVia Ostiense, ⓜPiramide) This easygoing bar was once a bakery, hence the name ('double zero' is a type of flour). But today the sleek, modern interior attracts hungry, trendy Romans who pile in here for its cheap, canteen-style lunches, pizza slices, famously lavish *aperitivo* (6pm to 9pm)

Bar in Trastevere (p175)

and abundant weekend brunch (12.30pm to 3.30pm). It's all wine bar after 9pm. There are pavement tables.

Neo Club   Club
(☎338 9492526; www.piovra.it; Via degli Argonauti 18; ☉11pm-late Fri & Sat; Ⓜ Garbatella)

This small, dark two-level club has an underground feel, and it's one of the funkiest choices in the zone, featuring a dancetastic mishmash of breakbeat, techno and old-school house.

SHOWTIME

Opera, jazz, theatre and more

Showtime

Enjoying Rome's colourful street life is often entertainment enough, but there's more to having a good time in the Eternal City than people-watching in its piazzas. The city's music scene runs the gamut, with opera divas, jazz masters, rock icons and underground rappers playing to passionate audiences. Theatres stage everything from Shakespearean drama to avant-garde dance; cinemas screen art-house flicks; and arts festivals turn the city into a stage. In summer performances play out against backdrops of spectacular Roman ruins.

In This Section

Tickets

Tickets for concerts, live music and theatrical performances are widely available across the city. Prices range enormously depending on the venue and artist. Hotels can often reserve tickets for guests, or you can contact the venue or organisation directly – check listings publications for booking details. Otherwise you can try the following:

Orbis Servizi (Map p245; ☑06 482 74 03; www.boxofficelazio.it; Piazza dell'Esquilino 37; ☺9.30am-1pm & 4-7.30pm Mon-Sat; ⓜTermini)

Vivaticket (☑892 234; www.vivaticket.it)

Previous page: Performance at Teatro dell'Opera di Roma (p186)
VINCENZO PINTO/AFP/GETTY IMAGES ©

Busker, Vatican City

Classical Venues

Auditorium Parco della Musica (p188) Great acoustics, top international classical musicians and multiple concert halls.

Teatro dell'Opera di Roma (p186) Red velvet and gilt interior for Rome's opera and dance companies.

Terme di Caracalla (p186) Wonderful outdoor setting for summer opera and ballet.

Chiesa di Sant'Agnese in Agone (p186) Chamber music in a baroque church overlooking Piazza Navona.

Live Gigs

Nuovo Cinema Palazzo (p190) Exciting creative happenings in San Lorenzo's former Palace Cinema.

Blackmarket Hall (p173) Two bars filled with vintage sofas and armchairs, great for eclectic, mainly acoustic, live music.

Caffè Letterario (p186) Live gigs in a postindustrial space: designer looks, gallery, coworking space, stage and lounge bar.

Lanificio 159 (p191) Ex-wool factory hosting underground live gigs alongside club nights.

✪ Classical Music & Opera

Teatro dell'Opera di Roma   Opera
(Map p245; ☎06 48 16 01; www.operaroma.
it; Piazza Beniamino Gigli 1; ⊗box office 10am-
6pm Mon-Sat, 9am-1.30pm Sun; MRepubblica)
Rome's premier opera house boasts a
dramatic red-and-gold interior, a fascist
1920s exterior and an impressive history:
it premiered both Puccini's *Tosca* and
Mascagni's *Cavalleria rusticana*. Opera
and ballet performances are staged between November and June.

Terme di Caracalla   Opera
(www.operaroma.it; Viale delle Terme di Caracalla 52; tickets from €30; ⊗Jun & Jul; ⎕Viale
delle Terme di Caracalla) The hulking ruins
of this vast 3rd-century baths complex
(p102) set the memorable stage for the
Teatro dell'Opera's summer season of
music and ballet, with shows by big-name
Italian and international performers. It's an
unforgettable setting in which to catch a
top-quality performance.

Chiesa di Sant'Agnese in Agone   Church
(Map p250; ☎06 6819 2134; www.santagnesein
agone.org; Piazza Navona; ⊗9am-1pm & 3-7pm
Tue-Fri, 9am-1pm & 3-8pm Sat & Sun; ⎕Corso del
Rinascimento) With its theatrical facade and
rich, domed interior, the Chiesa di Sant'Agnese in Agone is typical of Francesco Borromini's baroque style. The church, which
regularly hosts classical music concerts, is
said to stand on the spot where the martyr
Agnes performed a miracle before being
killed. Legend has it that after she was
stripped naked by her executioners her hair
miraculously grew to cover her body and
preserve her modesty.

✪ Live Music

Caffè Letterario   Live Music
(☎06 5730 2842; www.caffeletterarioroma.it;
Via Ostiense 95; ⊗10am-2am Tue-Fri, 4pm-2am
Sat & Sun; ⎕Via Ostiense, MPiramide) Caffè
Letterario is an intellectual hang-out
housed in the funky, somewhat underground, postindustrial space of a former

Ballet performance, Auditorium Consiliazione (p190)

garage. It combines designer looks, a bookshop, gallery, coworking space, performance area and lounge bar. There are regular gigs, usually starting around 10pm, ranging from soul and jazz to blues and Indian dance.

Gregory's Jazz Club Jazz

(Map p245; ☎06 679 63 86, 327 8263770; www. gregorysjazz.com; Via Gregoriana 54d; obligatory drink €15-20; ⊙7.30pm-2am Tue-Sun; ☜; MBarberini) If Gregory's were a tone of voice, it'd be husky: unwind over a whisky in the downstairs bar, then unwind some more on squashy sofas upstairs to slinky live jazz and swing, with quality local performers who also like to hang out here.

Fonclea Live Music

(Map p253; ☎06 689 63 02; www.fonclea.it; Via Crescenzio 82a; cover after 8pm €10; ⊙6pm-2am Sep-May, concerts 9.30pm; ☜; 🚇Piazza del Risorgimento) Fonclea is a great little pub venue, with nightly gigs by bands playing everything from jazz and soul to pop, rock and doo-wop. Get in the mood with a drink during happy hour (6pm to 8.30pm daily). There are several cocktail bars nearby with outdoor tables.

Alexanderplatz Jazz

(Map p253; ☎06 8377 5604; www.alexander platzjazzclub.com; Via Ostia 9; tickets €15-20; ⊙8.30pm-1.30am; MOttaviano-San Pietro) Intimate, underground and hard to find – look for the discreet black door near the corner – Rome's most celebrated jazz club draws top Italian and international performers and a respectful cosmopolitan crowd. Book a table for the best stage views or to dine here, although note that it's the music that's the star act. Performances begin at 10pm.

ConteStaccio Live Music

(www.facebook.com/contestaccio; Via di Monte Testaccio 65b; ⊙6pm-5am Wed-Sat; 🚇Via Galvani) A fixture on Rome's music scene, ConteStaccio is one of the top venues on the Testaccio clubbing strip. It's known for its free gigs which feature both emerging

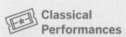

Classical Performances

Opera & Dance

Rome's opera house, the Teatro dell'Opera di Roma (p186), is a grandiose venue but its productions can be a bit hit and miss. It's also home to Rome's official Corps de Ballet and has a ballet season running in tandem with its opera performances. Both ballet and opera move outdoors for the summer season at the ancient Roman baths Terme di Caracalla (p186), which is an even more spectacular setting.

Rome's Auditorium Parco della Musica (p188) hosts classical and contemporary dance. The Auditorium Conciliazione (p190) is another good place to catch contemporary-dance companies.

Music

Rome's world-class Orchestra dell'Accademia Nazionale di Santa Cecilia (www. santacecilia.it) plays at the Auditorium Parco della Musica (p188). There are also concerts by the Accademia Filarmonica Romana at Teatro Olimpico (p190); at the Auditorium Conciliazione (p190), Rome's premier classical-music venue before the newer auditorium was opened and still a force to be reckoned with; and held by the Istituzione Universitaria dei Concerti (p188) in the Aula Magna of La Sapienza University.

Free classical concerts are held in many of Rome's churches; look out for information at Rome's tourist kiosks. The **Basilica di San Paolo Fuori le Mura** (www.basilicasanpaolo.org; Piazzale San Paolo 1; cloisters adult/reduced €4/3; ⊙7am-6.30pm; MBasilica San Paolo) hosts an important choral mass on 25 January, and the hymn 'Te Deum' is sung at the **Chiesa del Gesù** (Map p250; www.chiesadelgesu.org; Piazza del Gesù; ⊙6.45am-12.45pm & 4-7.30pm, St Ignatius rooms 4-6pm Mon-Sat, 10am-noon Sun; 🚇Largo di Torre Argentina) on 31 December.

What, When & Where

What's On?

Comune di Roma (www.060608.it)

Eventful (http://rome.eventful.com)

In Rome Now (www.inromenow.com)

Romeing (www.romeing.it)

Rome Opera Omnia (www.romaopera omnia.com)

Entertainment by Neighbourhood

Centro Storico Great for concerts in churches or theatres (usually in Italian).

Trastevere & Gianicolo A few blues and jazz live-music venues.

Monti, Esquilino & San Lorenzo Live-music venues and Rome's major opera house in Monti; alternative cultural venues in San Lorenzo.

San Giovanni & Testaccio Regular live gigs in the district's clubs and summertime opera in the Terme di Caracalla.

Southern Rome This area is home to a scattering of theatres and live-music venues.

Villa Borghese & Northern Rome Home to the great Auditorium Parco della Musica, as well as Rome's major sporting venues.

groups and established performers, spanning a range of styles – indie, pop, rock, acoustic, reggae, new wave. Also serves food.

Big Mama
Blues

(Map p254; ☎06 581 25 51; www.bigmama. it; Vicolo di San Francesco a Ripa 18; ☺9pm-1.30am, shows 10.30pm, closed summer; ☒Viale di Trastevere, ☒Trastevere/Mastai)

Head to this cramped basement for a mellow night of Eternal City blues. A long-standing venue, Big Mama also stages jazz, funk, soul and R & B acts, as well as popular cover bands.

Charity Café
Live Music

(Map p245; ☎06 4782 5881; www.charitycafe. it; Via Panisperna 68; ☺6pm-2am Tue-Sun; ⓂCavour) Think narrow space, spindly tables, dim lighting and laid-back vibe: this is a place to snuggle down and listen to some slinky live jazz or blues. Civilised, relaxed, untouristy and very Monti. Gigs usually take place from 10pm; *aperitivo* is between 6pm and 9pm. Check the website to see who's performing. It's closed on Sundays in summer.

Istituzione Universitaria dei Concerti
Live Music

(IUC; ☎06 361 00 51; www.concertiiuc.it; Piazzale Aldo Moro 5; ☒Verano) The IUC organises a season of concerts in the Aula Magna of La Sapienza University, including many visiting international artists and orchestras. Performances cover a wide range of musical genres, including baroque, classical, contemporary and jazz.

✪ Theatre & the Arts

Auditorium Parco della Musica
Concert Venue

(☎06 8024 1281; www.auditorium.com; Viale Pietro de Coubertin; ☒Viale Tiziano) The hub of Rome's thriving cultural scene, the Auditorium is the capital's premier concert venue. Its three concert halls offer superb acoustics, and together with a 3000-seat open-air arena, stage all manner of performances, from classical music concerts to jazz gigs, public lectures and film screenings.

The Auditorium is also home to Rome's world-class Orchestra dell'Accademia Nazionale di Santa Cecilia (www.santa cecilia.it).

Top Five for Jazz & Blues

Alexanderplatz (p187)

Auditorium Parco della Musica

Charity Café

Big Mama

Gregory's Jazz Club (p187)

Clockwise from left: Auditorium Parco della Musica;
Performance at Auditorium Parco della Musica;
Alexanderplatz (p187)

Isola del Cinema

Nuovo Cinema
Palazzo   Arts Centre

(Map p255; www.nuovocinemapalazzo.it; Piazza dei Sanniti 9a; ⊘hours vary; 🚇Via Tiburtina) Students, artists and activists are breathing new life into San Lorenzo's former Palace Cinema with a bevy of exciting creative happenings: think film screenings, theatre performances, DJs, concerts, live music, breakdance classes and other artsy events. In warm weather, the action spills outside on to the street terrace. Check the Facebook page for event details.

English Theatre of Rome   Theatre

(Map p250; ☑06 687 94 19; www.rometheatre. com; Teatro L'Arciliuto, Piazza Monte Vecchio 5; 🚇Corso del Rinascimento) The English Theatre of Rome stages a mix of contemporary and classic plays, comedies and bilingual productions at the Teatro L'Arciliuto near Piazza Navona. Check their Facebook page for news of upcoming performances.

> " *There are various atmospheric outdoor summer film festivals...* "

Auditorium
Conciliazione   Live Performance

(Map p253; ☑06 683 22 56; www.auditorium conciliazione.it; Via della Conciliazione 4; ⊘box office 9am-8pm Mon-Sat, to 5pm Sun; 🚇Piazza Pia) On the main approach road to St Peter's Basilica, this large auditorium plays host to a wide range of events – classical and contemporary concerts, cabarets, dance spectacles, theatre productions, film screenings, exhibitions and conferences.

Teatro Olimpico   Theatre

(☑06 326 59 91; www.teatroolimpico.it; Piazza Gentile da Fabriano 17; 🚇Piazza Mancini, 🚇Piazza Mancini) The Teatro Olimpico hosts a varied program of opera, dance, one-person shows, musicals and comedies, as well as classical-music concerts by the Accademia Filarmonica Romana.

✪ Clubbing

Lanificio 159   Club
(06 4178 0081; www.lanificio.com; Via Pietralata 159a; ☺club nights 11pm-4.30am Fri & Sat
Sep-May; ☷Via Pietralata) Occupying a former
wool factory in Rome's northeastern suburbs, this cool underground venue hosts
live gigs and hot clubbing action, led by top
Roman crews and international DJs. The
club is part of a larger complex that stages
more reserved events such as Sunday
markets, exhibitions and *aperitivi*.

✪ Cinema

Isola del Cinema   Outdoor Cinema
(Map p254; www.isoladelcinema.com; Piazza
San Bartolomeo all'Isola, Isola Tiberina; tickets
adult/reduced €6/5; ☺mid-Jun–Sep) Come

Cinema Under the Stars

There are various atmospheric outdoor
summer film festivals; check festival
websites for program and ticketing
details. The Isola del Cinema shows
independent films in the romantic
setting of the Isola Tiberina annually
from mid-June to September. This runs
in conjunction with the riverside Lungo
il Tevere festival (p175).

summer, the Isola Tiberina sets the stage
for a season of outdoor cinema, featuring Italian and international films, some
shown in their original language. There are
also meetings with actors and directors,
masterclasses and film-related events.

ACTIVE ROME

From football to cooking courses

Active Rome

Activities in Rome are tied up with the city's astonishing history and heritage: be it walking down cobbled lanes littered with Roman ruins, cycling past baroque fountains or jogging through the landscaped grounds of palatial villas, there's ample in the city to keep visitors both active and visually stimulated. Romans are passionate about sport. Just as crowds swarmed to the Colosseum to cheer on gladiators, so modern-day fans flock to the stadium to support the city's two premier football (soccer) teams. For those who prefer more hands-on pursuits, the capital cooks up courses and themed activity tours galore.

In This Section

Sports Seasons

Football is the main sport in Rome, with the season running from late August to May when Roma and Lazio fans flock to Stadio Olimpico to cheer on their team on home turf. Rugby fans can watch international matches on alternate weekends in February and March. Tennis enthusiasts follow the Internazionali BNL d'Italia in early May.

Segway tour crossing Piazza del Campidoglio (p21)

The Best Activities

Bici & Baci (p196) Explore the city by pedal-power.

Stadio Olimpico (p198) Join noisy Roma and Lazio fans supporting their team at a Sunday match.

Circo Massimo (p197) Where else can you jog at dawn around an ancient chariot racetrack?

Via Appia Antica (p76) Hike or bike along this ancient Roman road on the city's southern fringe.

A Friend in Rome (p197) Vintage-car drives and horse rides along Via Appia Antica.

The Best Tours & Courses

Casa Mia (p198) Food and wine tours with tastings and artisan-shop visits.

Latteria Studio (p198) Boutique food tours and cooking classes in a Trastevere food-photography studio.

Red Bicycle (p196) Experience Rome's sunset from a saddle with this bike outfit.

Arcult (p197) Contemporary architecture tours on foot.

Vino Roma (p199) Immerse yourself in the Roman world of wine.

✪ Cycling & Scootering

Navigating this traffic-clogged, partly cobbled city by bike isn't a popular local activity, but cycling remains popular with tourists keen to see the city from a different perspective. Several outlets rent wheels, with or without a guide; electric bicycles, Vespas and scooters are perhaps more suited to navigating Rome's seven hills.

If you want to dodge the traffic and simply pedal along quiet 'country' lanes laced with green fields and the odd scatter of Roman ruins, get a bus to Via Appia Antica, (p76) from where you can rent a bicycle to explore the Parco Regionale Appia Antica.

In town, a smoothly paved cycling path stretches along the River Tiber for some 9km from Ponte Guglielmo Marconi in Ostiense (south) to the Stadio Olimpico (north).

> *…simply pedal along quiet 'country' lanes laced with green fields and the odd scatter of Roman ruins…*

Cycling to the Catacombe di San Callisto (p78)

Red Bicycle   Cycling

(Map p246; ☎327 5387148; www.theredbicycle. org; Via Ostilia 4b; 🚇Via Labicana) A cycle outfit offering bike hire (€10/15 per half/full day) and a range of cycling tours taking in the city's main neighbourhoods and environs. Prices start at €45 for a three-hour sunset tour, rising to €99 for a full-day ride to Ostia Antica.

Bici & Baci   Tours

(Map p245; ☎06 482 84 43; www.bicibaci.com; Via del Viminale 5; bike tours from €30, Vespa tours from €145; ⏰8am-7pm; Ⓜ Repubblica) Bici & Baci runs a range of daily walking, bike and Segway tours taking in the main historic sites and Via Appia Antica; these are in English or Dutch. Also offers tours on vintage Vespas, classic Fiat 500 cars or funky three-wheeled Ape Calessinos.

✪ Walking & Running

Rome is a pleasurable city to explore by foot, if only for the astonishing littering of ancient Roman monuments pretty much everywhere you walk. Footpaths along the

SUN_SHINE/SHUTTERSTOCK ©

Tiber, sections of which are decorated with fantastic street art such as William Kentridge's monumental **Triumphs & Laments** (Map p250; Lungotevere della Farnesina; 🚇Lungotevere dei Tebaldi), provide the perfect jogging track for many a Roman who enjoys a morning run. Grassy routes, kinder to the knees and greener on the eyes, include **Circo Massimo** (Circus Maximus; Map p246; 📷06 06 08; Via dei Cerchi; adult/reduced €5/4; ⊘archaeological area 10am-4pm Sat & Sun, by reservation only Tue-Fri; MCirco Massimo), Villa Borghese (p58), the landscaped park of **Villa Doria Pamphilj** (⊘sunrise-sunset; 🚇Via di San Pancrazio), and out-of-town Parco della Caffarella in the Parco Regionale Appia Antica (p76).

The annual Rome Marathon (www.maratonadiroma.it) follows a 42km-long course starting and finishing near the Colosseum, taking in many of the city's big sights. There is, however, some doubt about the event's future – check the website for updates.

A Friend in Rome
Tours
(📷340 5019201; www.afriendinrome.it) Silvia Prosperi and her team offer a range of private tours covering the Vatican and main historic centre, plus areas outside the capital. They can also organise kid-friendly tours, food-and-wine itineraries, vintage-car drives and horse rides along Via Appia Antica. Rates start at €165 for a basic three-hour tour (up to eight people); add €55 for every additional hour.

Arcult
Walking
(📷339 6503172; www.arcult.it) Run by architects, Arcult offers excellent customisable group tours focusing on Rome's contemporary architecture. Prices depend on the itinerary but range from €250 to €370 for two to 10 people.

The Roman Guy
Tours
(📷06 9480 4747; www.theromanguy.com) Tip-top, small-group tours of Rome, including a 3½-hour 'locals' food' tour in Trastevere and the Jewish Ghetto (€90).

 Roma Afloat

Rome Boat Experience (Map p250; 📷06 8956 7745; www.romeboatexperience.com; adult/reduced €18/12; ⊘Apr-Oct) runs hop-on, hop-off cruises along the Tiber, as well as dinner (€65, 2½ hours) and aperitif (€30, 1½ hours) cruises. The main embarkation point is Molo Sant'Angelo, over the river from Castel Sant'Angelo.

⊙ Spectator Sports

Basketball
Basketball is a popular spectator sport in Rome, though it inspires nothing like the fervour of football. Rome's team, Virtus Roma (www.virtusroma.it), plays throughout the winter months at the **Palalottomatica** (📷06 54 09 01; www.palazzodellosportroma.it; Piazzale dello Sport 1; MEUR Palasport) in EUR.

Rugby Union
Italy's rugby team, the Azzurri (the Blues), entered the Six Nations tournament in 2000, although success has been scarce. The team currently plays home international games at the Stadio Olimpico (p198).

Tennis
Italy's premier tennis tournament, the **Internazionali BNL d'Italia** (www.internazionalibnlditalia.com), is one of the most important events on the European tennis circuit. Every May the world's top players meet on the clay courts at the monumental, fascist-era **Foro Italico** (Viale del Foro Italico; 🚇Lungotevere Maresciallo Cadorna). Tickets can usually be bought at the Foro Italico each day of the tournament, except for the final days, which are sold out weeks in advance.

Football Matches

In Rome you're either for AS Roma (*giallorossi* – yellow and reds) or Lazio (*biancazzurri* – white and blues), with both teams playing in Serie A (Italy's premier league). A striking new 52,500-seat stadium – a contemporary glass-and-steel structure inspired by the Colosseum – is planned for Roma at Tor di Valle in southwest Rome, but construction is yet to commence; current estimates have it opening in 2023 at the earliest.

September to May there's a game at home for Roma or Lazio almost every weekend: a trip to football stadium **Stadio Olimpico** (☑06 3685 7563; Viale dei Gladiatori 2, Foro Italico; ☒Lungotevere Maresciallo Cadorna) is unforgettable. Ticket-purchase regulations are strict. Tickets must bear the holder's name and passport or ID number, and you must present a photo ID at the turnstiles when entering the stadium. Two tickets are permitted per purchase for Serie A, Coppa Italia and UEFA Champions League games. Tickets cost from €10 to €750. Buy them online at the AS Roma website (www.asroma.com), from TicketOne (www.ticketone.it; telephone 89 21 01), at authorised TicketOne sales points (check its website) or at one of the A S Roma or Lazio shops around the city. To get to the stadium, take metro line A to Ottaviano–San Pietro, then bus 32.

AS Roma versus Lazio
GENNARO DI ROSA/SHUTTERSTOCK ©

Equestrian Events

Rome's top equestrian event is the Piazza di Siena showjumping competition (www.piazzadisiena.org), an annual international event held in May, gorgeously set in Villa Borghese.

❸ Food & Wine

Casa Mia   Tours
(☑346 8001746; www.italyfoodandwinetours.com; 3hr tour with tastings 1/2/3/4 people €410/450/480/510) Serious food and wine tours, including a Trastevere and Jewish Quarter neighbourhood tour, with tastings and behind-the-scene meetings with local shopkeepers, producers, chefs and restaurateurs. Bespoke tours, dining itineraries and reservations can also be arranged. Covers some of the best eating areas of Rome.

Latteria Studio   Cooking
(☑835 29990; https://latteriastudio.com; Via di Ponziano 29; ☒Viale di Trastevere, ☒Trastevere/Pascarella) Highly personalised market tours and cooking classes in a stylish food-photography studio in backstreet Trastevere. Prices vary, depending on the course. Count on around €140 for six hours of market shopping, pasta-making, feasting and more. The schedule varies, but there are usually tours twice a month.

GT Food & Travel   Tours
(☑320 7204222; www.gtfoodandtravel.com; 3hr tour with tastings per person around €130; ☺noon Thu-Tue) Small-group food-lover tours, including a themed 'Cucina Povera & Roman Cuisine' tour in Monteverde. Market tours, half- and full-day custom tours, cooking classes and in-home dining experiences are also on offer.

Katie Parla   Food & Drink
(https://katieparla.com; prices on application) New Jersey native Katie Parla, now a Roman resident, writes the city's best-known English-language food blog and also

Making pasta

conducts private walking tours for small groups of up to six people. These cover Testaccio, the *centro storico*, Prati, Trionfale and Esquilino.

Vino Roma   Wine

(Map p246; ☏328 4874497; www.vinoroma. com; Via in Selci 84g; 2hr tastings per person €50; Ⓜ Cavour) With beautifully appointed century-old cellars and a chic tasting studio, Vino Roma guides both novices and wine enthusiasts in the basics of Italian wine under the knowledgeable stewardship of sommelier Hande Leimer and her expert team. Also on offer are a wine-and-cheese dinner (€60) with snacks and cold cuts to accompany the wines, and bespoke three-hour food tours. Book online.

REST YOUR HEAD

From *pensioni* to hostels

Rest Your Head

Accommodation is plentiful in Rome – whether you yearn to splurge like royalty or bunk down in a hostel, you'll find somewhere to suit your style. At the top end of the market, opulent five-star hotels occupy stately palazzi (mansions) and chic boutique guesthouses boast discreet luxury. Family-run B&Bs and pensioni (guesthouses) offer character and a warm welcome, while religious houses cater to pilgrims and cost-conscious travellers. Hostel-goers can choose between party-loving hang-outs and quieter, more restrained digs.

In This Section

Accommodation Tax

Everyone overnighting in Rome pays the *tassa di soggiorno*, a room-occupancy tax on top of their bill:

- €3 per person per night in one- and two-star hotels

- €3.50 in B&Bs and room rentals

- €4/6/7 in three-/four-/five-star hotels

The tax applies for a maximum of 10 consecutive nights. Prices in reviews don't include tax.

Roman apartments

Reservations & Checking In/Out

○ Book ahead, especially in high season (Easter to September, and over the Christmas–New Year period) and during major religious festivals.

○ A *camera matrimoniale* is a room with a double bed; a *camera doppia* has twin beds.

○ When you check in, present your passport or ID card.

○ Checkout is usually between 10am and noon (around 9am in hostels).

○ Most guesthouses and B&Bs require you to arrange, in advance, a time to check in.

Websites

Lonely Planet (www.lonelyplanet.com/italy/rome/hotels) Author-reviewed accommodation options.

Cross Pollinate (www.cross-pollinate.com) Personally vetted rooms and apartments.

Bed & Breakfast Italia (www.bbitalia.it) Italian B&B network listing many Rome options.

Rome Accommodation.net (www.rome-accommodation.net) Apartment and vacation-home rentals.

Rome As You Feel (www.romeasyoufeel.com) Apartment rentals: studio flats to luxury apartments.

🛏 Accommodation Types

Rome doesn't have a low season as such, but rates are at their lowest from November to March (excluding Christmas and New Year) and from mid-July through August. Expect to pay top whack in spring (April to June) and autumn (September and October) and over the main holiday periods (Christmas, New Year and Easter).

Most midrange and top-end hotels accept credit cards. Budget places might, but it's always best to check in advance. Apartment rentals will require prepayment and a credit-card guarantee, and rarely offer flexible booking policies.

Pensions & Hotels

The bulk of Rome's accommodation consists of *pensioni* (pensions) and *alberghi* (hotels).

A *pensione* is a small, family-run hotel, often in a converted apartment. Rooms are usually fairly simple, though most come with a private bathroom.

Hotels are rated from one to five stars. Most hotels in Rome's historic centre tend to be three-star and up. As a rule, a three-star room will come with a hairdryer, a minibar (or fridge), a safe, air-con and wi-fi. Some have satellite TV and a tea/coffee set-up.

Roman hotel rooms tend to be small, especially in the *centro storico* and Trastevere. In these areas, many hotels are housed in centuries-old *palazzi*.

Apartment Rentals

An excellent option for families, groups of friends and those who like to self-cater, short-term apartment stays can often work out considerably less expensive than an extended hotel sojourn. Many booking services require a minimum stay (usually three or four nights). Cleaning service is rarely included and you will often need to pay a special cleaning levy when you leave.

Rentals can be found across the city. If you are keen to visit the major sights on foot, the *centro storico*, Tridente, Trevi, Monti and Trastevere are good choices; all are characterful neighbourhoods that are well connected with public transport. They also have supermarkets, bakeries and delis where you can source catering provisions. Note that many apartment buildings don't have elevators – those with limited mobility should check before booking. Check amenities (is there a washing machine and a dishwasher?), and if you're visiting in summer, make sure there is air-conditioning.

B&Bs & Guesthouses

Alongside traditional B&Bs, Rome has many boutique-style guesthouses offering chic, upmarket accommodation at midrange to top-end prices.

Breakfast in a Roman B&B usually consists of bread rolls, croissants, yogurt, ham and cheese. Some B&Bs offer breakfast (usually coffee and a pastry) in a nearby cafe; check when you make your booking.

Hostels

Rome's hostels cater to everyone from backpackers to budget-minded families. Many offer hotel-style rooms alongside traditional dorms.

The city's new breed of hostels are chic, designer pads with trendy bar-restaurants, bike rental, the occasional stunning rooftop garden and a fantastic array of organised tours and activities on offer.

Religious Institutions

Many of Rome's religious institutions offer cheap(ish) rooms. These often impose strict curfews and are fairly short on frills; some are single-sex only. Book well ahead.

Where to Stay

Rome is expensive and busy; book ahead to secure the best deal.

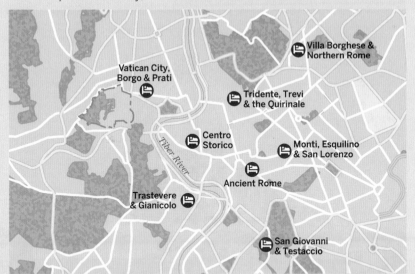

Neighbourhood	Atmosphere
Ancient Rome	Close to major sights such as Colosseum, Roman Forum and Capitoline Museums; quiet at night. Not cheap and has few budget options; restaurants are touristy.
Centro Storico	Atmospheric area with everything on your doorstep – Pantheon, Piazza Navona, restaurants, bars, shops. Most expensive part of town; few budget options; can be noisy.
Tridente, Trevi & the Quirinale	Good for Spanish Steps, Trevi Fountain and designer shopping; excellent midrange and top-end options; good transport links. Upmarket area with prices to match; subdued after dark.
Monti, Esquilino & San Lorenzo	Many hostels and budget hotels around Stazione Termini; top eating options in Monti and thriving nightlife in studenty San Lorenzo; good transport links. Some dodgy streets in Termini area.
San Giovanni & Testaccio	Authentic atmosphere with good eating and drinking options; Aventino is a quiet, romantic area; Testaccio is a top food and nightlife district. Not many big sights.
Trastevere & Gianicolo	Gorgeous, atmospheric area; party vibe with hundreds of bars, cafes, and restaurants; some interesting sights. Can be noisy, particularly in summer; try to stay in the 'quiet' side, east of Viale di Trastevere.
Vatican City, Borgo & Prati	Near St Peter's Basilica and Vatican Museums; decent range of accommodation; some excellent shops and restaurants; on the metro. Expensive near St Peter's; not much nightlife.
Villa Borghese & Northern Rome	Largely residential area good for the Auditorium and some top museums; quiet after dark. Out of the centre; few budget choices.

View to St Peter's Basilica (p46) from the Tiber

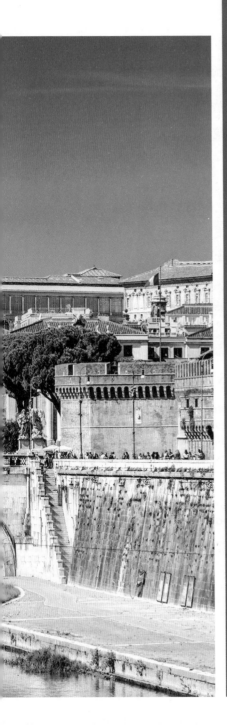

In Focus

Via Nazionale, Rome

Rome Today

For better and worse, Rome can't escape its history. While its ancient sites and great monuments continue to draw visitors in ever-increasing numbers, its streets and creaking infrastructure are showing undeniable signs of strain. Garbage and graffiti have become burning political issues as the city struggles to shake off the effects of years of cutbacks and political corruption.

Potholes, Boars & Burning Buses

Over the past year or so, the single most talked about subject in Rome has been the state of the city's streets and parks. From bar conversations to newspaper articles, everyone has had their say on the condition of the capital's potholed roads, unkempt parks and overflowing rubbish bins. Online, videos have been posted showing wild boars roaming down busy streets.

The city's public transport has also come under fire, quite literally in the case of a bus bursting into flames in May 2018. This was one of several cases of buses spontaneously combusting because of a lack of maintenance.

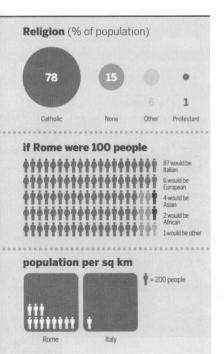

Religion (% of population)

78 Catholic | 15 None | 6 Other | 1 Protestant

if Rome were 100 people

87 would be Italian
6 would be European
4 would be Asian
2 would be African
1 would be other

population per sq km

= 200 people

Rome | Italy

The situation has sparked community action. Romans have been out on streets spray-painting potholes and cleaning up their local parks, while a mass sit-in saw thousands turn out in support of a recently formed protest movement, *Roma Dice Basta* (Rome Says Enough).

City Hall in the Spotlight

Mayor Raggi is not the only person who's been under the cosh. Over on the west bank of the Tiber, Pope Francis has come under intense scrutiny for his management of the Church's response to clerical abuse scandals and allegations of cover-ups. A former Vatican envoy even published a letter calling on him to resign, claiming the Argentinian pontiff had known of allegations against an American archbishop but had refused to act on them.

The pope did later defrock Theodore E McCarrick, an ex-cardinal and the former archbishop of Washington DC, but the letter provoked heated debate within the Vatican, highlighting the seemingly intractable division between the Church's conservatives and the more progressive-minded liberals.

On a lighter note, in January 2019 the world's press gleefully reported the launch of a Vatican athletics team. To endless 'Nuns on the Run' headlines, news emerged of the Athletica Vaticana and its team of priests, nuns, Swiss Guards and even a 62-year old library professor. Their goal, it was reported, was to participate in competitions such as the Mediterranean Games and the Games of the Small States of Europe.

Tourism Blooms

While it will undoubtedly be some time before a Vatican athlete wins gold, Rome continues to break records. A bumper crop of tourists visited the city in 2018, and a number of all-time highs were registered.

The city's two airports, Fiumicino and Ciampino, together welcomed a record 49 million travellers, while Rome itself drew 15 million tourists. Of these, around half – 7.6 million to be exact – visited the Colosseum, confirming it as Italy's most popular tourist attraction.

But while the numbers are impressive, they raise the problem of overtourism, an issue that has been affecting Rome and a number of Italian cities. A particular source of local exasperation has long been traffic congestion caused by tour buses, something the city authorities acknowledged in December 2018 when they banned tourist coaches from the city centre.

History

Rome's history spans three millennia, from the classical myths of vengeful gods to the follies of Roman emperors, from Renaissance excess to swaggering 20th-century fascism. Everywhere you go, you're surrounded by the past. Martial ruins, Renaissance palazzi (mansions) and flamboyant baroque basilicas evoke tales of family feuds, historic upheavals, artistic rivalries, dark intrigues and violent passions.

753 BC

According to legend, Romulus kills his twin brother Remus and founds Rome on the Palatino.

509 BC

The Roman Republic is founded, paving the way for Rome's rise to European domination.

15 March 44 BC

On the Ides of March, Julius Caesar is stabbed to death in the Teatro di Pompeo (on modern-day Largo di Torre Argentina).

Colonna Traiana and the Imperial Forums (p83)

KAVALENKAVOLHA/GETTY IMAGES ©

The Myth of Ancient Rome

As much a mythical construct as a historical reality, ancient Rome's image has been carefully nurtured throughout history.

Rome's original myth makers were the first emperors. Eager to reinforce the city's status as *caput mundi* (capital of the world), they turned to writers such as Virgil, Ovid and Livy to create an official Roman history. These authors, while adept at weaving epic narratives, were less interested in the rigours of historical research and frequently presented myth as reality. In the *Aeneid,* Virgil brazenly draws on Greek legends and stories to tell the tale of Aeneas, a Trojan prince who arrives in Italy and establishes Rome's founding dynasty.

Ancient Rome's rulers were sophisticated masters of spin; under their tutelage, art, architecture and elaborate public ceremony were employed to perpetuate the image of Rome as an invincible and divinely sanctioned power.

AD 67	**80**	**285**
St Peter and St Paul become martyrs as Nero massacres Rome's Christians in a ploy to win popularity after the great fire of AD 64.	The 50,000-seat Flavian Amphitheatre, better known as the Colosseum, is inaugurated by the emperor Titus.	Diocletian splits the Roman Empire in two. The eastern half later joins the Byzantine Empire; the western half falls to the barbarians.

The canopo, Villa Adriana (p117)

★ **Best Historical Sites**

Palatino (p60)

Roman Forum (p80)

Ostia Antica (p98)

Via Appia Antica (p76)

Villa Adriana (p117)

Legacy of an Empire

Rising out of the bloodstained remnants of the Roman Republic, the Roman Empire was the Western world's first great superpower. At its zenith under Emperor Trajan (r AD 98–117), it extended from Britannia in the north to North Africa in the south, from Hispania (Spain) in the west to Palestina (Palestine) and Syria in the east. Rome itself had more than 1.5 million inhabitants. Decline eventually set in during the 3rd century and by the latter half of the 5th century Rome was in barbarian hands.

In AD 285 the emperor Diocletian, prompted by widespread disquiet across the empire, split the empire into eastern and western halves – the west centred on Rome and the east on Byzantium (later called Constantinople) – in a move that was to have far-reaching consequences for centuries. In the west, the fall of the Western Roman Empire in AD 476 paved the way for the emergence of the Holy Roman Empire and the Papal States, while in the east Roman (later Byzantine) rule continued until 1453 when the empire was finally conquered by Ottoman armies.

Emergence of Christianity

The ancient Romans were remarkably tolerant of foreign religions. They themselves worshipped a cosmopolitan pantheon of gods, ranging from household spirits and former emperors to deities appropriated from Greek mythology such as Jupiter, Juno, Neptune and Minerva. Religious cults were also popular – the Egyptian gods Isis and Serapis enjoyed a mass following, as did Mithras, a heroic saviour-god of vaguely Persian origin, who was worshipped by male-only devotees in underground temples.

Christianity swept in from the Roman province of Judaea in the 1st century AD. Its early days were marred by persecution, most notably under Nero (r 54–68), but it slowly caught on, thanks to its popular message of heavenly reward.

However, it was the conversion of Emperor Constantine (r 306–37) that really set Christianity on the path to European domination. In 313 Constantine issued the Edict of Milan,

476
The fall of Romulus Augustulus marks the end of the Western Empire.

754
Pope Stephen II and Pepin, king of the Franks, cut a deal resulting in the creation of the Papal States.

1084
Rome is sacked by a Norman army after Pope Gregory VII invites them in to help him against the besieging forces of Henry IV.

officially legalising Christianity, and in 380, Theodosius (r 379–95) made Christianity Rome's state religion. By this time the Church had developed a sophisticated organisational structure based on five major sees: Rome, Constantinople, Alexandria, Antioch and Jerusalem. At the outset, each bishopric carried equal weight, but in subsequent years Rome emerged as the senior party. The reasons for this were partly political – Rome was the wealthy capital of the Roman Empire – and partly religious – early Christian doctrine held that St Peter, founder of the Roman Church, had been sanctioned by Christ to lead the universal Church.

Papal Control

But while Rome had control of Christianity, the Church had yet to conquer Rome. This it did in the dark days that followed the fall of the Roman Empire by skilfully stepping into the power vacuum created by the demise of imperial power. And although no one person can take credit for this, Pope Gregory the Great (r 590–604) did more than most to lay the groundwork. A leader of considerable foresight, he won many friends by supplying free bread to Rome's starving citizens and restoring the city's water supply. He also stood up to the menacing Lombards, who presented a very real threat to the city.

It was this threat that pushed the papacy into an alliance with the Frankish kings, resulting in the creation of the two great powers of medieval Europe: the Papal States and the Holy Roman Empire. In Rome, the battle between these two superpowers translated into endless feuding between the city's baronial families and frequent attempts by the French to claim the papacy for their own. This political and military fighting eventually culminated in the papacy transferring to the French city of Avignon between 1309 and 1377, and the Great Schism (1378–1417), a period in which the Catholic world was headed by two popes, one in Rome and one in Avignon.

Romulus & Remus

The most famous of Rome's legends is the story of Romulus and Remus and the foundation of the city on 21 April 753 BC.

According to myth, Romulus and Remus were the children of the Vestal Virgin Rhea Silva and the god of war, Mars. While babies they were set adrift on the Tiber to escape a death penalty imposed by their great-uncle who was battling their grandfather for control of Alba Longa. However, they were discovered by a she-wolf, who suckled them until a shepherd, Faustulus, found and raised them.

Years later they decided to found a city on the site where they'd originally been saved. Not knowing where this was, they consulted the omens. Remus, on the Aventino, saw six vultures; his brother, on the Palatino, saw 12. The meaning was clear but the two argued and Romulus ended up killing Remus before going on to found his city.

1300	**1378–1417**	**1527**
Pope Boniface VIII proclaims Rome's first ever Jubilee, offering a full pardon to anyone who makes the pilgrimage to the city.	Squabbling between factions in the Catholic Church leads to the Great Schism.	Pope Clement VII hides in Castel Sant'Angelo as Rome is sacked by troops loyal to Charles V, king of Spain and Holy Roman Emperor.

Laurence Olivier and John Gavin in *Spartacus*

SILVER SCREEN COLLECTION/GETTY IMAGES ©

★ Best Ancient Rome on Screen

Spartacus (1960; Stanley Kubrick)

Quo Vadis (1951; Mervyn LeRoy)

Gladiator (2000; Ridley Scott)

I, Claudius (1976; BBC)

Rome (2005–07; HBO, BBC)

As both religious and temporal leaders, Rome's popes wielded influence well beyond their military capacity. For much of the medieval period, the Church held a virtual monopoly on Europe's reading material (mostly religious scripts written in Latin) and was the authority on virtually every aspect of human knowledge.

Modern Influence of the Vatican

Almost a thousand years on and the Church is still a major influence on modern Italian life. Its rigid stance on social and ethical issues such as birth control, abortion, same-sex marriage and euthanasia informs much public debate, often with highly divisive results.

This relationship between the Church and Italy's modern political establishment is a fact of life that dates to the establishment of the Italian Republic in 1946. For much of the First Republic (1946–94), the Vatican was closely associated with Democrazia Cristiana (DC; Christian Democrat Party), Italy's most powerful party and an ardent opponent of communism. At the same time, the Church, keen to weed communism out of the political landscape, played its part by threatening to excommunicate anyone who voted for Italy's Partito Comunista Italiano (PCI; Communist Party). Today, no one political party has a monopoly on Church favour, and politicians across the spectrum tread warily around Catholic sensibilities.

The Renaissance: a New Beginning

Bridging the gap between the Middle Ages and the modern age, the Renaissance (*Rinascimento* in Italian) was a far-reaching intellectual, artistic and cultural movement. It emerged in 14th-century Florence but quickly spread to Rome, where it gave rise to one of the greatest makeovers the city had ever seen.

1798
Napoleon marches into Rome. A republic is announced, but it doesn't last long and in 1801 Pope Pius VII returns to Rome.

1870
Nine years after Italian unification, Rome's city walls are breached at Porta Pia and Pope Pius IX cedes the city to Italy.

1922
Some 40,000 fascists march on Rome. King Vittorio Emanuele III invites the 39-year-old Mussolini to form a government.

Humanism & Rebuilding

The movement's intellectual cornerstone was humanism, a philosophy that focused on the central role of humanity within the universe, a major break from the medieval world view, which had placed God at the centre of everything. It was not antireligious though. One of the most celebrated humanist scholars of the 15th century was Pope Nicholas V (r 1447–84), who is considered the harbinger of the Roman Renaissance.

When Nicholas became pope in 1447, Rome was not in a good state. Centuries of medieval feuding had reduced the city to a semideserted battleground. In political terms, the papacy was recovering from the trauma of the Great Schism and attempting to face down Muslim encroachment in the east.

Against this background, Nicholas decided to rebuild Rome as a showcase of Church power, setting off an enormous program that would see the building of the Sistine Chapel and St Peter's Basilica.

Roman Roads

The ancient Romans were the expert engineers of their day, and the ability to travel quickly was an important factor in their power to rule. The queen of all ancient roads was Via Appia Antica, which connected Rome with the southern Adriatic port of Brindisi, named after Appius Claudius Caecus, the Roman censor who initiated its construction in 312 BC. Via Appia survives to this day, as do many of the other consular roads, Via Aurelia, Via Cassia, Via Flaminia and Via Salaria among them.

Sack of Rome & Protestant Protest

But outside Rome an ill wind was blowing. The main source of trouble was the long-standing conflict between the Holy Roman Empire, led by the Spanish Charles V, and the Italian city states. This simmering tension came to a head in 1527 when Rome was invaded by Charles' marauding army and ransacked as Pope Clement VII (r 1523–34) hid in Castel Sant'Angelo. The sack of Rome, regarded by most historians as the nail in the coffin of the Roman Renaissance, was a hugely traumatic event. It left the papacy reeling and gave rise to the view that the Church had been greatly weakened by its own moral shortcomings. That the Church was corrupt was well known, and it was with considerable public support that Martin Luther pinned his famous 95 Theses to a church door in Wittenberg in 1517, thus sparking off the Protestant Reformation.

Counter-Reformation

The Catholic reaction to the Reformation was strong. The Counter-Reformation was marked by a second wave of artistic and architectural activity, as the Church once again turned to bricks and mortar to restore its authority. But in contrast to the Renaissance,

1929
The Lateran Treaty is signed, creating the state of Vatican City.

1946
The Italian republic is born after a vote to abolish the monarchy.

1978
Former prime minister Aldo Moro is kidnapped and shot by a cell of the extreme left-wing *Brigate Rosse* (Red Brigades).

Mafia Capitale

Rome's recent history has seen its fair share of scandal and controversy, most notably in the form of the Mafia Capitale case. This broke in 2014 when allegations surfaced that the city's municipal council had been colluding with a criminal gang to cream off public funds. The subsequent investigation, the largest anticorruption operation since the Mani Pulite campaign of the 1990s, resulted in hundreds of arrests and convictions for more than 40 people, including former politicians and city officials. The man held to be the ringleader, a one-eyed gangster and former member of a right-wing terrorist group, received a 20-year prison sentence.

the Counter-Reformation was a period of persecution and official intolerance. With the full blessing of Pope Paul III, Ignatius Loyola founded the Jesuits in 1540, and two years later the Holy Office was set up as the Church's final appeals court for trials prosecuted by the Inquisition. In 1559 the Church published the *Index Librorum Prohibitorum* (Index of Prohibited Books) and began to persecute intellectuals and freethinkers.

Despite, or perhaps because of, the Church's policy of zero tolerance, the Counter-Reformation was largely successful in reestablishing papal prestige. From being a rural backwater with a population of around 20,000 in the mid-15th century, Rome had grown to become one of Europe's great 17th-century cities, home to Christendom's most spectacular churches and a population of 100,000 people.

The First Tourists

While Rome has a long past as a pilgrimage site, its history as a modern tourist destination can be traced back to the late 1700s and the fashion for the Grand Tour. The 18th-century version of a gap year, the Tour was considered an educational rite of passage for wealthy young men from northern Europe, and Britain in particular.

Rome, enjoying a rare period of peace, was perfectly set up for this English invasion. The city was basking in the aftermath of the 17th-century baroque building boom, and a craze for all things classical was sweeping Europe. Rome's papal authorities were also crying out for money after their excesses had left the city coffers bare, reducing much of the population to abject poverty.

Thousands came, including German writer Goethe, who stopped off to write his travelogue *Italian Journey* (1817), and English poets Byron, Shelley and Keats, who all fuelled their Romantic sensibilities in the city's vibrant streets.

Artistically, rococo was all the rage. The Spanish Steps, built between 1723 and 1726, proved a major hit with tourists, as did the exuberant Trevi Fountain.

2005	2013	2014
Pope John Paul II dies after 27 years on the papal throne. He is replaced by his long-standing ally Josef Ratzinger (Benedict XVI).	Pope Benedict XVI becomes the first pope to resign since 1415. Argentinian cardinal Jorge Mario Bergoglio is elected as Pope Francis.	Ex-mayor Gianni Alemanno and up to 100 other public officials are investigated as the Mafia Capitale scandal rocks Rome.

Ghosts of Fascism

Rome's fascist history is a highly charged subject. Historians on both sides of the political spectrum have accused each other of recasting the past to suit their views: left-wing historians have criticised their right-wing counterparts for glossing over the more unpleasant aspects of Mussolini's regime, while right-wingers have attacked their left-wing colleagues for whitewashing the facts to perpetuate an overly simplistic antifascist narrative. In 2018 mayor Virginia Raggi announced that the city will rename streets still named after fascists.

Mussolini

Benito Mussolini was born in 1883 in Forlì, a small town in Emilia-Romagna. As a young man he was an active member of the Italian Socialist Party, rising through the ranks to become editor of the party's official newspaper. However, service in WWI and Italy's subsequent descent into chaos led to a change of heart and in 1919 he founded the Italian Fascist Party.

In 1921 Mussolini was elected to the Chamber of Deputies. His parliamentary support was limited, but on 28 October 1922 he marched on Rome with 40,000 black-shirted followers. The march was largely symbolic but it had the desired effect: King Vittorio Emanuele III, fearful of a civil war between the fascists and socialists, invited Mussolini to form a government. By the end of 1925 the king had seized complete control of Italy. In order to silence the Church Mussolini signed the Lateran Treaty in 1929, which made Catholicism the state religion and recognised the sovereignty of the Vatican State.

Abroad, Mussolini invaded Abyssinia (now Ethiopia) in 1935 and sided with Hitler in 1936. In 1940, from the balcony of Palazzo Venezia, he announced Italy's entry into WWII to a vast, cheering crowd. The good humour didn't last: Rome suffered, first at the hands of its own fascist regime, then, after Mussolini was ousted in 1943, at the hands of the Nazis. Rome was finally liberated from German occupation on 4 June 1944.

Postwar Period

Defeat in WWII didn't kill off Italian fascism, and in 1946 hard-line Mussolini supporters founded the Movimento Sociale Italiano (MSI; Italian Social Movement). For close on 50 years this overtly fascist party participated in mainstream Italian politics, while on the other side of the spectrum the PCI grew into Western Europe's largest communist party. The MSI was finally dissolved in 1994, when Gianfranco Fini rebranded it as the postfascist Alleanza Nazionale (AN; National Alliance). AN remained an important political player until it was incorporated into Silvio Berlusconi's Popolo della Libertà party in 2009.

Outside the political mainstream, fascism (along with communism) was a driving force of the domestic terrorism that rocked Rome and Italy during the *anni di piombo* (years of lead), between the late 1960s and the early '80s.

2016	**2017**	**2018**
Virginia Raggi, a 37-year-old lawyer, becomes Rome's first woman mayor and vows to fight corruption.	As Brexit shockwaves rock Europe, 27 EU leaders gather on the Capitoline Hill to celebrate the EU's 60th anniversary.	Giuseppe Conte is sworn in as PM, heading a populist coalition (Five Star Movement and hard-right League party).

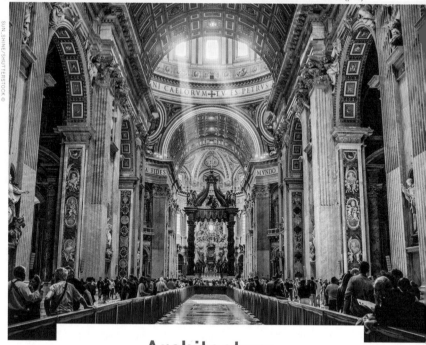

Interior, St Peter's Basilica (p46)

SUN_SHINE/SHUTTERSTOCK ©

Architecture

From ancient ruins and Renaissance basilicas to baroque churches and hulking fascist palazzi (mansions), Rome's architectural legacy is unparalleled. Michelangelo, Bramante, Borromini and Bernini are among the architects who stamped their genius on the city's urban landscape. More recently, contemporary 'starchitects', including Renzo Piano and Zaha Hadid, have left an imprint.

The Ancients

Architecture was central to the success of the ancient Romans. In building their great capital, they were pioneers in the use of architecture to tackle problems of infrastructure, urban management and communication. For the first time, architects and engineers designed houses, roads, aqueducts and shopping centres alongside temples, tombs and imperial palaces. To do this, the Romans advanced methods devised by the Etruscans and Greeks, developing construction techniques and building materials that allowed them to build on a massive and hitherto unseen scale.

Etruscan Roots

By the 7th century BC the Etruscans were the dominant force on the Italian peninsula, with important centres at Tarquinia, Caere (Cerveteri) and Veii (Veio). Little remains of their city states – they built with wood and brick, which didn't age well – and much of what we now know about them derives from findings unearthed in their impressive cemeteries. These were constructed outside the city walls and harboured richly decorated stone tombs covered by mounds of earth.

Roman Developments

When Rome was founded sometime around the 8th century BC, the Etruscans were at the height of their power and Greek colonists were establishing control over southern Italy. In subsequent centuries a three-way battle for domination ensued. Against this background, Roman architects borrowed heavily from Greek and Etruscan traditions, gradually developing their own styles and techniques.

Ancient Roman architecture was monumental in form and often propagandistic in nature. Huge amphitheatres, aqueducts and temples joined muscular and awe-inspiring basilicas, arches and thermal baths in trumpeting the skill and vision of the city's early rulers and the nameless architects who worked for them.

Temples

Early Republican-era temples were based on Etruscan designs, but over time the Romans turned to the Greeks for their inspiration. Whereas Greek temples had steps and colonnades on all sides, the classic Roman temple had a high podium with steps leading up to a deep porch.

The Roman use of columns was also Greek in origin, even if the Romans favoured the more slender Ionic and Corinthian columns over the plain Doric pillars. To see how these differ, study the exterior of the Colosseum, which incorporates all three styles.

Aqueducts & Sewers

One of the Romans' crowning architectural achievements was the development of a water-supply infrastructure.

To meet the city's water demand, the Romans constructed a complex system of aqueducts to bring water in from the hills of central Italy and distribute it around town. The first aqueduct to serve Rome was the 16.5km Aqua Appia, which became fully operational in 312 BC. Over the next 700 years or so, up to 800km of aqueducts were built in the city, a network capable of supplying up to one million cubic metres of water per day.

At the other end of the water cycle, waste water was drained away via an underground sewerage system known as the Cloaca Maxima (Great Sewer) and emptied downstream into the Tiber.

Residential Housing

While Rome's emperors and aristocrats lived in luxury on the Palatino (Palatine Hill), the city's poor huddled together in large residential blocks called *insulae*. These poorly built structures were sometimes up to six or seven storeys high, accommodating hundreds of people in dark, unhealthy conditions. Near the foot of the staircase leading up to the Chiesa di Santa Maria in Aracoeli, you can still see a section of what was once a typical city-centre *insula*.

Museo Nazionale delle Arti del XXI Secolo (p106)

PHOTO BERNARD TOUILLON
COURTESY FONDAZIONE MAXXI ©

★ Architectural Icons

Colosseum (p36)

Pantheon (p50)

St Peter's Basilica (p46)

Museo Nazionale delle Arti del XXI
Secolo (p106)

Concrete & Monumental Architecture

Most of the ruins that litter modern Rome are the remains of the ancient city's big, show-stopping monuments. The Colosseum, the Pantheon and the Forums are not only reminders of the sophistication and scale of ancient Rome – just as they were originally designed to be – but also monuments to the vision and bravura of the city's ancient architects.

One of the key breakthroughs the Romans made was the invention of concrete in the 1st century BC. Made by mixing volcanic ash with lime and an aggregate, often tufa rock or brick rubble, concrete was quick to make, easy to use and cheap. It allowed the Romans to develop vaulted roofing, which they used to span the Pantheon's ceiling and the huge vaults at the Terme di Caracalla.

Early Christian

The most startling reminders of early Christian activity are the catacombs, a series of underground burial grounds built under Rome's ancient roads. Christian belief in the resurrection meant that the Christians could not cremate their dead, as was the custom in Roman times, and with burial forbidden inside the city walls they were forced to go outside the city.

The Christians began to abandon the catacombs in the 4th century and increasingly opted to be buried in the churches the emperor Constantine was building in the city. The most notable of the many churches he commissioned is the Basilica di San Giovanni in Laterano, the model on which many subsequent basilicas were based. Other period show-stoppers include the Basilica di Santa Maria in Trastevere and the Basilica di Santa Maria Maggiore.

A second wave of church-building hit Rome in the period between the 8th and 12th centuries. As the early papacy battled for survival against the threatening Lombards, its leaders took to construction to leave some sort of historical imprint, resulting in churches such as the Chiesa di Santa Maria in Cosmedin, home of the Bocca della Verità (Mouth of Truth).

The Renaissance

Many claim it was the election of Pope Nicholas V in 1447 that sparked the Renaissance in Rome. Nicholas believed that as head of the Christian world Rome had a duty to impress, a theory that was endorsed by his successors, and it was at the behest of the great papal dynasties – the Barberini, Farnese and Pamphilj – that the leading artists of the day were summoned to Rome.

Bramante & the High Renaissance

It was under Pope Julius II that the Roman Renaissance reached its peak, thanks largely to a classically minded architect from Milan, Donato Bramante.

Considered the high priest of Renaissance architecture, Bramante arrived in Rome in 1499 and developed a hugely influential, refined classical style. His 1502 Tempietto, for example, perfectly illustrates his innate understanding of proportion. In 1506 Julius commissioned him to start work on his greatest project – the rebuilding of St Peter's Basilica. The fall of Constantinople's Aya Sofya (Church of the Hagia Sofia) to Islam in the mid-14th century had pricked Nicholas V into ordering an earlier revamp, but the work had never been completed and it wasn't until Julius took over the project that progress was made. Bramante died in 1514, however, and he never got to see how his original Greek-cross design was developed.

St Peter's Basilica occupied most of the other notable architects of the High Renaissance, including Giuliano da Sangallo, Baldassarre Peruzzi and Antonio da Sangallo the Younger. Michelangelo eventually took over in 1547, modifying the layout and creating the basilica's crowning dome. Modelled on Brunelleschi's cupola for the Duomo in Florence, this is considered the artist's finest architectural achievement and one of the most important works of the Roman Renaissance.

Rococo Frills

In the early days of the 18th century, as baroque fashions began to fade and neoclassicism waited to make its 19th century entrance, the rococo burst into life. Drawing on the excesses of the baroque, it was a short-lived, theatrical fad but one that left several iconic monuments.

The Spanish Steps, built between 1723 and 1726 by Francesco de Sanctis, provided a focal point for the many Grand Tourists who were busy discovering Rome's classical past. A short walk to the southwest, Piazza di Sant'Ignazio was designed by Filippo Raguzzini to provide a suitably melodramatic setting for the Chiesa di Sant'Ignazio di Loyola, Rome's second most important Jesuit church. Most spectacular of all was the Trevi Fountain, one of the city's most exuberant and enduringly popular monuments. It was designed in 1732 by Nicola Salvi and completed three decades later.

The Baroque

As the principal motor of the Roman Renaissance, the Catholic Church became increasingly powerful in the 16th century. But with power came corruption and calls for reform. These culminated in the far-reaching Protestant Reformation, which prompted the Counter-Reformation, a vicious campaign to get people back into the Catholic fold. In the midst of this great offensive, baroque art and architecture emerged as an effective form of propaganda. Stylistically, baroque architecture aims for a dramatic sense of dynamism, often achieved by combining spatial complexity with clever lighting and flamboyant painting or sculpture.

One of the first great Counter-Reformation churches was the Jesuit Chiesa del Gesù, designed by leading architect Giacomo della Porta. In a move away from the style of earlier Renaissance churches, the facade has pronounced architectural elements that create a contrast between surfaces and a play of light and shade.

The late 16th-century papacy of Sixtus V marked the start of major urban-planning schemes. Domenico Fontana and others created a network of thoroughfares to connect previously disparate parts of the sprawling medieval city. Fontana also designed the main facade of Palazzo del Quirinale, the pope's summer residence for almost three centuries.

Fontana dei Quattro Fiumi (p66)

KIRK FISHER/SHUTTERSTOCK ©

Bernini Versus Borromini

No two people did more to fashion the face of Rome than Gian Lorenzo Bernini and Francesco Borromini, the great figures of the Roman baroque. Naples-born Bernini, confident and suave, is best known for his work in the Vatican, where he designed St Peter's Square and was chief architect at St Peter's Basilica from 1629.

Under the patronage of the Barberini pope Urban VIII, Bernini was given free rein to transform the city, and his churches, *palazzi,* piazzas and fountains remain landmarks to this day. His fortunes nosedived, however, when the pope died in 1644. Urban's successor, Innocent X, wanted as little contact as possible with the favourites of his hated predecessor, and instead turned to Borromini.

Borromini, a solitary, peculiar chap from Lombardy, created buildings involving complex shapes and exotic geometry, including Piazza Navona's Chiesa di Sant'Agnese in Agone.

Rationalism & Fascism

Rome entered the 20th century in good shape. During the late 19th century it had been treated to one of its periodic makeovers – this time after being made capital of the Kingdom of Italy in 1870. Piazzas such as Piazza Vittorio Emanuele II and Piazza della Repubblica were built, and roads were laid. To celebrate unification, and pander to the ruling Savoy family, the ostentatious Vittoriano monument was built.

The 1920s saw the emergence of architectural rationalism. Its main Italian proponents, the Gruppo Sette, combined classicism with modernism, which tied in perfectly with Mussolini's vision of fascism as the modern bearer of ancient Rome's imperialist ambitions. Mussolini's most famous architectural legacy is Rome's southern EUR district, an Orwellian quarter of wide boulevards and huge linear buildings, built for the Esposizione Universale di Roma in 1942.

Modern Rome

The 21st century has witnessed a flurry of architectural activity in Rome by world-class 'starchitects': Italy's foremost architect, Renzo Piano, designed the Auditorium Parco della Musica; American Richard Meier built a controversial new pavilion for the 1st-century-AD Ara Pacis; and Anglo-Iraqi Zaha Hadid won plaudits for the Museo Nazionale delle Arti del XXI Secolo (MAXXI). In the Forum Boarium area, French architect Jean Nouvel completed a contemporary-arts gallery, hotel and restaurant at Palazzo Rhinoceros in 2018 for the Fondazione Alda Fendi – Esperimenti; and much-delayed construction is set to start on a new 52,500-capacity, €400 million stadium, the Stadio della Roma, in the city's southern reaches

Laocoön (p41), Museo Pio-Clementino, Vatican Museums

ANDROVER/SHUTTERSTOCK ©

The Arts

Rome has long provided inspiration for painters, sculptors, film-makers, writers and musicians. The great works of Roman antiquity fuelled the imagination of Renaissance artists; Counter-Reformation persecution led to baroque art; the trauma of Mussolini and WWII found expression in neorealist cinema. More recently, urban art has flourished and film-making has returned to the streets of Rome.

Painting & Sculpture

Home to some of the Western world's most recognisable art, Rome is a visual feast. Its churches alone contain more masterpieces than many small countries, and the city's galleries are laden with works by world-famous artists.

Etruscan Groundwork

Laying the groundwork for much later Roman art, the Etruscans placed great importance on their funerary rites and they developed sepulchral decoration into a highly sophisticated art form. Elaborate stone sarcophagi were often embellished with a reclining figure or a couple, typically depicted with a haunting, enigmatic smile. An important example is the

Basilica di Santa Maria in Trastevere (p110)

Sarcofago degli sposi (Sarcophagus of the Betrothed) in the Museo Nazionale Etrusco di Villa Giulia. The Etruscans were also noted for their bronze work and filigree jewellery. One of Rome's most iconic sculptures, the 5th-century-BC *Lupa capitolina* (Capitoline Wolf), held in the Capitoline Museums, is an Etruscan bronze.

Roman Developments

In terms of decorative art, the Roman use of mosaics and wall paintings was derived from Etruscan funerary decoration. By the 1st century BC, floor mosaics were a popular form of home decor. Typical themes included landscapes, still lifes, geometric patterns and depictions of gods. In the Museo Nazionale Romano: Palazzo Massimo alle Terme, you'll find some spectacular wall mosaics and 1st-century-BC frescoes.

Sculpture was an important element of Roman art, and was largely influenced by Greek styles. Indeed, early Roman sculptures were often made by Greek artists or were copies of Greek works. They were largely concerned with the male physique and generally depicted visions of male beauty – the *Apollo Belvedere* and the *Laocoön* in the Vatican Museums are classic examples.

In terms of function, Roman art was highly propagandistic and from the time of Augustus (r 27 BC–AD 14), art was increasingly used to serve the state. This new narrative art often took the form of relief decoration – the *Ara Pacis Augustae* is a stunning example.

Early Christian Art

The earliest Christian art in Rome is the traces of biblical frescoes in the Catacombe di Priscilla and the Catacombe di San Sebastiano.

With the legalisation of Christianity in the 4th century, these images began to move into the public arena, appearing in mosaics across the city and in churches such as the Basilica di Santa Maria Maggiore. Eastern influences became much more pronounced between the 7th and 9th centuries, when Byzantine styles swept in from the east, leading to a brighter, golden look. Typical of the style are the mosaics in the Basilica di Santa Maria in Trastevere.

The Renaissance

The Renaissance arrived in Rome in the latter half of the 15th century, and was to have a profound impact on the city, as the top artists of the day were summoned to decorate the many new buildings going up around town.

Rome's most celebrated works of Renaissance art are Michelangelo's paintings in the Sistine Chapel – his cinematic ceiling frescoes, painted between 1508 and 1512, and the *Giudizio Universale* (Last Judgment), which he worked on between 1536 and 1541.

Renaissance art, inspired by humanism, focused heavily on the human form. This led artists to develop a far greater appreciation of perspective. But while early Renaissance painters made great strides in formulating rules of perspective, they still struggled to paint harmonious arrangements of figures. And it was this that Raffaello Sanzio (Raphael; 1483–1520) tackled in his great masterpiece La Scuola di Atene (The School of Athens; 1510–11) in the Vatican Museums.

Counter-Reformation & the Baroque

The baroque burst on to Rome's art scene in the early 17th century. Combining a dramatic sense of dynamism with highly charged emotion, it was enthusiastically appropriated by the Catholic Church, which used it as a propaganda tool in its persecution of Counter-Reformation heretics. The powerful popes of the day eagerly championed the likes of Caravaggio, Gian Lorenzo Bernini, Domenichino, Pietro da Cortona and Alessandro Algardi.

Unsurprisingly, much baroque art has a religious theme and you'll often find depictions of martyrdoms, ecstasies and miracles.

One of the key painters of the period was Caravaggio (1573–1610), whose realistic interpretations of religious subjects often outraged his patrons. In contrast, the exquisite sculptural works of Gian Lorenzo Bernini (1598–1680) proved an instant hit.

Neoclassicism

Emerging in the late 18th and early 19th centuries, neoclassicism signalled a departure from the emotional abandon of the baroque and a return to the clean, sober lines of classical art. Its major exponent was the sculptor Antonio Canova (1757–1822), whose study of Paolina Bonaparte Borghese as Venere vincitrice (Venus Victrix) in the Museo e Galleria Borghese is typical of the mildly erotic style for which he became known.

Street Art

Street art in Rome is edgy, exciting, progressive and a fabulous excuse to delve into the city's gritty southern suburbs when you need a break from Ancient Rome's tourist crowds. Tourist kiosks have maps marked up with key street-art works, and 15 street-art itineraries can be found under 'Itineraries' at the official tourism website, www.turismoroma.it. Ephemeral artworks range from a William Kentridge frieze on the Tiber embankment to the fading murals of Bolognese artist Blu and stencil work of Sten & Lex in off-beat Ostiense.

Literature

Rome has a rich literary tradition, encompassing everything from ancient satires to dialect poetry, antifascist prose and contemporary thrillers.

Classics

Famous for his blistering oratory, Marcus Tullius Cicero (106–43 BC) was the Roman Republic's preeminent author of philosophical works and speeches. His contemporary, Catullus (c 84–54 BC) cut a very different figure with his epigrams and erotic verse.

On becoming emperor in 27 BC, Augustus encouraged the arts, and Virgil (70–19 BC), Ovid, Horace and Tibullus all enjoyed freedom to write.

Rome as Inspiration

Rome has provided inspiration for legions of foreign authors. In the 18th century the city was a hotbed of literary activity as historians and Grand Tourists poured into Rome from northern Europe. The German author Goethe captures the elation of discovering ancient

Sergio Leone

Best known for almost single-handedly creating the spaghetti western, Roman-born Sergio Leone (1929–89) is a cult hero. The son of a silent-movie director, Leone cut his teeth as a screenwriter, before working as assistant director on *Quo vadis?* (1951) and *Ben-Hur* (1959). He made his directorial debut three years later on *Il colosso di Rodi* (The Colossus of Rhodes; 1961).

But it was with his famous dollar trilogy – *Per un pugno di dollari* (A Fistful of Dollars; 1964), *Per qualche dollari in piu* (For a Few Dollars More; 1965) and *Il buono, il brutto, il cattivo* (The Good, the Bad and the Ugly; 1966) – that he really hit the big time. Stylistically, he introduced innovations that later became trademarks, most notably his use of musical themes to identify characters (calling on old schoolmate, the composer Ennio Morricone, to assist).

Rome in his travelogue *Italian Journey* (1817). The city was also a magnet for English Romantic poets: John Keats, Lord Byron, Percy Bysshe Shelley, Mary Shelley and other writers all spent time here. More recently, Rome has provided settings for many a literary blockbuster, including Dan Brown's thriller *Angels & Demons* (2001).

Writing Today

Rome-born Niccolò Ammaniti is one of Italy's best-selling authors. In 2007 he won the Premio Strega, Italy's top literary prize, for his novel, *Come Dio comanda* (As God Commands), although he's best known internationally for *Io non ho paura* (I'm Not Scared; 2001), the book on which the 2003 film of the same name is based.

Cinema

Rome has a long cinematic tradition, spanning the works of the postwar neorealists and film-makers as diverse as Federico Fellini, Sergio Leone, Nanni Moretti, and Paolo Sorrentino, the Oscar-winning director of *La grande belleza* (The Great Beauty).

The golden age of Roman cinema was the late 1940s, when Roberto Rossellini (1906–77) produced a trio of neorealist masterpieces, most notably *Roma città aperta* (Rome Open City; 1945). Also important was Vittorio de Sica's 1948 *Ladri di biciclette* (Bicycle Thieves).

Federico Fellini (1920–94) took the creative baton from the neorealists, producing his era-defining hit *La dolce vita* in 1960. Idiosyncratic and whimsical, Nanni Moretti continues to make films that fall outside of mainstream tradition, including *Habemus Papam*, his 2011 portrayal of a pope having a crisis of faith.

Villa Borghese and the Terme di Caracalla were among the locations for Ben Stiller's *Zoolander 2;* the Tiber riverside and Via della Conciliazione appeared in the James Bond outing *Spectre;* and in the city's southern reaches, a remake of *Ben-Hur* was recently filmed at the Cinecittà studios, the very same place where the original was shot in 1959.

Music

Despite austerity-led cutbacks, Rome's music scene is bearing up well. International orchestras perform to sell-out audiences, jazz greats jam in steamy clubs, and rappers rage in underground venues.

Jazz has long been a mainstay of Rome's music scene, while recent decades have seen the emergence of a vibrant rap and hip-hop culture. Opera is served up at the Teatro dell'Opera and, in summer, at the spectacular Terme di Caracalla.

Villa Borghese (p58)

The Roman Way of Life

As a visitor, it's often difficult to see beyond Rome's spectacular veneer to the large, modern city that lies beneath: a living, breathing capital that's home to almost three million people. So how do the Romans live in their city? Where do they work? Who do they live with? How do they let their hair down?

Work

Employment in the capital is largely based on Italy's bloated state bureaucracy. Every morning armies of suited civil servants pour into town and disappear into vast ministerial buildings to keep the machinery of government ticking over. Other important employers include the tourism sector, finance, media and culture.

But as Italy's economy continues to stagnate, it's tough for young people to get a foot on the career ladder. To land it lucky, it helps to know someone. Official figures are impossible to come by, but it's a widely held belief that personal or political connections are the best way of landing a job.

Like workplaces everywhere in Italy, Rome's workplace remains predominantly male. Female unemployment is an ongoing issue and Italian women continue to earn less than

Campo de' Fiori (p96)

★ **Best Local Haunts**

Doppiozeroo (p180)

Stadio Olimpico (p198)

Mercado de Porta Portese (p96)

Villa Borghese (p58)

their male counterparts. That said, recent signs have been positive. Half of Prime Minister Matteo Renzi's 2014 cabinet were women, and in June 2016 Rome elected its first-ever female mayor.

Home Life & Family

Romans, like most Italians, live in apartments, which are often small and expensive. House prices in central Rome are among the highest in the country and many first-time buyers are forced to move out of town or to distant suburbs. Rates of home ownership are relatively high in Rome and properties are commonly kept in the family, handed down from generation to generation. People do rent, but the rental market is largely targeted at Rome's huge student population.

It's still the rule rather than the exception for Romans to stay at home until they marry, which they typically do at around age 30. But while faith in the family remains, the family unit is shrinking – Italian women are giving birth later than ever and having fewer children.

Play

Despite the high cost of living in Rome, few Romans would swap their city for anywhere else, and they enjoy it with gusto. You only have to look at the city's pizzerias and trattorias to see that eating out is a much-loved local pastime. Drinking, in contrast, is not a traditional Roman activity and an evening out in Rome is as much about flirting and looking gorgeous as it is about consuming alcohol.

Clothes shopping is a popular Roman pastime, alongside cinema-going and football (soccer); a trip to the Stadio Olimpico to watch a Sunday football game is considered an afternoon well spent. Romans are inveterate car-lovers, and on hot summer weekends they will often drive out to the coast or surrounding countryside.

Religion

Rome is packed with churches. And with the Vatican in the centre of town, the Church is a constant presence in Roman life. Yet the role of religion in modern Roman society is an ambiguous one. On the one hand, most people consider themselves Catholic, but on the other, church attendance is in free fall, particularly among the young.

Catholicism's hold on the Roman psyche is strong, but an increase in the city's immigrant population has led to a noticeable Muslim presence. Friction has flared on occasion, and there were violent scenes in early 2018 when far-right anti-immigration protesters clashed with police.

Castel Sant'Angelo (p49)

BLUE PLANET STUDIO/SHUTTERSTOCK ©

Survival Guide

Directory A–Z

Accessible Travel

o Cobbled streets, paving stones, blocked pavements and tiny lifts are difficult for the wheelchair-bound, while the relentless traffic can be disorienting for partially sighted travellers or those with hearing difficulties.

o All stations on metro line B have wheelchair access and lifts except for Circo Massimo, Colosseo and Cavour. On line A, Cipro and Termini are equipped with lifts. Note, however, that just because a station has a lift that doesn't mean it will necessarily be working.

o Bus 590 covers the same route as metro line A and is one of 22 bus and tram services with wheelchair access. Routes with disabled access are indicated on bus stops.

o Contact **ADR Assistance** (www.adrassistance.it) for help at Fiumicino or Ciampino airports.

o Taxi company **Fausta Trasporti** (06 540 33 62; http://accessibletransportation rome.com) has a fleet of wheelchair-accessible vehicles that can carry up to seven people, including three wheelchair users.

o Download Lonely Planet's free Accessible Travel guide from http://lptravel.to/ AccessibleTravel.

Customs Regulations

o Entering Italy from another EU country you can bring, duty-free: 10L spirits, 90L wine and 800 cigarettes.

o If arriving from a non-EU country the limits are 1L spirits (or 2L fortified wine), 4L still wine, 60ml perfume, 16L beer, 200 cigarettes and other goods up to a value of €300/430 (travelling by land/sea); anything over this must be declared on arrival and the duty paid.

o On leaving the EU, non-EU residents can reclaim value-added tax (VAT) on expensive purchases.

Dangers & Annoyances

Rome is a safe city but petty theft can be a problem. Use common sense and watch your valuables.

o Pickpockets are active in touristy areas such as the Colosseum, Piazza di Spagna, Piazza Venezia and St Peter's Square.

o Be alert around Stazione Termini and on crowded public transport – the 64 Vatican bus is notorious.

Electricity

Type F
230V/50Hz

Type L
230V/50Hz

Emergency & Important Numbers

Ambulance	☎118
Fire	☎115
Police	☎112, ☎113

Internet Access

• Free wi-fi is widely available in hostels, B&Bs and hotels, though with signals of varying quality. Many bars and cafes also offer wi-fi.

• There are many public wi-fi hotspots across town run by **WiFimetropolitano** (www.cittametropolitana roma.gov.it/wifimetropoli tano). To use these, register online using a credit card or Italian mobile phone.

Legal Matters

The most likely reason for a brush with the law is to report a theft. If you have something stolen and you want to claim it on insurance, you must make a statement to the police. Insurance companies won't pay up without official proof of a crime.

LGBT+ Travellers

Homosexuality is legal (over the age of 16) and even widely accepted, but Rome is fairly conservative in its attitudes and discretion is still wise.

The city has a thriving, if low-key, gay scene. There are relatively few queer-only venues but the Colosseum end of Via di San Giovanni in Laterano is a favourite hang-out and many clubs host regular gay and lesbian nights.

Medical Services

Italy has a public health system that is legally bound to provide emergency care to everyone. EU nationals are entitled to reduced-cost, sometimes free, medical care with a European Health Insurance Card (EHIC), available from your home health authority; non-EU citizens should take out medical insurance.

For emergency treatment, you can go to the *pronto soccorso* (casualty department) of an *ospedale* (public hospital). For less serious ailments call the **Guardia Medica Turistica** (Map p254; ☎06 7730 6650; Via Emilio Morosini 30; ◷24hr; ▣Viale di Trastevere, ▣Viale di Trastevere).

English-speaking doctors are available for house calls or appointments at the private clinic **Doctors in Italy** (Map p250; ☎370 1359521, 06 679 06 95; www. doctorsinitaly.com; 3rd fl, Via Frattina 48; ◷10am-8pm Mon-Fri; Ⓜ Spagna).

Money

• Italy uses the euro. There are seven euro notes, which come in denominations of €500, €200, €100, €50, €20, €10 and €5. Euro coins are in denominations of €2 and €1, and 50, 20, 10, five, two and one cents.

• You can change your money in banks, at post offices or at a *cambio* (exchange office). There are exchange booths at Stazione Termini and at Fiumicino and Ciampino airports.

ATMs

• ATMs (known in Italy as *bancomat*) are widely available in Rome and most will accept cards tied into the Visa, MasterCard, Cirrus and Maestro systems.

• Most ATMs impose a daily cash-withdrawal limit of €250.

Credit Cards

• Virtually all midrange and top-end hotels accept credit cards, as do most restaurants and large shops. Some cheaper *pensioni* (pensions), trattorias and pizzerias only accept cash.

Discount Cards

Roma Pass (www.romapass.it; €38.50). Valid 72 hours, the Roma Pass includes free admission to two museums or sites, as well as reduced entry to extra sites, unlimited city transport and discounted entry to other exhibitions and events. The 48-hour Roma Pass (€28) is a more limited version.

Omnia Card (www.omniakit.org; adult/reduced €113/80) Also valid 72 hours, this card includes fast-track entry to the Vatican Museums and admission to St Peter's Basilica, Basilica di San Giovanni in Laterano, and Carcere Mamertino. Free travel on hop-on hop-off Open Bus Vatican & Rome, plus unlimited public transport within Rome. Free entry to two sites, then 50% discount to extra sites. A 24 hour version is also available (€55).

Don't rely on credit cards at museums or galleries.

○ Major cards such as Visa, MasterCard, Eurocard, Cirrus and Eurocheques are widely accepted. Amex is also recognised, although it's less common.

Opening Hours

Banks 8.30am–1.30pm and 2.45–4.30pm Monday to Friday

Bars & cafes 7.30am–8pm, sometimes until 1am or 2am

Shops 9am–7.30pm or 10am–8pm Monday to Saturday, some 11am–7pm Sunday; smaller shops 9am–1pm and 3.30–7.30pm (or 4pm–8pm) Monday to Saturday; some shops are closed Monday morning

Clubs 10pm–4am or 5am

Restaurants noon–3pm and 7.30–11pm (later in summer)

Public Holidays

Most Romans take their annual holiday in August. Many businesses and shops close for at least part of the month, particularly around 15 August.

Public holidays include the following:

Capodanno (New Year's Day) 1 January

Epifania (Epiphany) 6 January

Pasquetta (Easter Monday) March/April

Giorno della Liberazione (Liberation Day) 25 April

Festa del Lavoro (Labour Day) 1 May

Festa della Repubblica (Republic Day) 2 June

Festa dei Santi Pietro e Paolo (Feast of Sts Peter & Paul) 29 June

Ferragosto (Feast of the Assumption) 15 August

Festa di Ognisanti (All Saints' Day) 1 November

Festa dell'Immacolata Concezione (Feast of the Immaculate Conception) 8 December

Natale (Christmas Day) 25 December

Festa di Santo Stefano (Boxing Day) 26 December

Telephone

○ Rome's area code is 06, which must be dialled even when calling locally.

○ Mobile-phone numbers begin with a three-digit prefix starting with a 3.

○ To call abroad from Italy dial 00, then the country and area codes, followed by the full number.

Mobile Phones

○ Italian mobile phones operate on the GSM 900/1800 network, which is compatible with the rest of Europe and Australia but not always with the North American GSM or CDMA systems – check with your service provider.

○ The cheapest way of using your mobile is to buy a prepaid (prepagato) SIM card. TIM (www.tim.it), Wind (www.wind.it), Vodafone (www.vodafone.it) and Tre (www.tre.it) all offer SIM cards and have retail outlets across town.

○ Under Italian law all SIM cards must be registered, so take your passport or ID card when you buy one.

Time

Italy is in a single time zone, one hour ahead of GMT. Daylight-saving time, when clocks move forward one hour, starts on the last Sunday in March. Clocks are put back an hour on the last Sunday in October.

Italy operates on a 24-hour clock, so 6pm is written as 18:00, for instance.

Toilets

Public toilets are not widespread but you'll find them at St Peter's Square (free) and Stazione Termini (€1). If you're caught short, the best thing to do is to nip into a cafe or bar.

Tourist Information

There are tourist information points at **Fiumicino** (International Arrivals, Terminal 3; ◷8am-8.45pm) and **Ciampino** (Arrivals Hall; ◷8.30am-6pm) airports, and locations across the city:

Castel Sant'Angelo (www.turismoroma.it; Piazza Pia; ◷9.30am-7pm summer, 8.30am-6pm winter; 🚌Piazza Pia)

Imperial Forums (Via dei Fori Imperiali; ◷9.30am-7pm, to

8pm Jul & Aug; 🚌Via dei Fori Imperiali)

Piazza delle Cinque Lune (Map p250; ◷9.30am-7pm; 🚌Corso del Rinascimento) Near Piazza Navona.

Stazione Termini (Map p255; ☎06 06 08; www.turismoroma.it; Via Giovanni Giolitti 34; ◷8am-6.45pm; Ⓜ️Termini) In the hall adjacent to platform 24.

Via Marco Minghetti (Map p250; ☎06 06 08; www.turismoroma.it; Via Marco Minghetti; ◷9.30am-7pm; 🚌Via del Corso) Between Via del Corso and the Trevi Fountain.

For information about the Vatican, contact the **Ufficio Pellegrini e Turisti** (Map p253; ☎06 6988 1662; www.vatican.va; St Peter's Sq; ◷8.30am-6.30pm Mon-Sat; 🚌Piazza del Risorgimento, Ⓜ️Ottaviano-San Pietro).

The **Comune di Roma** (☎06 06 08; www.060608.it; ◷9am-7pm) runs a free multilingual tourist information telephone line providing info

on culture, shows, hotels, transport etc. Its website is also an excellent source of information.

Rome's official tourist website, **Turismo Roma** (www.turismoroma.it), has comprehensive information about sights, accommodation and city transport, as well as itineraries and up-to-date listings.

Visas

● Italy is one of the 26 European countries to make up the Schengen area. There are no customs controls when travelling between Schengen countries, so the visa rules that apply to Italy apply to all Schengen countries.

● EU citizens do not need a visa to enter Italy – a valid ID card or passport is sufficient.

Practicalities

Newspapers Key national dailies include centre-left *la Repubblica* (www.repubblica.it) and its right-wing rival *Corriere della Sera* (www.corriere.it). For the Vatican's take on affairs, *L'Osservatore Romano* (www.osservatoreromano.va) is the Holy See's official paper.

Smoking Banned in enclosed public spaces, which includes restaurants, bars, shops and public transport. It's also banned in Villa Borghese and other public parks between June and September.

Television The main terrestrial channels are RAI 1, 2 and 3 run by Rai (www.rai.it), Italy's state-owned national broadcaster, and Canale 5, Italia 1 and Rete 4 run by Mediaset (www.mediaset.it), the commercial TV company founded and still partly owned by Silvio Berlusconi.

Weights & Measures Italy uses the metric system.

○ Nationals of some other countries, including Australia, Canada, Israel, Japan, New Zealand, Switzerland and the USA, do not need a visa for stays of up to 90 days.

Women Travellers

○ Sexual harrassment can be an issue in Rome. If you feel yourself being groped on a crowded bus or metro, a loud *'che schifo!'* (how disgusting!) will draw attention to the incident.

○ Take all the usual precautions you would in any large city and, as in most places, avoid wandering around alone late at night, especially in the area around Termini station.

Transport

Arriving in Rome

Most people arrive in Rome by plane, landing at one of its two airports: Leonardo da Vinci, better known as Fiumicino; or Ciampino, hub for European low-cost carrier Ryanair. Flights from New York take around nine hours, from London 2¾

hours, from Sydney at least 22 hours.

As an alternative to short-haul flights, trains serve Rome's main station, Stazione Termini, from several European destinations, including Paris (about 15 hours) and cities across Italy.

Ferries serve Civitavecchia, some 80km north of Rome, from a number of Mediterranean ports.

Flights, cars and tours can be booked online at lonelyplanet.com/bookings.

Leonardo da Vinci Airport

Rome's main international airport, **Leonardo da Vinci** (06 6 59 51; www.adr.it/fiumicino), aka Fiumicino, is 30km west of the city.

The easiest way to get into town is by train, but there are also buses and private shuttle services.

Train

FL1 (www.trenitalia.com; 1 way €8) Connects to Trastevere, Ostiense and Tiburtina stations, but not Termini. Departures from the airport every 15 minutes (half-hourly on Sundays and public holidays) between 5.57am and 10.42pm, from Tiburtina every 15 minutes between 5.01am and 10.01pm.

Leonardo Express (www.trenitalia.com; 1 way €14) Runs to/from Stazione Termini. Departures from the airport every 30 minutes between 6.08am and 11.23pm, and from Termini between 5.20am and 10.35pm. Journey time is 30 minutes.

Bus

Cotral (800 174471, from a mobile 06 7205 7205; www.cotralspa.it; 1 way €5, purchased on bus €7) Runs between Fiumicino and Stazione Tiburtina via Termini. Four to six daily departures including night services from the airport at 1.45am, 3.45am and 5.45am, and from Tiburtina at 12.30am, 2.30am and 4.30am. Journey time is one hour.

Schiaffini Rome Airport Bus

(06 713 05 31; www.romeairportbus.com; Via Giolitti; 1 way/return €6.90/9.90) Regular services from the airport to Stazione Termini between 6.05am and midnight; from Termini between 5.10am and 1am. Allow about an hour for the journey.

SIT Bus (06 591 68 26; www.sitbusshuttle.com; 1 way/return €6/11) Regular departures to Stazione Termini (Via Marsala) from 7.15am to 12.40pm; from Termini between 4.45am and 8.30pm. All buses stop near the Vatican (Via Crescenzio 2) en route. Tickets are available on the bus. Journey time is approximately one hour.

Private Shuttle

Airport Connection Services
(338 9876465; www.airportconnection.it) Transfers to/from the city centre start at €22 per person (€28 for two).

Airport Shuttle (06 4201 3469; www.airportshuttle.it) Transfers to/from your hotel for €25 for one person, then €6 for each additional passenger up to a maximum of eight.

Taxi

The set fare to/from the city centre is €48, which is valid for up to four passengers including luggage. Note that taxis registered in Fiumicino charge more, so make sure you catch a Comune di Roma taxi – these are white with a taxi sign on the roof and Roma Capitale written on the door along with the taxi's licence number. Journey time is approximately 45 to 60 minutes depending on traffic.

Ciampino Airport

Ciampino (⏚06 6 59 51; www.adr.it/ciampino), 15km southeast of the city centre, is used by Ryanair for European and Italian destinations. It's not a big airport but there's a steady flow of traffic and at peak times it can get extremely busy.

To get into town, take one of the dedicated bus services. Alternatively, take a bus to Ciampino station then pick up a train to Termini or bus to Anagnina metro station (on line A).

Bus

Atral (www.atral-lazio.com) Runs buses between Ciampino Airport and Anagnina metro station (€1.20) and Ciampino train station (€1.20), where you can get a train to Termini (€1.50).

Schiaffini Rome Airport Bus (⏚06 713 05 31; www.romeair portbus.com; Via Giolitti; 1 way/ return €5.90/9.90) Regular departures to/from Via Giolitti outside Stazione Termini.

From the airport, services are between 4am and 11.45pm; from Via Giolitti, buses run from 4.20am to midnight. Buy tickets on board, online, at the airport, or at the bus stop. Journey time is approximately 40 minutes.

SIT Bus (⏚06 591 68 26; www. sitbusshuttle.com; to/from airport €6/5, return €9) Regular departures from the airport to **Via Marsala** (Map p245; Via Marsala 5) outside Stazione Termini between 7.45am and 12.15am, and from Termini between 4.30am and 9.30pm. Get tickets on the bus. Journey time is 45 minutes.

Terravision (Map p255; www. terravision.eu) Runs from the airport to Stazione Termini between 8.15am and 12.15am; from Termini between 4.30am and 9.20pm. Bank on 45 minutes for the journey.

Taxi

The set rate to/from the airport is €30. Journey time is approximately 30 minutes depending on traffic.

Termini Train Station

Rome's main station and principal transport hub is **Stazione Termini** (Map p245; www.romatermini.com; Piazza dei Cinquecento; ⓂTermini). It has regular connections to other European countries, all major Italian cities and many smaller towns.

Train information is available from the customer service area on the main concourse to the left of the ticket desks. Alternatively, check www.trenitalia.com or phone 89 20 21.

From Termini, you can connect with the metro or take a bus from Piazza dei Cinquecento out front. Taxis are outside the main entrance/exit.

Left Luggage (Map p255; 1st 5hr €6, 6-12hr per hour €1, 13hr & over per hour €0.50; ⏱6am-11pm) is available by platform 24 on the Via Giolitti side of the station.

Civitavecchia Port

The nearest port to Rome is at Civitavecchia, about 80km north of town. Ferries sail here from Barcelona and Tunis, as well as Sicily and Sardinia. Check www.traghettiweb.it for route details, prices, and to book.

Bookings can also be made at the Termini-based **Agenzie 365** (Map p255; ☏06 4782 5179; www.agenzie365.it; Stazione Termini, Via Giolitti 34; ☺8am-9pm; ⓂTermini), at travel agents or directly at the port.

From Civitavecchia there are half-hourly trains to Stazione Termini (€4.60 to €16, 45 minutes to 1½ hours). Civitavecchia's station is about 700m from the entrance to the port.

Getting Around

Rome is a sprawling city, but the historic centre is relatively compact. Distances are not great and walking is often the best way of getting around.

Public transport includes buses, trams, metro and a suburban train network. The main hub is Stazione Termini.

Metro

○ Rome has two main metro lines, A (orange) and B (blue), which cross at Termini.

○ Trains run between 5.30am and 11.30pm (to 1.30am on Fridays and Saturdays).

○ Take line A for the Trevi Fountain (Barberini), Spanish Steps (Spagna) and St Peter's (Ottaviano–San Pietro).

○ Take line B for the Colosseum (Colosseo).

Bus

○ The **main bus station** (Map p245) is in front of Stazione Termini on Piazza dei Cinquecento, where there's an **information booth** (Map p245; ☺8am-8pm).

○ Other important hubs are at Largo di Torre Argentina and Piazza Venezia.

○ Buses generally run from about 5.30am until midnight, with limited services throughout the night.

○ For route planning and real time information, **Roma Bus** is a useful phone app.

○ Rome's night bus service comprises more than 25 lines, many of which pass Termini and/or Piazza Venezia. Night buses are marked with an 'n' before the number and their bus stops have a blue owl symbol. Departures are usually every 15 to 30 minutes, but can be much slower. The most useful routes:

n1 Follows the route of metro line A.

n2 Follows the route of metro line B.

n7 Piazzale Clodio, Piazza Cavour, Via Zanardelli, Corso del Rinascimento, Corso Vittorio Emanuele II, Largo di Torre Argentina, Piazza Venezia, Via Nazionale and Stazione Termini.

Car & Motorcycle

○ Driving around Rome is not recommended. Riding a scooter or motorbike is faster and makes parking easier, but Rome is no place for learners, so if you're not an experienced rider, give it a miss. Hiring a car for a day trip out of town is worth considering.

○ Most of Rome's historic centre is closed to unauthorised traffic from 6.30am to 6pm Monday to Friday, from 2pm to 6pm Saturday, and from 11pm to 3am Friday and Saturday. Evening restrictions also apply in Trastevere, San Lorenzo, Monti and Testaccio, typically from 9.30pm or 11pm to 3am on Fridays and Saturdays (also Wednesdays and Thursdays in summer).

○ All streets accessing the Limited Traffic Zone (ZTL) are monitored by electronic-access detection devices. If you're staying in this zone and have a vehicle, contact your hotel. For further information, check www.agenziamobilita.roma.it.

Hire

To hire a car you'll require a driving licence (plus IDP if necessary) and credit card. Age restrictions vary but generally you'll need to be 21 or over.

Major car-rental companies have desks at both of

Rome's airports and Stazione Termini. Reckon on from €20 per day for a small car. Note also that most Italian hire cars have manual gear transmission.

To hire a scooter, prices range from about €30 to €120 depending on the size of the vehicle. Reliable operators:

Eco Move Rent (⏺06 4470 4518; www.ecomoverent.com; Via Varese 48-50; bike/scooter/Vespa per day from €11/40/45; ⏺8.30am-7.30pm; Ⓜ Termini)

On Road (⏺06 481 56 69; www.scooterhire.it; Via Cavour 80a; scooter rental per day from €44; ⏺9am-7pm; Ⓜ Termini)

Treno e Scooter (Map p245; ⏺342 7693291; www.trenoescooter.com; Piazza dei Cinquecento; scooter rental per day €28-79; ⏺9am-7pm Mon-Sat, 9am-2pm & 4-7pm Sun; Ⓜ Termini)

Parking

● Blue lines denote pay-and-display parking – get tickets from meters (coins only) and *tabacchi* (tobacconist's shops).

● Expect to pay up to €1.20 per hour between 8am and 8pm (11pm in some places). After 8pm (or 11pm) parking is free until 8am the next morning.

● Traffic wardens are vigilant and fines are not uncommon. If your car gets towed away, call the **traffic police** (⏺06 6 76 91).

● Useful car parks:

Piazzale dei Partigiani (per hour €0.77; ⏺6am-11pm; Ⓜ Piramide)

Stazione Termini (Map p245; Piazza dei Cinquecento; per hour/day €2.20/18; ⏺6am-midnight; 🚇 Piazza dei Cinquecento)

Villa Borghese (⏺06 322 59 34; www.sabait.it; Viale del Galoppatoio 33; per hour/day €2.30/22; ⏺24hr; 🚇 Via Pinciana)

Train

Apart from connections to Fiumicino airport, you'll probably only need the overground rail network if you head out of town.

Public Transport Tickets

Public-transport tickets are valid on all buses, trams and metro lines, except for routes to Fiumicino airport. Tickets:

BIT (a single ticket valid for 100 minutes; in that time it can be used on all forms of transport, but only once on the metro) €1.50

Roma 24h (24 hours) €7

Roma 48h (48 hours) €12.50

Roma 72h (72 hours) €18

CIS (weekly ticket) €24

Children under 10 travel free.

Buy tickets from *tabacchi* (tobacconist's shops), news stands, and vending machines at main bus stops and metro stations. Validate in machines on buses, at metro entrance gates or at train stations. Ticketless riders risk a fine of at least €50.

● Train information is available from the customer service area on the main concourse in Stazione Termini. Alternatively, check www.trenitalia.com or phone 89 20 21.

● Buy tickets on the main station concourse, from automated ticket machines, or from an authorised travel agency – look for an FS or *biglietti treni* sign in the window.

● Rome's second train station is **Stazione Tiburtina**, four stops from Termini on metro line B. Of the capital's eight other train stations, the most important are **Stazione Roma-Ostiense** and **Stazione Trastevere**.

Language

Italian pronunciation isn't difficult as most sounds are also found in English. The pronunciation of some consonants depends on which vowel follows, but if you read our pronunciation guides below as if they were English, you'll be understood just fine. Just remember to pronounce double consonants as a longer, more forceful sound than single ones. The stressed syllables in words are in italics in our pronunciation guides.

To enhance your trip with a phrasebook, visit **lonelyplanet.com**. Find Lonely Planet iPhone phrasebooks in the Apple App store.

Basics

Hello.
Buongiorno./Ciao. (pol/inf)   bwon·jor·no/chow

How are you?
Come sta?   ko·me sta

I'm fine, thanks.
Bene, grazie.   be·ne gra·tsye

Excuse me.
Mi scusi.   mee skoo·zee

Yes./No.
Sì./No.   see/no

Please. (when asking)
Per favore.   per fa·vo·re

Thank you.
Grazie.   gra·tsye

Goodbye.
Arrivederci./Ciao. (pol/inf)   a·ree·ve·der·chee/chow

Do you speak English?
Parla inglese?   par·la een·gle·ze

I don't understand.
Non capisco.   non ka·pee·sko

How much is this?
Quanto costa?   kwan·to ko·sta

Accommodation

I'd like to book a room.
Vorrei prenotare   vo·ray pre·no·ta·re
una camera.   oo·na ka·me·ra

How much is it per night?
Quanto costa per   kwan·to kos·ta per
una notte?   oo·na no·te

Eating & Drinking

I'd like ..., please.
Vorrei . . ., per favore.   vo·ray . . . per fa·vo·re

What would you recommend?
Cosa mi consiglia?   ko·za mee kon·see·lya

That was delicious!
Era squisito!   e·ra skwee·zee·to

Bring the bill/check, please.
Mi porta il conto,   mee por·ta eel kon·to
per favore.   per fa·vo·re

I'm allergic (to peanuts).
Sono allergico/a   so·no a·ler·jee·ko/a
(alle arachidi). (m/f)   (a·le a·ra·kee·dee)

I don't eat ...
Non mangio . . .   non man·jo . . .

fish	pesce	pe·she
meat	carne	kar·ne
poultry	pollame	po·la·me

Emergencies

I'm ill.
Mi sento male.   mee sen·to ma·le

Help!
Aiuto!   a·yoo·to

Call a doctor!
Chiami un medico!   kya·mee oon me·dee·ko

Call the police!
Chiami la polizia!   kya·mee la po·lee·tsee·a

Directions

I'm looking for (a/the) ...
Cerco . . .   cher·ko . . .

bank
la banca   la ban·ka

... embassy
la ambasciata de . . .   la am·ba·sha·ta de . . .

market
il mercato   eel mer·ka·to

museum
il museo   eel moo·ze·o

restaurant
un ristorante   oon rees·to·ran·te

toilet
un gabinetto   oon ga·bee·ne·to

tourist office
l'ufficio del turismo   loo·fee·cho del too·reez·mo

Behind the Scenes

Writer Thanks

Nicola Williams

As with every Italian title I work on, gratitude goes to Italophiles I have met on my travels and continue to share my passion for *la vita bella* with: art historian Molly McIlWrath, professional Roman foodies Gina Tringali & Eleonora Baldwin, 'treasure hunt' queen Daisy de Plume @ ThatMuse (next stop: the Vatican) and my very own pseudo-Italian Matthias Luefkens.

Alexis Averbuck

It was a true joy to research Rome, a return to one of my first and most magical travel writing spots; this is thanks in large part to the fabulous company and comradery of my beloved Ryan Ver Berkmoes. And the delightful reunion with our dear Hydriot friends, Sergei and Mina. Many thanks are also due to Anna Tyler who helmed the project with superb attention to detail, guidance and grace.

Duncan Garwood

A big thank you to fellow authors Virginia Maxwell and Alexis Averbuck for their suggestions and to Anna Tyler at Lonely Planet for all her support. In Rome *grazie* to Alexandra Bruzzese for her foodie tips and Richard McKenna for his ever-entertaining lunch company. As always, a big, heartfelt hug to Lidia and the boys, Ben and Nick.

Virginia Maxwell

I had a number of excellent travelling companions on this research trip who walked, ate and drank their way through the city with me: thanks to Peter Handsaker, Catherine Hannebery and Pat Yale. Thanks also to Anna Tyler for her expert briefing and project guidance, and to Rome-based Duncan Garwood and Alexandra Bruzzese for their tips.

Acknowledgements

Cover image: Pantheon, Hercules Milas/Alamy©

Climate map data adapted from Peel MC, Finlayson BL & McMahon TA (2007) 'Updated World Map of the Köppen-Geiger Climate Classification', *Hydrology and Earth System Sciences*, 11, 1633–44.

Illustration pp84–5 by Javier Zarracina.

This Book

This 4th edition of Lonely Planet's *Best of Rome* guidebook was curated by Nicola Williams, and researched and written by Alexis Averbuck, Duncan Garwood and Virginia Maxwell. The previous two editions were also written by Duncan Garwood and Nicola Williams. This guidebook was produced by the following:

Destination Editor Anna Tyler

Senior Product Editor Elizabeth Jones

Regional Senior Cartographer Anthony Phelan

Product Editor Kate Mathews

Book Designer Ania Bartoszek

Assisting Editors Imogen Bannister, Emma Gibbs, Jennifer Hattam, Kate James, Alison Morris, Susan Paterson, Simon Williamson

Cartographers Julie Dodkins, Rachel Imeson

Cover Researcher Brendan Dempsey-Spencer

Thanks to Alexandra Bruzzese, Gemma Graham, Martin Heng, Brana Vladisavljevic

Send Us Your Feedback

We love to hear from travellers – your comments keep us on our toes and help make our books better. Our well-travelled team reads every word on what you loved or loathed about this book. Although we cannot reply individually to postal submissions, we always guarantee that your feedback goes straight to the appropriate authors, in time for the next edition. Each person who sends us information is thanked in the next edition, the most useful submissions are rewarded with a selection of digital PDF chapters.

Visit lonelyplanet.com/contact to submit your updates and suggestions or to ask for help. Our award-winning website also features inspirational travel stories, news and discussions.

Note: We may edit, reproduce and incorporate your comments in Lonely Planet products such as guidebooks, websites and digital products, so let us know if you don't want your comments reproduced or your name acknowledged. For a copy of our privacy policy visit lonelyplanet.com/privacy.

Index

A

B

000 Map pages

C

D

CATARINA BELOVA/SHUTTERSTOCK ©

Rome Maps

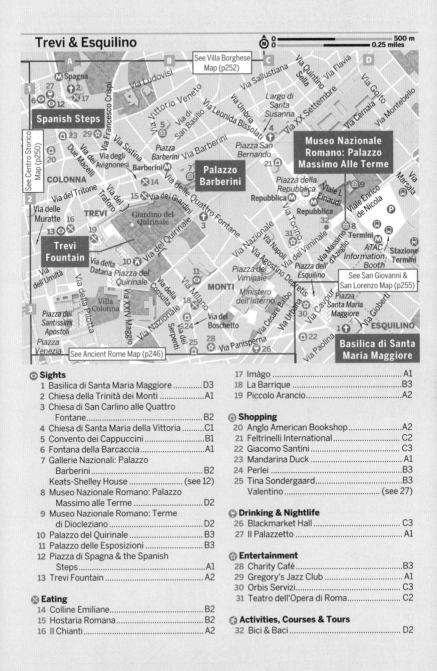

Trevi & Esquilino

See Villa Borghese Map (p252)

See Centro Storico Map (p250)

See Ancient Rome Map (p246)

See San Giovanni & San Lorenzo Map (p255)

0 — 500 m
0 — 0.25 miles

Spanish Steps

Museo Nazionale Romano: Palazzo Massimo Alle Terme

Palazzo Barberini

Trevi Fountain

Basilica di Santa Maria Maggiore

Ancient Rome

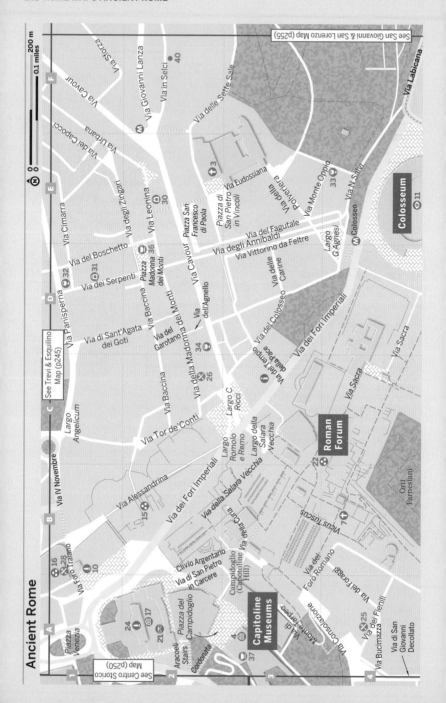

See Centro Storico Map (p250)

See Trevi & Esquilino Map (p245)

See San Giovanni & San Lorenzo Map (p255)

Piazza Venezia

Largo Angelicum

Via IV Novembre

Via Foro Traiano

Aracoeli Stairs

Cordonata

Piazza del Campidoglio

Clivio Argentario

Via di San Pietro in Carcere

Campidoglio (Capitoline Hill)

Capitoline Museums

Monte Tarpeo

Via di Consolazione

Via del Tempio di Giove

Via di San Giovanni Decollato

Via Bucimazza

Via dei Fienili

Via del Foro Romano

Vicus Tuscus

Orti Farnesiani

Roman Forum

Via Sacra

Via della Salara Vecchia

Largo della Salara Vecchia

Largo Romolo e Remo

Via Tor de' Conti

Via Alessandrina

Via dei Fori Imperiali

Via della Salara Vecchia

Largo C Ricci

Via Baccina

Via Cavour

Via della Madonna dei Monti

Via del Garofano

Via di Sant'Agata dei Goti

Via Panisperna

Via dei Serpenti

Via del Boschetto

Via Cimarra

Via degli Zingari

Piazza Madonna dei Monti

Via Leonina

Via Urbana

Via del Capocci

Via Cavour

Via Giovanni Lanza

Via Sforza

Via in Selci

Via delle Sette Sale

Via Eudossiana

Piazza di San Pietro in Vincoli

Piazza San Francesco di Paola

Via delle Polveriera

Via del Fagutale

Via degli Annibaldi

Via Vittorino da Feltre

Via delle Carine

Via del Colosseo

Via del Tempio della Pace

Via dei Fori Imperiali

Via Sacra

Largo G Agnesi

Via Monte Oppio

Via N Salvi

Via Labicana

Colosseum

200 m
0.1 miles

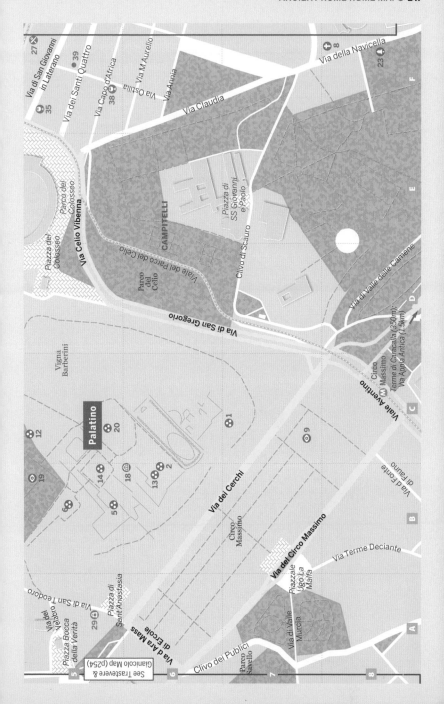

CAMPITELLI

Palatino

Parco del Colosseo

Via Celio Vibenna

Parco del Celio

Viale del Parco del Celio

Via di San Gregorio

Vigna Barberini

Piazza del Colosseo

Piazza di SS Giovanni e Paolo

Clivo di Scauro

Via di Valle delle Camene

Via Claudia

Via di San Giovanni in Laterano

Via dei Santi Quattro

Via Capo d'Africa

Via Ostilia

Via M Aurelio

Via Annia

Via della Navicella

Viale Aventino

Circo Massimo

Terme di Caracalla (350m);
Via Appia Antica (1.5km)

Via di Fonte di Fauno

Via dei Cerchi

Circo Massimo

Via del Circo Massimo

Via Terme Deciante

Piazzale Ugo La Malfa

Via di Valle Murcia

Via di Valle

Parco Savello

Clivo dei Publici

Via d'Ara Mass di Ercole

Piazza di Sant'Anastasia

Via di San Teodoro

Via del Velabro

Piazza Bocca della Verità

See Trastevere & Gianicolo Map (p254)

27
39
35
38
23
8
1
12
19
20
14
18
13
2
5
6
9
29

Ancient Rome

Centro Storico

Centro Storico

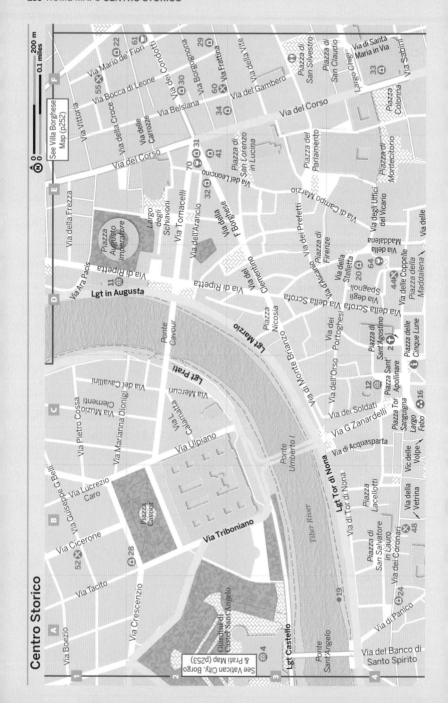

See Vatican City, Borgo
& Prati Map (p253)

See Villa Borghese
Map (p252)

200 m
0.1 miles

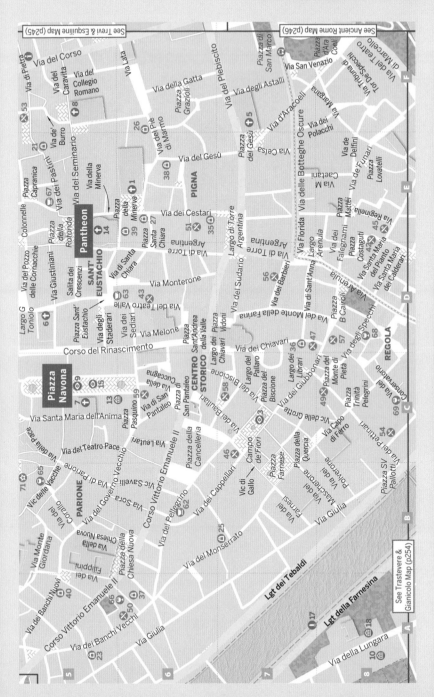

Villa Borghese

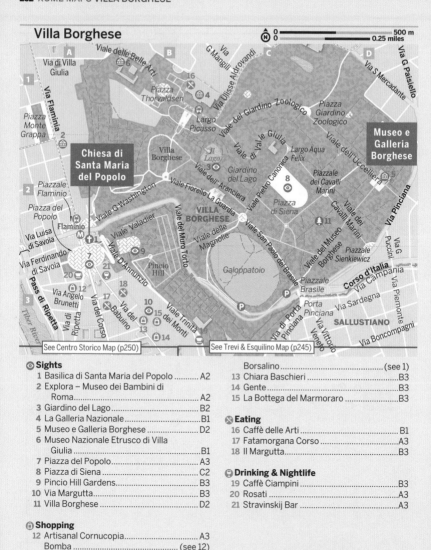

Vatican City, Borgo & Prati

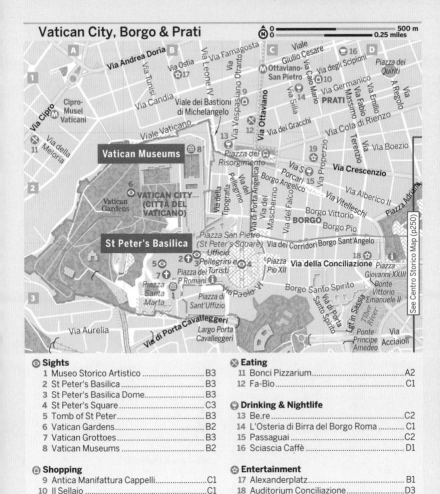

◎ Sights
1 Museo Storico Artistico	B3
2 St Peter's Basilica	B3
3 St Peter's Basilica Dome	B3
4 St Peter's Square	C3
5 Tomb of St Peter	B3
6 Vatican Gardens	B2
7 Vatican Grottoes	B3
8 Vatican Museums	B2

ⓐ Shopping
9 Antica Manifattura Cappelli	C1
10 Il Sellaio	C1

⊗ Eating
11 Bonci Pizzarium	A2
12 Fa-Bìo	C1

🍷 Drinking & Nightlife
13 Be.re	C2
14 L'Osteria di Birra del Borgo Roma	C1
15 Passaguai	C2
16 Sciascia Caffè	D1

🎭 Entertainment
17 Alexanderplatz	B1
18 Auditorium Conciliazione	D3
19 Fonclea	C2

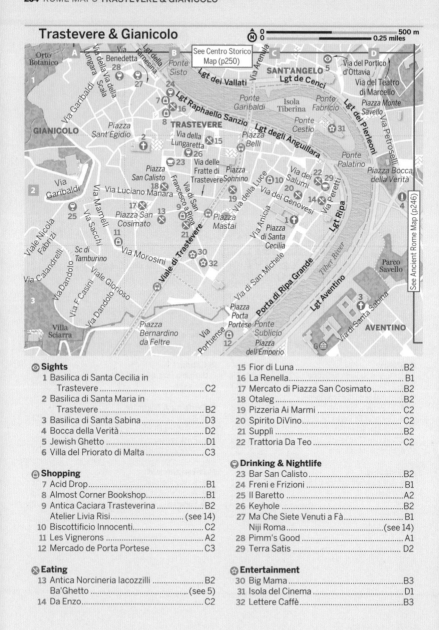

Trastevere & Gianicolo

0   500 m
0   0.25 miles

See Centro Storico Map (p250)

See Ancient Rome Map (p246)

San Giovanni & San Lorenzo

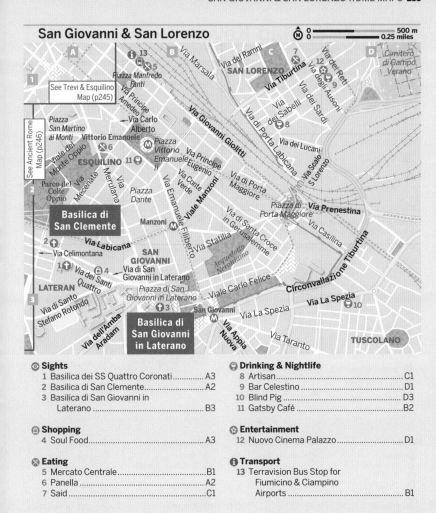

◎ Sights
1 Basilica dei SS Quattro Coronati	A3
2 Basilica di San Clemente	A2
3 Basilica di San Giovanni in Laterano	B3

🛍 Shopping
4 Soul Food	A3

✕ Eating
5 Mercato Centrale	B1
6 Panella	A2
7 Said	C1

● Drinking & Nightlife
8 Artisan	C1
9 Bar Celestino	D1
10 Blind Pig	D3
11 Gatsby Café	B2

✦ Entertainment
12 Nuovo Cinema Palazzo	D1

● Transport
13 Terravision Bus Stop for Fiumicino & Ciampino Airports	B1

Symbols & Map Key

Look for these symbols to quickly identify listings:

◉ Sights
✈ Activities
⊜ Courses
☉ Tours
✪ Festivals & Events

✪ Eating
☕ Drinking
✪ Entertainment
🔒 Shopping
ℹ Information & Transport

These symbols and abbreviations give vital information for each listing:

🍃 Sustainable or green recommendation
FREE No payment required

☏ Telephone number
🕓 Opening hours
Ⓟ Parking
🚭 Nonsmoking
❄ Air-conditioning
@ Internet access
📶 Wi-fi access
🏊 Swimming pool

🚌 Bus
⛴ Ferry
🚊 Tram
🚆 Train
📋 English-language menu
🥗 Vegetarian selection
👪 Family-friendly

Find your best experiences with these Great For... icons.

 Art & Culture
 Beaches
 Budget
 Cafe/Coffee
🚲 Cycling
🔜 Detour
🍷 Drinking
 Entertainment
 Events
 Family Travel
🍽 Food & Drink

 History
 Local Life
 Nature & Wildlife
📷 Photo Op
🔭 Scenery
🛍 Shopping
 Short Trip
 Sport
 Walking
 Winter Travel

Sights
- Beach
- Bird Sanctuary
- Buddhist
- Castle/Palace
- Christian
- Confucian
- Hindu
- Islamic
- Jain
- Jewish
- Monument
- Museum/Gallery/Historic Building
- Ruin
- Shinto
- Sikh
- Taoist
- Winery/Vineyard
- Zoo/Wildlife Sanctuary
- Other Sight

Points of Interest
- Bodysurfing
- Camping
- Cafe
- Canoeing/Kayaking
- Course/Tour
- Diving
- Drinking & Nightlife
- Eating
- Entertainment
- Sento Hot Baths/Onsen
- Shopping
- Skiing
- Sleeping
- Snorkelling
- Surfing
- Swimming/Pool
- Walking
- Windsurfing
- Other Activity

Information
- Bank
- Embassy/Consulate
- Hospital/Medical
- Internet
- Police
- Post Office
- Telephone
- Toilet
- Tourist Information
- Other Information

Geographic
- Beach
- Gate
- Hut/Shelter
- Lighthouse
- Lookout
- Mountain/Volcano
- Oasis
- Park
- Pass
- Picnic Area
- Waterfall

Transport
- Airport
- BART station
- Border crossing
- Boston T station
- Bus
- Cable car/Funicular
- Cycling
- Ferry
- Metro/MRT station
- Monorail
- Parking
- Petrol station
- Subway/S-Bahn/Skytrain station
- Taxi
- Train station/Railway
- Tram
- Tube Station
- Underground/U-Bahn station
- Other Transport

Virginia Maxwell

Although based in Australia, Virginia spends at least half of her year updating Lonely Planet destination coverage across the globe. The Mediterranean is her major area of interest – she has covered Spain, Italy, Turkey, Syria, Lebanon, Israel, Egypt, Morocco and Tunisia for Lonely Planet – but she also covers Finland, Bali, Armenia, the Netherlands, the US and Australia. Follow her @maxwellvirginia on Instagram and Twitter.

Our Story

A beat-up old car, a few dollars in the pocket and a sense of adventure. In 1972 that's all Tony and Maureen Wheeler needed for the trip of a lifetime – across Europe and Asia overland to Australia. It took several months, and at the end – broke but inspired – they sat at their kitchen table writing and stapling together their first travel guide, *Across Asia on the Cheap*. Within a week they'd sold 1500 copies. Lonely Planet was born.

Today, Lonely Planet has offices in Franklin, London, Melbourne, Oakland, Dublin, Beijing and Delhi, with more than 600 staff and writers. We share Tony's belief that 'a great guidebook should do three things: inform, educate and amuse'.

Our Writers

Nicola Williams

Border-hopping is a way of life for British writer, runner, foodie, art aficionado and mum-of-three Nicola Williams, who has lived in a French village on the southern side of Lake Geneva for more than a decade. Nicola has authored more than 50 guidebooks on Paris, Provence, Rome, Tuscany, France, Italy and Switzerland for Lonely Planet and covers France as a destination expert for the *Telegraph*. She also writes for *The Independent*, *The Guardian*, lonelyplanet.com, *Lonely Planet Magazine*, *French Magazine*, Cool Camping France and others. Catch her on the road on Twitter and Instagram at @tripalong.

Alexis Averbuck

Alexis Averbuck has travelled and lived all over the world, from Sri Lanka to Ecuador, Zanzibar and Antarctica. In recent years she's been living on the Greek island of Hydra and exploring her adopted homeland; sampling oysters in Brittany and careening through hill-top villages in Provence; and adventuring along Iceland's surreal lava fields, sparkling fjords and glacier tongues. A travel writer for over two decades, Alexis has lived in Antarctica for a year, crossed the Pacific by sailboat and written books on her journeys through Asia, Europe and the Americas. She's also a painter (visit www.alexisaverbuck.com) and promotes travel and adventure on video and television.

Duncan Garwood

From facing fast bowlers in Barbados to side-stepping hungry pigs in Goa, Duncan's travels have thrown up many unique experiences. These days he largely dedicates himself to the Mediterranean and Italy, his adopted homeland where he's been living since 1997. He's worked on more than 30 Lonely Planet titles, including guidebooks to Rome, Sardinia, Sicily, Spain and Portugal, and has contributed to books on food and epic drives. He's also written on Italy for newspapers, websites and magazines.

More Writers

STAY IN TOUCH LONELYPLANET.COM/CONTACT

AUSTRALIA The Malt Store, Level 3, 551 Swanston St, Carlton, Victoria 3053
☏ 03 8379 8000,
fax 03 8379 8111

IRELAND Digital Depot, Roe Lane (off Thomas St), Digital Hub, Dublin 8, D08 TCV4, Ireland

USA 124 Linden Street, Oakland, CA 94607
☏ 510 250 6400,
toll free 800 275 8555,
fax 510 893 8572

UK 240 Blackfriars Road, London SE1 8NW
☏ 020 3771 5100,
fax 020 3771 5101

 twitter.com/
lonelyplanet

 facebook.com/
lonelyplanet

 instagram.com/
lonelyplanet

 youtube.com/
lonelyplanet

 lonelyplanet.com/
newsletter